THE SALE

25

High Performance Selling Skills
To Master *Before Your Competitors Do!*

By
Don Hutson

Published by
Executive Books
P.O. Box 1044, Harrisburg, PA 17108

Published by Executive Books
P.O. Box 1044, Harrisburg, PA 17108
(717) 691–0400

Distributed by Publishers Distribution Service
121 E. Front St., Suite 203
Traverse City, MI 49684
(616) 929–0733

Book Design and make–up:
Electronic Publishing Services, Inc.

Printed in the United States of America
ISBN: 0–937539–18–X

DEDICATION

To the loving memories of…

My father, Marvin Lee Hutson, who inspired me early to appreciate the selling opportunity in our free enterprise system and later created the intrigue and desire in me to develop the skill of public speaking.

And, my mother, Sara Summers Hutson, who was blind enough to think I could do little wrong, and yet visionary enough to know that I needed her counsel.

Acknowledgments

Many people are instrumental in the publishing of a book. I've listed the people who have made the greatest contributions to this book becoming a reality.

My editor, Dolores Bell of Write House Communications did a yeoman's job, with excellence and professionalism. Special thanks, too, to my valued associate Linda Hightower for her transcribing and proofing.

My peers, the members of Speakers Roundable who have had a great impact on my thinking and my success: Ken Blanchard, Ty Boyd, Dan Burrus, Jim Cathcart, Danny Cox, Patricia Fripp, Christopher Hegarty, Art Holst, Allan Hurst, Charlie Jones, Jim Newman, Charlie Plumb, Nido Qubein, Brian Tracy, Herb True, Jim Tunney, Tom Winninger. And, of course, the "elder statesmen" of our group from whom I have learned much - Bill Gove, Ira Hayes, and Cavett Robert.

My mentors, Dr. Kenneth McFarland, a great patriot and orator, and Arthur H. "Red" Motley, who coined the phrase "Nothing Happens Until Somebody Sells Something." They both helped mold my early values.

My educator, Dr. Wayland Tonning, who spearheaded the first (and currently only) Sales major which I received at Memphis State University in 1967.

Last, but not least, I wish to express my gratitude to the late Dick Gardner who hired me at age 20 and taught me many basic and advanced skills in selling and presenting.

Don Hutson's
<u>THE</u> <u>SALE</u>

Section One   1
Sales Success Through Self-Empowerment:
Mastering the Mind Game

Skill 1: Using Positive Thinking With Balance and Insight   3

Skill 2: Understanding Self-Image Psychology   15

Skill 3: Mastering "The Numbers Game"   27

Skill 4: Getting "Up" For High Performance   37

Skill 5: Dealing with Rejection, Stress and Worry   49

Skill 6: Imagination and Creativity: Go For the Big Ones!   65

Section Two   81
Sales Strategies That Work...If You Do

Skill 7: The Process of Building Trust   83

Skill 8: Learning to Ask Questions and Listen   103

Skill 9: Needs-Analysis Selling   117

Skill 10: The Needs-Based Presentation   127

Skill 11: Developing Business: From Suspect to Confidant   141

Skill 12: Building Value Rather Than Cutting Price   151

Skill 13: Understanding Human Behavior in Selling   161

Skill 14: Selling With Adaptable Strategies   175

Skill 15: Presenting Your Proposal   187

Skill 16: Closing the Sale: Earning the Right   203

Skill 17: Closing the Sale: Getting the "Yes"   213

SECTION THREE   239
The Excellence Dimension:
Getting The Most Out Of You

SKILL 18: Enthusiasm in Selling   241

SKILL 19: Goal Setting   249

SKILL 20: Goal Achievement   271

SKILL 21: Your Personal Image of Excellence   283

SKILL 22: Handling Conflict, Problems and Feedback 297

SKILL 23: Common Sense Sales Ideas   313

SKILL 24: Dedication to Training   335

SKILL 25: Gaining Career Progress   349

INDEX   360

Quotes Regarding Speaker and Author Don Hutson...

"Don Hutson's new sales book has value for training and employee motivation."

> Jerry McMorris, President
> NW Transport Services, Inc.
> Denver, CO

"Don Hutson did more for the attitudes and skills of our sales people in one hour than I could have imagined. He is a rare talent!"

> John Kluge, Chairman of the Board
> Metromedia, Inc.
> New York, NY

"Your talk, 'Leadership Makes The Difference', was a perfect way to end our meeting. The personal touches you added about our goals and specific problems really caught the attention of our managers."

> Ronald H. Doerr, President and CEO
> National Steel Corporation
> Pittsburgh, PA

"Don has managed to convey the enthusiasm of his personal presentations into written word with this book. I plan on reading it once a year to re-energize myself!"

> Joseph S. Viland, President
> Wabash Alloys
> Wabash, IN

"I think I've heard them all in the past forty years including legends like Elmer Wheeler and "Red" Motley, but never one better than Don Hutson!"

> Walter C. Fisher, Chairman of the Board (retired)
> Zenith Corporation
> Chicago, IL

"Thank you for the terrific training program, 'High Performance Management'. You captured the hearts and minds of a very tough audience. I now have a turned-on-to-training employee population who are eager to attend upcoming sessions."

> Arlene G. Douglas
> Training, Human Resources Department
> American College of Physicians
> Philadelphia, PA

"We are all looking for value and Don Hutson's The Sale certainly delivers it! The chapter on 'Building Value Rather than Cutting Price' is very timely – we plan to reference it in subsequent training classes."

> Roger Loeffelbein, President and CEO
> Bryan Foods Division of Sara Lee Corporation
> Chicago, IL

"Worldclass! Don Hutson reveals the keys to unlocking individual potential and offers useful ideas for developing excellence in sales. Definitely a valuable tool for any business."

> Gary D. Sasser, President and CEO
> Averitt Express
> Cookeville, TN

"Your presentation, 'The Challenge of Managerial Excellence', was one of the most informative, interesting and well-liked presentations delivered to a KCMA convention!"

> C. Richard Titus, Executive Vice President
> Kitchen Cabinet Manufacturers Association
> Reston, VA

"Don Hutson's advice in The Sale is on point even to the most professional salespeople... and entertaining!"

> James L. Mann, President and CEO
> Sungard Data Systems, Inc.
> Wayne, PA

"Don Hutson's contribution in helping our organization and our people grow has been tremendous! His devotion to thorough research enables him to develop a personalized, high impact program that gets results. The response of our people to Don has been outstanding."

> Frederick F. Avery, President and CEO
> Kraft Food Ingredients
> Memphis, TN

"The Sale is a barrier-busting dictionary of skills and applications for anyone serious about achieving success... geared to those who strive for superior performance. I am a Don Hutson ENTHUSIAST!"

> Dr. Lawrence T. Markson, President
> Markson Mgmt.
> Lake Success, NY

"Don Hutson's The Sale will transfer Don's superb skills of selling and mastering competition to salespeople everywhere. If you want to be the best, read it."

> Jack Watson, CLU, President
> Franklin Life
> Springfield, IL

Introduction

"There's nothing new in selling" is a statement I still hear occasionally—and it's one that I will debate with anybody, anywhere. Successful sales professionals today sell quite differently from the salespeople of the past. This book is a collection of sales ideas and techniques that I believe work effectively in today's competitive selling marketplace.

As recently as a few years ago, selling was perceived as something you did *to* somebody, often in a less than honorable way. Today, the authentic high performance salesperson is seen as one on the cutting edge of sales excellence, a pro who makes his client's problems his own problems. Today's high performance pros give needs-based presentations, not hype-based pitches. Yes, today there is a new breed of sensitive, inquisitive, knowledgeable, strategic salespeople whose high incomes reflect the valuable services they perform for their clients – not the dollars they manipulatively bilk out of someone.

While writing this book has been a lengthy task that has stretched through several years of my life, it has been one of the greatest pleasures of my training career. Developing the book has afforded me the opportunity to study the craft of selling and to interview some great sales professionals, many of whom are part of these pages. I've written about millionaires and even some billionaires; I've shared with you suggestions and strategies from a number of insightful, hard-working sales professionals; I've even mentioned a number of people I know you've never heard of but who have achieved some uncommon and, in some cases, extraordinary things. The stories of all these people have, I believe, contributed in measurable and meaningful ways to this book.

The current sales environment is one in which buyers are more sophisticated and demanding than at any time in the past. Buyers today demand maximum value at a reasonable price. Though there are exceptions, I find that generally people are more willing to pay for quality today then ever before. People are no longer willing to buy schlock; they want quality products and services with effective applications, accompanied by terrific service. Buyers today appreciate salespeople who focus creatively on their needs rather than just trying to move products.

As a result of these changes in the selling environment, organizations who may have previously shunned any reference to *sales* are now developing and utilizing aggressive sales postures to enhance their business base. For example, ten years ago you would never have heard accountants discussing a sales effort on behalf of their firm. Today they may call their effort "practice development," but most of them will readily admit they have indeed become sales oriented. (As a matter of fact, a couple of years ago my biggest customer was the world-wide accounting firm Arthur Andersen and Company). Banks are another example of the burgeoning sales cultures developing. I have recently done sales training programs for Sun Bank (FL), the Huntington Bank (OH), Chase Manhattan (NY), AmSouth (AL) and the Eastern Bank (MA), and I expect to be working with other banks in the future. Accountants, bankers – today *everybody* needs to sell themselves and their ideas just to keep their jobs!

Today everybody, at one time or another, is trying to sell something. If it isn't a product, it is an idea or a premise.

Several years ago my good friend Don Clanton, Senior Vice President and Managing Director of Commerce Investments, was sitting at the bar in TGI Friday's with two of his associates having a drink. The evening was progressing normally when they were startled to see a man walk into the restaurant dressed in full scuba gear, diving mask and all.

The alien-like fellow walked up to the bar, pulled a large diving knife from the scabbard on his leg, slammed the sharp blade into the wooden bar, and ordered a drink.

It's hard to rattle Don Clanton. He turned to the man and said, "Nice outfit. Is that what you normally wear when you're going out for drink?" The diver responded, "Don't tell anybody, but my divorce trial is coming up in two weeks, and if I can sell somebody on the idea of declaring me crazy, it's gonna save me thousands!"

I recently was interviewed by Bonnie Churchill in Beverly Hills for her nationwide radio show. An idea I set forth in that interview and that I believe in wholeheartedly is that one of the best things anyone can do to enjoy career progress today – regardless of what line of work they are in – is to study the latest communications and persuasive skills. These skills will be beneficial to everyone, especially if you work in a traditional sales job, but also if you work in a field in which you sell indirectly.

I agree with my good friend and client, Tony Piazza, Senior Vice President and General Manager of SONY Consumer Sales Company, who said "Sales is neither specifically an act nor a science but a combination of both. However, true success in sales is directly proportional to one's passion for achievement." Great salespeople today find the successful mix of skills that work, along with energies to be expended to become high producers.

In my 25-year career, I have made over 20,000 sales calls and none of them were ever just alike. There's a great variance in customers' needs and priorities, just as there is variance in customers' behavior. So we need a variety of sales approaches to be successful in various situations. We need to arm ourselves with the skills that will enable us to be at our best with people we call on, whatever the circumstances.

This book contains a smorgasbord of ideas. Some will help you become more productive. Some will help you find creative new approaches to plug into your success strategy. Some may be inappropriate to your situation but may provide amusing reading anyway, and they should give you a different perspective on what worked for someone else in selling. Perhaps the most valuable ideas in this book will be those that pique your imagination and stimulate you to create a similar but different technique that will work great for you. If my words spark a new strategy or your rediscovery and improvement of an existing skill that makes your tomorrows better than your yesterdays and todays, I will feel rewarded.

The 25 sales skills presented in this book are not intended to enable you to hammer people into saying "Yes." Those tactics are gone. The skills I've included are designed to enhance your repertoire of client-based selling skills – the only kind of skills that are effective today. I've also included some time-tested basic skills that we need to periodically review and brush up on. And you will notice that several of the 25 high performance selling skills do not center around what you say or do in your relationship with a prospect or client; instead, they center around what you can do about *yourself* to increase your opportunities for sales success.

Like any other tape you hear, seminar you attend or book you read, this book will only be as good as what you do with what you've learned. There's little or no value in a learning experience that does not result in a behavior change. As you absorb this material, ask yourself, "What am I going to do differently as a result of what I've learned reading this book?"

I ask of you only this: Open your mind. Absorb the ideas in this book and mentally prepare yourself, not only for the enhancement of your sales skills, but for behavior changes as well. I hope you get a great many quality ideas from these pages but, at the very minimum, I hope you get at least one *gem* of an idea, technique or strategy that will make your life and your career better than ever before.

Don Hutson
P.O. Box 172181
Memphis, TN 38187–2181
(901) 767-0000

SECTION ONE

Sales Success Through Self-Empowerment: Mastering the Mind Game

SKILL 1: Using Positive Thinking With Balance and Insight

SKILL 2: Understanding Self-Image Psychology

SKILL 3: Mastering "The Numbers Game"

SKILL 4: Getting "Up" For High Performance

SKILL 5: Dealing with Rejection, Stress and Worry

SKILL 6: Imagination and Creativity: Go For the Big Ones!

Skill #1

◆◆◆◆◆

Using Positive Thinking With Balance and Insight

❝One cannot directly choose his circumstances, but he can choose his thoughts and indirectly, yet surely, shape his circumstances.❞

— JAMES ALLEN

A major attribute of the high performance sales professional is that he or she always has a proper perspective on what I call the *mental profile*. The well-balanced individual does not get out of touch with reality. They never reach the point where they substitute positive thinking for *thinking*.

Is the projection of a balanced, positive demeanor something others have learned to expect of you? If so, that's good. It demonstrates that you have cultivated a very positive habit. Confucius said, "He who cannot smile should not keep shop." I say, "He who does not smile often does not sell often." In selling any product, service, or idea, your disposition will have an impact on the response to your proposition!

Reflexive Responses

When someone asks you "How are you?" or "How's it going?" what do you say? Most people never stop to think about the impact their answer to that simple question will have. An optimistic answer, accompanied by a pleasant smile, not only helps you build rapport quicker, it also makes you more of a pleasure to do business with. No one wants to have to carry a pessimistic burden on their shoulders. Be a carrier of sunshine, not sorrow!

The mental attitude you display to others becomes much like an invisible magnet; it can pull you up to the heights of high achievers who expect good things from life, or it can pull you down among the grovelling pessimists.

Let's think about some of the ways you might respond to the question, "How's it going?"

(1) *"Terrible!"*

That response is usually followed by elaboration. It's wasted breath. Believe me, they really don't want to hear about it. To tell people everything that's wrong in your life is rather like a verbal expression of mental halitosis. Cavett Robert has said, "Don't tell people your problems! Seventy-five percent of them could care less, and the other twenty-five percent are actually glad to hear that you've got more problems than they do!"

(2) *"Not too bad..."*

I think this remark is often a person's way of saying that things are really pretty good in their life, but since they are basically negatively programmed, they feel a need to make a downtrodden remark. Do they think an expression of wholesome optimism is unsophisticated?

(3) *"Pretty good."*

That's trying harder. Remember, people want to do business with winners, so don't tell them you're losing by giving a negative response to a simple surface question.

(4) *"Great!"*

That word is Ira Hayes's trademark.
"How are you, Ira?" "Great!"
"How's your wife?" "Great!"
"How's the speaking tour?" "Great!"
"How's your sore throat?" "Great!" With Ira, it's a positive reflex that sets up a positive beginning for any interaction.

(5) *"Terrific!"*

I think Ed Foreman may have copyrighted that word. With Ed, everything is terrific. He admits that on a day when everything isn't terrific, it's tough to say the word the first few times, but he's found that if you say it anyway, within a short time, you'll find your day is terrific because you've programmed it (and yourself) that way.

(6) *"Perfect!"*

Carol Prentiss, wife of well-known philanthropist and restauranteur Jim Prentiss, smiles and confidently says "Perfect!" every time. She has an unstoppable optimistic attitude that makes her a pleasure to be around. Carol confesses that she probably gets more out of positive comments than any listener does.

(7) *"Like a Million!"*

Medical sales executive Lew Bennett came up with this one. It's filled with optimism and positive energy. I'm not sure exactly what it means, but it sure sounds good every time I hear Lew say it.

5

(8) *"Outstanding, but I'll get better!"*

This is a Zig Ziglar original. If you want to go to the pinnacle of optimism, Zig Ziglar is your ticket. He is simply the best for internalized personal optimism.

(9) *"Unbelievable!"*

My friend Tom Hopkins says this is the best response because, whether things are unbelievably good or unbelievably bad, you're covered either way!

I know I've used lots of ink to delve into this simple concept, but in selling, if we're to get positive results, we must say and do things that contribute to the kind of positive environment that is conducive to successful selling. Another vital reason for a positive response to this simple question is that you are not only setting the stage for the interaction, you are participating in positive self-talk that can intensify *your* conviction.

Categories of Mental Profile

Let's take a look at three basic categories of mental profile and see if you recognize yourself among them. First, consider this grid outlining various factors that affect the mental profile.

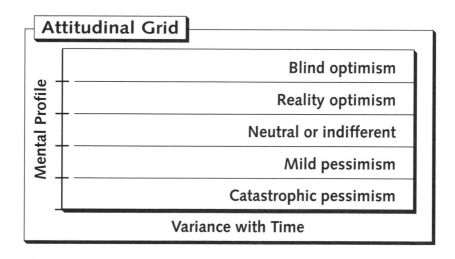

In the first category, we find the *blind optimist*. You've met the blind optimist before. That's the salesperson who is so high and ebullient that you wonder when and if they will ever come in for a landing. This individual is so overwhelmingly optimistic that he or she has difficulty handling problems and routine negative events when they occur.

Don't get me wrong. I really appreciate an individual with a wholesome attitude and an optimistic demeanor. The problem with blind optimists is that their brand of optimism is loud and shallow. When the blind optimist meets with rejection, very often they don't just come in for a landing – they crash!

Predictable attitude variance of the *Blind Optimist*

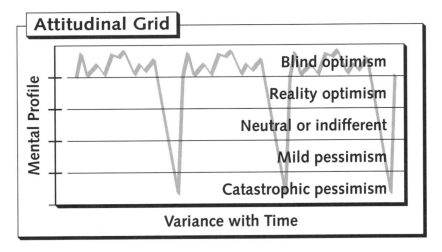

In earlier years, I was a blind optimist. Let me share with you an experience that matured my attitudinal genes.

For 10 years, I pursued the fun and rewarding hobby of collecting classic, antique, and exotic cars. I sometimes had 20 to 30 motorcars at a time, from Rolls Royces, Jaguars, Cadillacs, Packards, Ferraris, various vintages of Mercedes and others. I secured some from other collections, but I often purchased these collectibles at classic car auctions throughout the United States, many staged by the Kruses of Kruse Auction Company. Dean and Daniel have been great, long-time friends.

During this chapter in my life, I made an amusing discovery: A blindly optimistic participant in a classic car auction can get his financial knees knocked out from under him in short order. I learned the hard way the subtle and discreet clues to look for in evaluating a motorcar. *What you see is not always what you get!* Unfortunately, I paid handsomely for this learning experience.

While high performance salespeople project a positive demeanor, they aren't blind optimists. Top pros know that no matter how hard they try and how well prepared they are, they are not going to make a sale every time. This fact is simply a reality of the marketplace. Top pros seem to be mentally prepared for any eventuality.

The high performer may miss one sale, but then goes on and makes three more sales that day to make up for the one that got away. The blind optimist may be so overwhelmed by one "No" that he or she simply can't get going again. This is non-productive, peak-and-valley behavior. Don't allow yourself to be so optimistic that you are emotionally ill-equipped to deal with reality, which invariably deals us rejection, periodic discontent and unavoidable problems along with the joy we are entitled to.

The Reality Optimist

In the second category of mental profiles we find the *reality optimist.* This is the category in which most high performance sales professionals are found.

Reality optimists think rationally when they go out into the marketplace. They say to themselves, "My closing percentage has been X lately. Now I'm going to try to reach 100 percent, but after I've given it my best shot, if I don't make a sale, I'm not going to let that ruin my day."

As a salesperson, you can listen to tapes, you can read books, you can pick the brains of your sales manager – all these things you can do to try to improve your closing percentage. While these factors can have an impact on it, you can never control the behavior of your prospective clients. When a client declines to buy, the reality optimist says to himself, "Okay, I'll get the sale next time!" and then goes right on to the next client. You may not be in control of a client's decision, but you *can* be in control of how you will let rejection affect your attitude.

I have never met a high performance professional who did not have belief and optimism. These individuals are well balanced and organized, so that when they do experience rejection, it's like water off a duck's back. The blind optimist, by contrast, sets himself or herself up for failure due to an inability to handle negative events of the marketplace.

Predictable attitude variance of the *Reality Optimist*

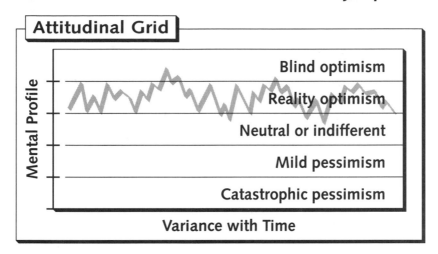

Attitudinal Grid

Mental Profile

Blind optimism

Reality optimism

Neutral or indifferent

Mild pessimism

Catastrophic pessimism

Variance with Time

The Pessimist

In the third category of mental profile we find the *pessimist*. This is the person who cheers everyone up when he leaves the room.

Let me tell you a story about a pessimist. Once a salesman and sales manager were riding down the road together, making calls. The manager said, "Hey, that looks like a great prospect over there! We've never called on that company. Let's make a cold call on them right now."

The pessimistic salesman said, "Might as well skip it. They're lousy prospects. I haven't called on them, but I've heard about them. They're not going to buy anything from us."

The sales manager came unglued. He said, "What kind of attitude is that? If you're going to be successful in the profession of selling, you've got to be positive!"

The salesman replied, "OK boss, I'm *positive* they ain't gonna buy anything from us!"

Given the choice, I can't imagine why anyone would prefer to think negatively, but many do. I believe negative thinking is usually a carelessly-acquired bad habit rather than a well-thought-out decision. My advice is to choose, instead, to vigorously nurture the habit of reality optimism.

Predictable attitude variance of the *Pessimist*

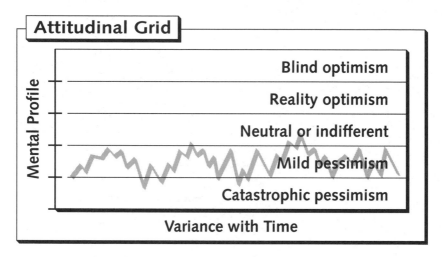

One of the worst attributes of the pessimist is that they limit their own performance by devoting valuable energy to feeling sorry for themselves. The pessimist stacks the cards against himself. The reality optimist not only stacks the cards in his favor; some would say he controls the game. A pessimist who cannot change his or her mental outlook, either through self-induced or management-induced behavior changes, really ought to choose some career other than selling.

Authentic Reality Optimism – The Guru

The best of the reality optimists, in my opinion, is the man known by many as the Patriarch of Positive Thinking, the legendary Dr. Norman Vincent Peale.

I first met Dr. Peale in 1968 as a 23-year-old salesman in the training business who was trying to master my chosen craft. In the following years, as I began to gain momentum as a professional speaker, I met Dr. Peale several times. Each time I saw him, Dr. Peale was gracious and inquired genuinely about me and my career. I will always remember, after my first interaction with Dr. Peale, saying to myself, "If this great man is a product of positive thinking, I'm all for it!" I read his books, listened to his tapes, and became a proponent of his philosophies, which have served me well.

Throughout my career, as I have been on convention programs and appeared at rallies with Dr. Peale, he has continued to be an inspiration to me. Most people talked about what was *wrong,* and it was refreshingly different to run into someone who focused on the positive and preferred discussing what was *right* about things.

Dr. Peale has mentioned that early positive thinker and prolific author Orison Swett Marden was one of his mentors. The positive philosophies of these two men nurture belief, endurance and self-confidence. The classic speech, "Why Positive Thinkers Get Positive Results," still moves me each time Dr. Peale delivers it.

In the late 1970's, I had the privilege of being on the speaker's staff of the Positive Thinking Rallies along with Dr. Peale, Paul Harvey, Zig Ziglar, Dr. Robert Schuller, Art Linkletter, Earl Nightingale, W. Clement Stone, Ira Hayes and Cavett Robert. We staged over 100 Positive Thinking Rallies in a period of about three years, routinely having audiences of 12,000 to 18,000 people.

I remember vividly an evening in Vancouver preceding a rally. Several of us were at dinner in a posh restaurant, including Dr. and Mrs. Peale. He was seated across from me and, after the usual proper greetings, Dr. Peale began to ask how I had been and how my career was progressing. He also solicited my opinion on a couple of items.

I realized, at that moment, that I was not only talking to the guru of positive thinking, but one of the most skilled communicators I had ever encountered. He possesses to a remarkable degree the skill of showing a genuine interest in the person he is talking with, and he always sets up the conversational flow to be positive and authentic, a rare talent which assures good communication and, in most cases, a positive outcome.

Dr. Peale, more than anyone I've ever met, has earned the right to talk about positive thinking and positive results. His longevity and endurance serve as evidence that positive thinking works. A few months ago I was on a program with Dr. Peale who, at age 94, was as positive as ever!

Positive thinking can be a valuable asset. It cannot supplant skill, knowledge and in-depth business acumen in our chosen field, but having a positive attitude will complement and enhance the other skills we develop. It will usually make a great contribution to one's success.

Outlook Affects Outcomes

Our thinking processes control our life, and the image we have of ourselves certainly affects our sales performance. Orison Swett Marden said, "A one-talent person with an overmastering self-faith often accomplishes infinitely more than a ten-talent person who does not believe in himself."

A study conducted several years ago by the University of Chicago supports the theory that your outlook can actually affect your life. The study even revealed that people who are ill but don't think of themselves as sick often enjoy better health than people who are not sick but believe they are!

What causes people to be negative and pessimistic anyway? I am convinced it's their personal choice. Pessimistic people experience what they perceive as a negative event or situation and they choose to become depressed. Perhaps it's a subconscious choice, but that's the result – depression. We are born to win but so often conditioned to lose.

We also *attract* what we think. Negative thoughts produce negative results. On the other hand, positive thoughts are the basis for successful attitudes and successful habits, habits that lead directly to positive results in everything we do.

High performance salespeople realize the importance of keeping a positive, realistic, wholesome frame of reference. They know that positive expectations lead to positive results.

The image and attitude you project are largely developed by habit. If you have the habit of projecting negative thoughts and feelings, reevaluate your behavior and make a conscious effort to change. The payoff could be great.

Remember that fear, doubt, and continuous procrastination are symptoms of the disease called *lack of confidence,* and lack of confidence is nurtured by negative thinking and the absence of an action plan. In the words of the late William James, "It is our attitude at the beginning of a difficult undertaking which, more than anything else, will determine its successful outcome."

The pessimist sees the problems in each opportunity, while the optimist sees the opportunities in each problem. High performance salespeople see themselves as professional problem-solvers. They capitalize on each opportunity with a positive belief in the results they can gain and the people they can help.

You control your mental attitude. If you want to succeed in selling, choose to vigorously nurture the habit of reality optimism. That choice will be a big step in the direction of higher sales performance and greater prosperity.

Successful Application 1

Featuring: Randolph W. Jones, President, Veterinary, Institutional, and Medical Divisions of Henry Schein, Inc.; Port Washington, NY

Submitted by: Michael Brown, Vice President of Sales, Birtcher Medical; Irvine, CA

Shortly after acquiring Deseret Medical, our sales management team at Warner Lambert Corporation was faced with a dangerous morale slump. Old-line salespeople began grumbling about having been "taken over" by a large corporation and having lost the free-spirited, entrepreneurial atmosphere that had made their company a sales-driven success in the past. They were afraid that their skills and individuality would be buried in the quagmire of corporate structure.

I was president of the management unit for sales and was faced with the task of keeping our sales force positive in the midst of the massive changes that they considered so threatening. Complaints ran a wide gamut, from new report forms and procedures to different designs for business cards. The declining situation boiled over when another new policy mandating smaller company cars was introduced, driving the field sales force into a frenzy.

Our management staff listened closely to the sales representatives, then devised a program that we hoped would turn negatives into positives. We felt we had come up with a winner.

We introduced a special six-month sales contest in which each of the top 10 sales achievers in our 96-person sales team would receive a Mercedes Benz on a two-year lease as their company car. Result? An *immediate* turnaround in morale and a 15 percent increase in average per-person sales productivity! We no longer heard complaints about company cars, since such comments would naturally yield a discussion on performance – i.e., get into the top 10 and earn yourself a real prestige company car!

Everyone had a shot at this great incentive program, and it worked. We simply impacted a negative situation with a positive program. The sales force recognized that management was neither too stilted nor too stuffy to have a little fun and that maybe things could actually get better than during "the good old days."

DON'S PARTING THOUGHT

Let's not be the victim of negative happenstance, but the architect of positive circumstance! Those who wish to sing always find a song.

Skill #2

✦✦✦✦✦

Understanding Self–Image Psychology

❝If one advances confidently in the direction of his own dreams and endeavors to live the life which he has imagined, he will meet with a success unexpected in common hours.❞

—HENRY DAVID THOREAU

I stayed broke all the way through college because I couldn't stay out of an airplane. I had aspirations in those days of becoming either a commercial airline pilot or an aircraft salesman.

Back then I was fortunate to be able to do some flying with the father of a close friend. Mike Ryan was a senior captain for Delta Airlines and had over 20,000 hours of flying time.

One day Mike and I were practicing take offs and landings in a small single-engine aircraft at a small airport just outside of Memphis. At the time, I had 30 hours of flying time. Any pilot will tell you that 30 hours flying time is nothing. I was a real greenhorn among aviators.

I was in the left seat at the controls of the aircraft and Mike was in the right seat as my instructor. On one particular pattern, we turned from base leg to final approach to land. When we turned final and I looked at the runway, I knew something was wrong.

The problem was, I didn't know *what* was wrong. We all know that step number one in problem solving is defining the problem, and I was so inexperienced that I couldn't even do that.

In retrospect, I know what was wrong on that day. My problem was that I was coming in "high and hot." That means my altitude and air speed were more than they should have been.

Most experienced pilots know that if you're coming in high and hot, and you lower the nose of the aircraft to decrease your altitude, you will simultaneously increase your air speed unless you know exactly how to handle it – which I did not. If you're coming in high and hot and you don't know how to handle it, there is a fair degree of predictability that you will "land long," as they say (which might be half way down the runway.)

I was very nervous. All I could think about was that at any minute Mike was going to say, "Don, we're not going to make it. Better add power and go around." But he didn't say anything, and his silence made me even more uptight.

There we were, getting closer and closer to the ground, the beads of perspiration popping off my forehead. I finally said to myself, "If Mike doesn't say go around, you will have to land this plane. If and when you do, you better hit those brakes with all the strength you can muster or you're going to have a major problem!" What I didn't want was a crumpled plane at the end of the runway!

Now we're about two feet off the ground and my stress level is high. Meanwhile Mike, with all his hours flying time, is sitting next to me in the right seat with his arms crossed, grinning.

After what seemed an eternity, Mike looked at me, still wearing his big grin, and said, "Don, do you know what the most useless thing in the world is?" What a time for philosophy, I thought. Mike said, "The most useless thing in the world is all that dang runway back there behind us!"

I don't think I'll ever forget that one! And it's a lesson we can apply to our sales careers. We all have some extra runway. Nobody functions at 100 percent of their potential. And that runway represents an opportunity for all of us to grow and be better than we've ever been before. Few things are sadder than opportunities not capitalized on.

The skill we'll be discussing in this chapter deals with where you think you are and where you think you are going with your life and your career. One of the opportunities for growth most often overlooked by salespeople can come through enhancing your self-image and programming your subconscious for greater levels of achievement. In this chapter, we'll look at both your present self image and your *projected* self image.

As a professional salesperson, your skills are valuable. You and those skills are appreciated and considered important by more people than you may have imagined. When *Fortune* magazine surveyed over 2,800 executives and asked what determines our success in business today, more than 85 percent agreed on this characteristic: the ability to confidently sell oneself and one's ideas to others. Your skill is a valuable commodity, and you should feel good about that skill and your demonstrated ability to use it.

Your Present Self Image: A Powerful Force

First let's define the term "present self image." Your present self image is your perception of your strengths and your weaknesses at this time.

The most powerful force you possess is what you say to yourself and truly believe. Positive self-talk not only enhances your present self image; I'm convinced it also expands your productive capacity. It programs you for more action and results!

I hope your present self image is always improving, because it's consistent with the growth process. The image you have had of yourself in the past has delivered you to where you are today, and your self image each day in the future will take you to where you are going to be.

Charisma transplants and success implants still aren't available, so we must look for other avenues to enhance our self image and how we display it to others. I know three excellent ways you can help yourself build a strong self image, and I'll outline them for you now.

One: Write down your personal positive affirmations

In the Goals and Values section of my daily planner, I currently have two written examples of positive affirmations. One is, "I have become a better person than I've ever been, and I continue to grow all of the time." Another is, "My program for optimum health is working. I'm exercising and watching food and nutritional intake better than ever, and I'm getting healthier every day."

Examples of career-related positive affirmations for professional sales-people might be "I am performing my Needs Analysis better each time I do it" or "I am eagerly and successfully making more cold calls than I ever have."

Positive affirmations help you feel better about yourself at present, and they pave the way for growth and progress in the future. Frequently reviewed positive affirmations, whether personal or professional, tend to enhance what you expect and get from yourself. Remember this maxim: "Whatever the mind of man can conceive and believe, it can achieve."

Two: Constantly analyze your strengths and weaknesses

Self assessment is extremely valuable, especially when we also get input from others whose opinions we respect. Successful people identify their human strengths and build on those strengths as their foundation for success. Simultaneously, they identify their personal weaknesses, eliminating as many weaknesses as they can and at least managing those weaknesses that can't be easily eliminated.

Your plan of action for a better life should be built on the foundation of your strengths. Remember, however, that you should never make someone else's opinion of you more important than your opinion of yourself.

Consider this question: If you had achieved your life's goals, professionally and personally, would your behavior and lifestyle be extraordinarily different from what they are right now? If your answer is no, then you are so successful and content that you are the envy of 99 percent of the rest of the world.

But if you answered yes and agreed that your behavior would be extraordinarily different, then consider what behavior patterns have put you where you are right now. Just as important, consider what different behaviors will be required to take you from where you are now to where you truly want to be.

During a recent National Speakers Association address, Les Brown said, "If greatness is possible, then good intentions, good follow-through, even periodic excellence are insufficient." We must diligently and constantly pursue personal excellence. Sometimes significant behavior changes are in order, but in many instances if you feel good about yourself, only minor changes may be needed to get you to where you truly want to be.

What level of success do you currently see for yourself? I once heard a successful general agent of one of the major life insurance companies tell his agents this: "The income level you expect to enjoy should be reflected by the income level of the clients you comfortably converse with." I guess that was his way of asking, "Are you a $40,000 salesperson talking to $40,000 clients, or are you a $200,000 salesperson talking to $200,000 clients?"

Your self image will determine your level of expectations. Mutt Easley, a buddy in high school told me he was sure he'd never get married. When I asked why, he said, "Because any woman who would marry me isn't good enough for me." The guy needed to work on his self image.

Walt Disney said, "The more you are like yourself, the less you are like anyone else, thus approaching uniqueness." Embrace your own individuality. Be yourself, be proud of who and what your are, but never usurp your opportunities to grow.

Three: Have a strong vision to reach toward

What is the rest of your life going to be like? Do you believe you are either destined to succeed or destined to fail in your life? What you visualize is what you will attract.

I submit that your future will be more of a decision than a destiny. Your present thoughts and plans will largely determine your future. And since you control your thoughts and your plans, you control your own future.

"Projected self image" is the phrase I use to refer to your vision of yourself in the future. Your projected self image is comprised of your strengths, your weaknesses, your levels of success and attainment as you imagine them to be at some future point. Intense, detailed visualization is required to program the subconscious mind for a better life and higher sales production.

Your Projected Self Image: Set Your Thermostat!

The power of the human visualization process is truly awesome. Once you program your conscious mind with definitive data from that powerful imagination, your subconscious mind goes to work to make it happen.

Just remember, though, that if the conscious mind never gets the data, it cannot be passed along to the subconscious mind for action. My good friend and fellow speaker, Dr. Tom Haggai, in his excellent book *How The Best Is Won,* said this: "Visions can't be taught. They have to be sought, and at the beginning are usually expensive."

Let's return to my premise that your future as a high performance salesperson is more of a decision than a simple destiny. What can you do to make the right decisions that will result in the vision, then the reality, of high performance? Set your thermostat!

Your most powerful goal-achieving mechanism is your subconscious mind. When you get your vision intact and your goals set in writing, you are postured for achievement.

It may sound like an over-simplification, but programming your subconscious mind is almost as simple as setting the thermostat in your home. You can turn it up or turn it down, but don't ever fool yourself into thinking that you haven't set it! Most people have their thermostats set far too low. They may have let the negative influence of other people psyche them out. Many will go to their graves with their music still inside them because they never turned up their *expectation and achievement thermostat.*

Want $7 Million? Turn Up Your Thermostat!

One of my most gratifying moments as a speaker came recently when I was addressing Healthco International for Healthco Regional Manager Gerry Mundy. Following my three-and-one-half hour sales and personal development seminar, Gerry got up and said to his sales force, "After hearing this program, I'm convinced our $93 million annual goal is too low. Should we go for $100 million?" The salespeople responded resoundingly, so they raised their goal. I learned later that they hit it.

Preparing for Opportunities

As we know, there is much more than luck in high performance selling. Dr. Kenneth McFarland said years ago, "Success can only occur when opportunity and preparation meet." Opportunity without preparation is useless, just as being well prepared but lacking opportunity is of little value.

Sales opportunities are out there in great abundance. Some people wouldn't recognize an opportunity if it bit them on the backside. Other people have a nose and an eye for it. How can you recognize and deal maturely with this thing called "opportunity"?

There are three types of opportunity. First, there is the obvious opportunity. Most people get their share of *obvious opportunities,* though some people who fail will vehemently deny that good opportunities have come their way.

Secondly, there is the *spontaneous opportunity*. We must be alert and ready when this type of opportunity presents itself, because it usually comes along at the least likely moment. Be ready to pounce on a spontaneous opportunity, since it will probably disappear as quietly and unobtrusively as it appeared.

Third and most importantly, there is the *visionary opportunity.* We create these ourselves in our own mind. This is what your projected self image is all about. Imagine great things and you've taken the first step to making great things happen.

The only substantive difference between your yesterdays and your tomorrows will be imagination accompanied by a plan to bring it into the present. Couple imagination with innovation and you have the dynamic duo that can lead to success. Without the two, your future will be like that of 99 percent of the populi – predictable and unexciting.

The Bird's Eye View: Dreams Abounding

Don't have a bug's eye view of the future. Have a bird's eye view. I first heard this analogy used by speaker and friend Heartsill Wilson. See the bigger picture. Think of the people you can help, the lives you can positively touch, the joys you can share with others.

A well-considered projected self image will be the thermostat by which you set your future lifestyle and achievement level. Too many people allow others to set their thermostats. Don't do it. This is no dress rehearsal. Today is the real thing.

Life itself is usually a self-fulfilling prophecy. You can make it work to your benefit rather than to your detriment. I agree with Gregory Baum who said, "Every person is called upon to create his future." Unleash your imagination, key on a noble vision, and go for it!

A New View of Goals

As we think of creating our own future, let me share with you an idea from a fellow speaker. Several years ago I was speaking at an international trade association convention in New Orleans and the speaker preceding me was Jerry Bresser. I had met Jerry a few years earlier at a National Speakers Association convention. Have you ever been to a speaker's convention? Interesting experience. Nobody can get a word in edgewise.

I would like to interject here my philosophy of listening to other speakers. If I am going to invest my time and possibly my money in hearing a speaker, that speaker had better give me one good idea. I require only one, but I require *at least one!* I hope for an idea of such quality that I immediately institute a behavioral change which improves me, my business, or my self-management process in some way.

At any rate, I wanted to hear what Jerry had to say. So I joined his audience, finding a seat near the back of the room. Jerry Bresser wasn't five minutes into his speech when he said something I'll never forget. It was a great line, it has made me a lot of money, and it has had a lasting impact on my thinking. He said, "The most beautiful thing about living in a free enterprise system and working in the great profession of selling is that there is no such thing as an unrealistic goal, there are only unrealistic time frames."

What an inspiring thought! Consider it carefully. No unrealistic goals, only unrealistic time frames means that, given a reasonable period of time, we can make just about anything happen that we truly want to make happen. My question to you is this: What do you want to happen in your future? What is your projected self image? It can be anything you want it to be.

Private Jets and 'Maltuition'

When I first heard this idea from Jerry, I started thinking about it and I want you to know that I really got carried away. I leaned back in my chair, I closed my eyes and all I could think about was how exciting my future could be. Let me tell you more specifically about my thoughts, which were admittedly quite materialistic.

Remember that I am a pilot. Also, I do some 140 appearances a year including speeches and seminars throughout the world. So I often find myself at the mercy of the airlines.

The thought occurred to me, as I let my imagination roam free, that if there is no such thing as an unrealistic goal, only unrealistic time frames, that someday…yes, some great day…I could have my own personal jet! As that idea struck me, I leaned further back in my chair and I mentally pictured myself completing an appearance in one city, out to the airport, climbing into my own small jet, me behind the controls, taxiing out onto the runway, adding power, down that runway, climbing out off into the sunset to the next city. What a vision! I got really excited.

This experience took place in my life just a few years ago and I want you to know that right now, today, you are reading the words of a guy who *still doesn't have a jet!* Have you priced one lately? I can't handle it. Not right now. At this writing, I still have kids in college and I'm suffering from maltuition!

But you know, the exciting thing is that there's nobody who can say that if I want it badly enough, I can't have my own personal jet in two years. Or five years. Or twenty years, or sometime further in the future. You could have one too! Remember: There's no such thing as an unrealistic goal, only unrealistic time frames.

High performance salespeople erase their barriers. They enhance their expectations, they dig a little deeper, they bite the bullet, they make it happen better than they have ever made it happen before. These great things happen because high performance salespeople *expect* great things to happen!

The best way to ensure yourself a high performance future is to expand your projected self image. Demand more of yourself. Stretch your horizons. Insightful and ambitious planning is in essence bringing the future into the present so that you can do something about it today. Don't procrastinate. Make it happen!

Successful Application 2

Featuring: Pat Moynihan, Agent, Allstate Insurance Company; Munster, IN office

Submitted by: Steve Westervelt, Market Sales Manager, Allstate Insurance Co.; Carmel, IN

Most articles on successful women in sales mention the woman's family life just in passing. After telling all about the woman's achievements, the article might say, "And by the way, she's married and has children."

My story starts with my family. Because the biggest question for me has always been how to keep my family intact and keep the same quality of life along the way to being successful in my career. I had to have peace of mind if I was going to be working; I had to know that the children would be taken care of in my absence.

I started working when my youngest child started kindergarten. Back then I had five children between the ages of 5 and 13. My husband Dan worked at a steel mill, and my goal was to make $100 a week to supplement his income.

We began with a simple arrangement. I would work 9 to 5. Dan would work the 4 p.m. to midnight shift and accept no overtime. This way, he would be home if one of the children was ill and also during the summer school break.

My first job was with an insurance agency a half mile from my home, close enough that I could get home quickly if there was an emergency. I worked in that office for five years, then moved to another company to get more experience in outside sales.

While I was at that company, I had an opportunity to interview with Allstate. When I went for that interview, I knew exactly what my goals were:

1. To keep my family going the same way as before.
2. To make more money and use my salary to afford a better way of life for the family. That would include a nicer home in a better neighborhood. I wanted to trade in our camper for a swimming pool in our backyard. And I wanted to help the children through college.
3. To do a good job at the work I do.
4. To further my education past high school.
5. To hire a full-time cleaning person.

It was not one of my goals to become independent. I wanted to be a partner with my husband in maintaining and improving our family's quality of life. When I set my goals, my family was always first. Money and success were on my list, but they were not Number One.

There are certain obstacles a working woman must overcome. I conquered the Guilt Obstacle early. I never felt guilty if I brought home fast food for the family's dinner. I never felt guilty if I couldn't see all the baseball or basketball games, wrestling competitions, or dance classes. I went to events around my work schedule and appointments.

I told myself that I was no longer competing with full-time homemakers or women who worked but knew exactly what time they would be home. I was competing with myself, with my sales from last month compared to this month. As long as I was doing my best and meeting my goals, I would not try to be Superwoman.

Through the years, some of my goals have changed. After 10 years with Allstate, I now plan on making $2,000 a week instead of $100. After I achieved the goal of making *Life Millionaire,* I concentrated on building my casualty business.

My four oldest children have all graduated from college, all with a B average or above. They all worked part-time jobs from the time they were 16 and while they were in college. Everyone of them can cook and do their own washing and ironing because I was not around to do these things for them. I feel good about the life they had growing up, and I know that putting family life first on my list of goals was right for me and for them.

In my work, I have had more success that I ever dreamed was possible. Sure, it has been hard work, but the rewards have made the effort worthwhile.

Thirteen years ago, I had flown in an airplane only once. Now my husband and I have been on Allstate trips to Hawaii, Mexico, the Bahamas, Bermuda, San Francisco and many other places. We have stayed in hotels where the room for one night cost more than we would have been able to spend on a whole week's vacation if I had not worked. We have a house full of prizes that I've won in sales contests. And there's another reward. I've not had to overcome the challenge of how to fix two pounds of hamburger a different and exciting way every night for 20 years!

I think I owe my success, both as a salesperson and as a wife and mother, to deciding what was most important to me, setting goals I could feel good about, having a determined game plan for achievement of those goals, and then working hard to have the things I wanted.

Don's Parting Thought

Most failures use up as much energy failing as successful people do succeeding. Plan your success with a vengeance. Remember, you are probably not as good today as you are going to be someday. Accelerate your achievement rate *now*. There is no reason to wait!

Skill #3

✦✦✦✦✦

Mastering "The Numbers Game"

"If a salesperson does not know statistically and productively exactly where he has been, it will be impossible to intelligently and accurately project where he is going."

—DICK GARDNER

Our ultimate success in selling is determined by the number of contacts we make and how good we are when we get there. Occasionally, obstacles rear their ugly heads and slow us down or get us off track. These are the times that separate the cream of the crop from the rest of the field.

The subject matter in this skill is difficult to learn and internalize but disastrous to ignore. High performance salespeople understand the essence of numbers in the selling profession. They know that nobody makes a sale every time. Maybe you've noticed this common fact of selling. Once in awhile, people say "No." Sometimes they scream it!

Nobody Sells Everybody

Nobody sells everybody. Not even high performance salespeople. Nobody's *that good*. But may I also suggest that there is no salesperson who can miss everybody either. Nobody's *that bad*, especially when you have a great product. Somebody could fumble all over themselves and still sell a great product from time to time. Even a blind hog finds an acorn once in a while.

I don't know what your closing percentage is, but I hope you know. (What is your conversion rate of prospects to confirmed sales?) Get a handle on your closing percentage, and then never let your guard down. Keeping up with your numbers can have a tremendous impact on your level of sales excellence. You can work to convert that closing percentage from 21 to 30 percent, or from 71 to 75 percent. Then you can get it from 75 to 80 percent.

One day while conducting a training session, I made the statement that nobody can sell everybody. A man in the back of the room stood up and interrupted me. He said, "I beg to differ with you, Don. I want you to know that I sell everybody I talk to!"

I thought I misunderstood him. So I walked back and I said, "Pardon me. I'm not sure I understood you correctly." And again he said, "I sell everybody I talk to. I never miss."

I said, "Obviously you aren't making enough calls!" Here was a guy who probably made two calls a month for two months and got lucky four times. Big producers have bigger numbers, and some rejection is always part of their success formula. The fact is, winners know that losing is an integral part of the success process.

It's easy once in a while to lean back and rely 100 percent on leads rather than doing any creative prospecting. It's easy to let our guard down. Remember, success in selling is determined by how many people we talk to and what our closing percentage is when we get there.

The numbers game can be a powerful force for personal growth and motivation. The salesperson who doesn't understand percentages will be utterly discouraged when the door doesn't open for him or her. But a mature salesperson will realize that when a door doesn't open, he or she is still better off than before the call because they are statistically that much closer to a "Yes."

Understanding The Numbers Game

To fully understand this philosophy, let's consider an example. The figures I use here may not fit your selling situation perfectly, but for the sake of simplicity, let's go with them.

Assume that your averages are such that you have to make ten calls to give four presentations…you must give four presentations to close one sale…and your average income is $1,000 per sale. That means, in hard numbers, that each presentation earned you $250, even if they said "No." And each call made you $100, even if they wouldn't listen to you.

Sound absurd? It's not – it's the Numbers Game. If you accept this basic philosophy, you will understand that ultimately you must maximize contact with people who can say "Yes" and be effective when you do. This rational reflection of simple numbers will philosophically serve you very well, because you will never again feel that your success or failure as a professional salesperson is on the line with any one prospect! An understanding of this principle will also keep most of the negative emotion out of your sales activities.

High performers have a special ability to fail successfully. They learn from experience and have no negative hang-ups that their image has been tarnished. They're already too busy on their next achievement to allow that destructive thought line to enter their minds.

Another aspect of the numbers game is to continually analyze your personal sales cycles. Your "sales cycle" is defined as the length of time required to close a sale from the first verbal contact with a given prospective buyer.

High performance salespeople are students of their own sales cycles. These pros are always evaluating their sales process, trying to figure out how they can build trust more proficiently so they can gain closure quicker. The sales cycle numbers they endlessly evaluate pertain to such vital statistics as number of contacts during a given time frame, number of days in the sales cycle, average length of a sales cycle during a three or six month period, average income per sale, percentage of customers who buy repeatedly versus one-time buyers, etc.

Your Best Shot on Every Call

High performance salespeople know their numbers. They know their own track record. This enables them not to be bothered by a periodic "No." If you ever reach a point in your career when you hang your feelings of self worth on one call or one customer, you're on the way out.

Successful salespeople realize that one who gives a half-hearted presentation because he or she is talking to what's perceived as only a "fair" prospect is shooting himself or herself in the foot. The empirical data is in and it supports the premise that extraordinary presentations delivered by salespeople with above-average levels of belief, sincerity and enthusiasm can and often do convert "fair" prospects into buyers! Pros give their best shot to every interaction with every prospect every time.

Does playing the Numbers Game and keeping score in your sales career seem too unimportant to fool with? Have you rationalized the old cliche you heard years ago that good salespeople are lousy on detail? If so, you are playing an old tape and need to erase it or throw it away.

The updated philosophy that high performers live by is this: Keep score. Know your numbers. Don't fall prey to the belief that business is good or bad because of circumstances beyond your control. Buy into the idea that business is good or bad when you *make it* so!

Just as a good pilot would not consider taking off without consulting his checklist, don't try to succeed without having your numbers down cold. If you don't know your numbers, you will ultimately work for less income per hour and per day, and you'll experience much more stress and frustration. And it will be much harder to give it your *best shot* on every call.

If You're Down, Get Up (And Keep Score!)

Many salespeople find that when their productivity is down, for whatever reason, they become "de-motivated." Being de-motivated invariably tends to decrease one's activity level. The salesperson makes fewer calls when he or she should be making more.

If you ever find yourself in another slump, you have to make a choice. You can wallow slovenly in a sea of self-pity, or you can turn on your afterburner and make something happen!

Here's my basic formula for getting out of a slump:

1. Identify the degree to which your business is off. (Example: down 21 percent from this time last month or last quarter)

2. Identify the three or four things that have contributed the most to your success, uniqueness and performance in the past.

3. Develop a plan to immediately get in contact with 21 percent more people than you've been calling on thus far this month or quarter.

4. When making those contacts, concentrate on the positive behaviors and techniques that you identified in Number Two above.

5. Evaluate your existing customer base for additional potential sales, either more volume in like items or the sale of additional products.

Simple? Yes. Does it work? You bet! Try it and I predict you will see immediate improvement. As Orison Swett Marden said, "The stream of plenty will not flow toward stingy, parsimonious, doubting thought. Wealth must be created mentally first."

Know Your Numbers And Fill The Pipeline

If you want to become a high performance salesperson, you *must* do your homework. Know your closing percentage. Know your average size order for each customer's. Research and project the potential of each customer additional business in the future.

When you make prospecting calls, know exactly how many are required to reach your goals. Know at all times the number of Needs Analyses you've performed and have in progress, and the number of sales closed within a given time frame. Until and unless you know your numbers, you will never be able to set goals with a credible procedure or function with maximum confidence.

Remember the pipeline concept. If we know our numbers, and we continue to fill the pipeline (make new calls), good things happen. Sales will result over a given period of time. It's foolproof.

If you know your numbers and give a high-quality presentation every time, you will never be at the mercy of momentary emotion during your career. You'll know what must be done for your next piece of business to come together.

You don't have to be a mathematical expert to profit from this philosophy of high performance selling. Speaking of mathematical experts, did you hear about Clarence? Clarence was the fellow voted "Most Likely to Fail" in high school. You've heard about people who don't know what's happening? Clarence didn't even suspect anything. Yes, he was slow.

Clarence finally graduated from high school at age 24. Only three years away from the 10-year class reunion! But during that three-year period, Clarence got his act together and became a multimillionaire.

Clarence made a fortune in the widget business. He went to his 10-year class reunion in a chauffeur-driven limousine, wearing an impeccably-tailored suit. As soon as he walked inside, people rushed up to him and said, "Clarence, how did you do it? You're the guy voted Most Likely to Fail and now you've got more money than all the rest of us combined."

Clarence grinned sheepishly and said, "Nothing to it. I'm in the widget business. We just buy these little widgets for a dollar, turn around and sell them for four dollars. Man, that's three percent profit!" You and I could use a little of that three percent action, couldn't we?

Most salespeople who have "emotional highs" that they capitalize on also have "emotional lows" that they suffer from. Understanding and practicing the Numbers Game can take the emotional lows out of the picture without destroying our emotional highs!

Successful Application 3

Featuring: Jerry Anzalone, General Sales Manger, Sylvan Pools; Phoenix, AZ office

Submitted By: Don Thoren, President, Thoren Consulting Group; Tempe, AZ

Phoenix is a great market for swimming pools. In fact, there are more pools per capita in the Phoenix area than anywhere else in the world. That's great for those of us in the pool business. What's not so great is that there are about 90 pool companies working my territory! So you'd better believe I have to stay optimistic and stay on my toes.

When it's 110 degrees, everybody is a prospect for a pool. The problem is they are not all financially qualified. I learned years ago not to pre-judge prospects. This day and age, you never know who can afford one and who can't. Just when you think you've got it all figured out is when an old boy in beat-up boots and torn jeans pays you with a big stack of hundred dollar bills. Our philosophy is simply to talk to as many people as we can and do everything we can to sell them.

Awhile back I was in the office late one afternoon doing some paperwork. It was about 5:30, and everyone had gone but me and one salesman. He was new on our team and still learning how to sell.

A call came in from a woman who wanted to know if someone could come by her house that evening and explain about buying a pool. I said, "Let me check to see if a salesman is free, and I'll call you back."

"John," I called to the salesman, "why don't you go out and sell this lady a pool?" He checked his chart. Nothing scheduled. Then he said to me, "Where's the call coming from? What's her neighborhood?"

"South Phoenix," I replied.

John's face fell. "Those people down there can't pass for credit," John said with a grimace. "They're low income. They can't afford swimming pools." Here is a prospective pool buyer calling us and John is trying to find something wrong with the opportunity!

Well, I can tell you that John's response wasn't what I like to hear from our salespeople. Pessimism has killed many a sale, primarily because the salesperson gives less than 100 percent effort. I could see that John had already killed this sale in his mind.

I put the lady on hold, turned to John and said, "Some people live in South Phoenix who aren't low income. And some low income people do buy swimming pools. But nobody sells swimming pools when they negatively pre-judge a prospect."

John heaved a sigh. I could tell he already believed that this sales call would be a big waste of his time. I knew if I sent John out with that attitude, he would fail. During my 29 years in sales, I've learned that, if you don't create a desire in someone to buy something, he or she won't buy. And you can only create that desire if you're optimistic about your chances. It's all in your attitude and your willingness to give every sales opportunity your best effort.

I decided to go on the sales call with John. I closed down the office, and we both got in John's car to drive out to South Phoenix.

John was new to sales, but he wasn't new to the swimming pool business. Actually, he knew the business quite well because he had owned a pool company that went bankrupt. John knew all the technical details about how pools work, but he lacked the ingredients of a good salesman. Especially a positive attitude.

As we drove toward South Phoenix, I kept telling John, "We're going to sell a pool here today. We *are* going to sell a pool here today…" I slapped my hand on the dashboard in rhythm to the positive chorus I was chanting.

We entered the neighborhood where our prospect lived. Graffiti was everywhere, covering walls and fences. The houses were small, most of them were run down, and they all looked a lot alike. But we found the right address.

Our knock was answered by an attractive woman in her early 30's. We stepped inside, and it was like entering Shangri La. Neat and beautiful. You could have eaten off the floor.

The woman told us that she had been born in the house across the street. Her hard-working parents had bought this house for her. It was paid for. No mortgage. I was sure she could see my eyes brighten with every sentence she spoke.

I told her that since she owned the house with no mortgage, financing should be easy to arrange. "I'm not going to finance it," she said. "I'm going to pay cash."

She made a pitcher of lemonade, and we talked about the design of the pool she wanted. I told her we could give her an estimate to compare with other prices. Her response should have taught John more about negative pre-judging than any lecture I might have prepared.

She wasn't planning to talk to any other company, she said. She had called five other pool companies that day before calling us. As soon as she gave them her name and address, they started backing up.

The first two said they would mail credit applications and come out after the credit cleared. The next two said they were too busy and would send someone later. The fifth company said they never came to her area at night.

"You were the only person who responded instantly, without prejudice or reservation," she said. "I felt then that you'd be a good person to work with. Now I'm convinced." We had blitzed the competition and had this sale in the bag, all because we had an open mind and a desire to sell a pool to anybody we could!

By 10 p.m., we had signed a contract at full price, no discounts. As we got back into the car, John was already counting his commission. On the way back, John talked about how we had gotten lucky. I disagreed. "We sold that pool because of a positive attitude and a willingness to make one more call," I maintained.

Not too long after that day, John left us to go with another pool company. He said the other company provided "better leads." I guess John didn't learn the good lesson that was there for him to learn in South Phoenix. A positive attitude and going for the numbers can help you succeed. It works when you have good leads, and it even works when you don't. You've got to believe you can succeed on every call.

Before every call, I tell myself this: "The best thing that can happen is that I'm going to make this sale! And the worst thing that can happen is that I'm going to get in some very good practice."

DON'S PARTING THOUGHT

Take care of your numbers and
your numbers will take care of you!

Skill #4

◆◆◆◆◆

Getting "Up" for High Performance

❝There is a legend that, when God was equipping man for his long life journey of exploration, the attendant good angel was about to add the gift of contentment and complete satisfaction. The Creator stayed his hand. 'No,' He said, 'if you bestow that upon him, you will rob him forever of all joy of self-discovery.'❞

—ORISON SWETT MARDEN
(CIRCA 1917)

I'm convinced that high performance salespeople have some special attributes that make a big difference in their sales production. Simply stated, they develop an impenetrable attitude for success.

They are people with a hunger for knowledge. They keep themselves open to new ideas. They're innovative, always looking for better ways to sell their products and services. They get excited about solving problems and satisfying needs.

On the other hand, many salespeople out there limit their professional growth by the fact that they have upstairs, in that human computer between their ears, a lot of garbage. They are still carrying around with them a collection of data that is outdated and useless. I'll tell you a little story to illustrate my point.

Cooking With The Latest Technology?

A couple was having a party, and the next door neighbors came over a little early to lend a hand with preparations. Betty slipped into the kitchen to help Margaret.

"Almost ready," Margaret said. "All I have to do is take the ham out of the oven, slice it and arrange it on the serving tray." She motioned for Betty to have a seat and keep her company.

As Margaret took the ham from the oven, Betty said to her, "I've noticed that when you cook a ham, you always cut off both ends of the ham. Why? With the cost of meat today, that's a pretty expensive technique."

Margaret stopped, looked at Betty, looked at the ham, and then said, "You know, I've never really thought about it. The truth is, I learned everything I know about cooking from my mother, and she always sliced off both ends of the ham. But your question makes me curious. I think I'll call Mother right now and ask her why." So Margaret telephoned her mother.

"Why, Margaret," her mother said, "you know that everything I know about cooking I learned from grandma – and she always sliced off the ends of the ham before cooking it."

Now Margaret's curiosity was really stirred up. She forgot about finishing the hors d'ouvres. The party was no longer on her mind. She just wanted to talk to grandma.

The phone rang a few times, but finally grandma heard it. "Grandma!" Margaret exclaimed. "I've got an important question for you. My neighbor Betty asked me why I sliced off the ends of the ham before cooking it. I told her I did it because mother always did, and mother says she always did it because you did. So I'm asking you, the expert, why do you slice off the ends of a ham before cooking it?"

And Grandma said, "Gosh, Margaret, I quit doing that 25 years ago. But I used to do it *because my pan was too small!*"

The "Garbage" We Carry Around

Are you, like Margaret, still carrying around garbage in your head? Are you needlessly hauling around excess baggage in the form of outdated sales ideas and preconceived limits on your abilities? Are you doing things because that's the way someone said they should be done or because that's the way they've always been done?

If you want to be a higher performer, you must throw out the garbage. Knock down the barriers. Get rid of the hangups. You've got to believe in yourself and your abilities and use the latest proven skills.

Which came first, the chicken or the egg? That's an age-old question that's fun to consider. But let me ask you a similar question that's more pertinent to our topic: Are high performance sales people *up* because they are good…or, are they *good* because they are up?

The word "up," in this usage, means optimistic, confident, filled with meaningful expectations. In sales terms, we're talking about salespeople who consistently possess and display a positive, refreshing attitude toward career and task.

By "good," we mean skilled salespeople who are above average and consistent in personal sales performance. You've probably heard of the 80/20 rule – that in the average sales organization, 20 percent of the salespeople make 80 percent of the sales, and the other 80 percent of the salespeople make 20 percent of the sales. High performance salespeople are among that 20 percent who make things happen. They throw their garbage out in a timely manner and keep themselves primed for consistent above-average production.

"Up" And "Good": The Snowball Effect

Back to our question: Are high performance salespeople up because they are good, or good because they are up? I submit that the answer to both these questions is Yes!

High performance pros stay up because they are good. And being good helps them to stay optimistic, confident, up. These two constructive traits feed on each other. There is a geometric or snowball effect when you are both up and good that causes sales to soar.

When performance is good, we have reason to be "up." But have you noticed that things don't always go just right when you're selling? This is a test! High performers stay up even when roadblocks get in their way. How do they do it?

I believe that for high performance professionals, being up is a developed habit. It's a decision you make, not destiny or an event that just happens in your life.

Getting ourselves up is easier some days than others. But the basic axiom remains the same: We have within ourselves the power to decide whether we are going to be a success or a failure. Motivation is an internalized power we give ourselves, as a gift, or deny ourselves to a fault.

If you want to stay up and good, momentum will play a strategic role. Momentum, whether it's positive or negative, impacts significantly on your production and ultimately your income.

Have you heard the old adage that when salespeople are good, they get better, and when they are bad, they get worse? Well, I agree with the first part of that statement. When they're good, they often do get better. However, when salespeople have a poor sales record or their performance is down, they don't have to get worse. Positive momentum is something we create for ourselves with desire and determination. Make the decision to get positive momentum and keep it.

Believe And Achieve!

A salesperson with marginal belief in self, product, service and end result for the customer can be quarterbacked out of that belief by any skilled communicator.

One reason above-average salespeople perform consistently is because their strong belief is unswerving. When belief doesn't waiver, performance seldom does. Strong belief enables a salesperson to comfortably give each call and each presentation his best shot. He never compromises the quality of his presentation; he knows if a prospect is worth investing time in, that prospect is worth the best presentation he has to offer! The pros never negatively pre-judge prospects. They know that if they simply perform at their best in every interaction, the law of averages and the laws of success will take great care of them.

Remember, your behavior is the result of your belief system. What you truly believe has impact on your behavior and results each day. Believe you are a winner, work for a great company, sell great products and services, and you will develop a stronger work ethic and higher income than ever.

Disciplined Self-Motivation

I don't know what motivates you, but I hope that you know. Once you discover which motivational factors really excite you, you can use them to stay inspired, active and productive. Knowing what is important to you, what fires you up and gets you excited, is a major step toward your destination of greater success.

Notice I said it's a step; it's not the entire journey. In order to be truly successful, you need more than motivation alone. You must add to motivation the quality of self-discipline. Self-discipline will give you the desire and commitment to stay the course if you lose a little of the original excitement that inspired you.

Take a sheet of paper and, for the next several days, write down those things that turn you on and turn you off. Maybe you don't want another plaque to hang on the wall or a trip or even a car. Maybe you want a jet or a condo! Note the things that cause you to want to succeed, because once you have clarified what motivates you, it's likely you will develop a stronger sense of mission in your life. Ask yourself: Why am I working?

What am I determined to achieve? Use your turn-ons as a constant source of power and energy, and treat the turn-offs as plagues to avoid.

For some people, it's as basic as keeping the wolves away. The more sophisticated person may be motivated by the desire to experience life to the fullest. Well-thought-out, significant goals serve as one of the most powerful sources of motivation. They intensify our vision and propel us to action.

Spend some time now, in the next few days, thinking about what salary you'd like to earn, what position you'd like to hold, what you'd like to achieve in the future. Then let the things you dream of become the impetus that keeps you motivated.

What you could have done, or should have done, in the past is now absolutely immaterial. The question is: What are you doing about today to make it better than your yesterdays? What is your plan for tomorrow?

Energy Decisions

Have you ever had an occasion when you were dog-tired, only to become totally energized when an appealing option came along? Fatigue can disappear when someone calls for an exciting golf outing or a tennis match.

We make important *energy decisions* daily. The energy we have to pursue a task is based on our mental perception of payoff or pleasure to be gained. Don't fool yourself – energy is largely a head game! The more skilled you are and the more determined you are to achieve a written sales goal, the easier it is to find the energy to go for it.

Several years ago when "A Chorus Line" was a new Broadway production and getting rave reviews, my wife and I got off a London-to-New York flight, quickly checked into our hotel, changed clothes, and went excitedly to the theatre. We decided to worry about sleep later. We were tired enough to drop, suffering from jet lag and a grueling trip, but we were energized with anticipation. And we enjoyed every moment of that great musical.

Unlike time, energy is not a commodity of which we have a set daily amount at our disposal. Positive, rejuvenating attitudes, coupled with character, discipline and various incentives, can renew your energy supply anytime.

Motivation Defined

The best definition of motivation I've ever heard came from the late Bob Bale, who was a true pro at understanding motivation in the sales environment. He was not only skilled and renowned in addressing sales organizations, but he was also one of the most talented humorous speakers who ever graced a platform.

I was having lunch with Bob one day back in 1975 at our National Speaker's Association Convention in Phoenix, and I said, "Bob, since you know so much about sales motivation, tell me your definition of motivation."

He said, "Don, I'll be happy to share it with you, and you can use it until you find one better." That was years ago, and I haven't found one half as good, much less one any better.

Bob Bale said, "Motivation is an idea, emotion or need from within a person which incites or impels that person to act or not to act." What does that definition imply? It implies a major point: that all motivation is self-motivation.

Motivation must come from within. It's got to be internalized if it's going to work, if it's going to last. We cannot rely on other people to motivate us. It's great if and when it periodically happens, but our primary motivation must come from deep within ourselves.

From time to time, you will be exposed to people who set positive examples and inspire you to want to succeed at some particular project or goal. But don't count on that happening frequently. Don't depend on others to jump-start you into action. Plan on internalizing your own impetus of motivation.

Tennis In Atlanta Anyone?

A few years ago I was conducting a management seminar in Atlanta. It was a morning program, and I was in the ballroom early setting up my visuals and preparing for the presentation. I thought I was alone, but I glanced up and noticed that coming down the center aisle toward me was a guy wearing a tennis shirt and shorts, sweatband around his forehead, tennis racket in hand. I certainly didn't assume that this guy was an early arrival for my seminar. Then I learned that I was indeed the first stop on his itinerary that morning.

He walked up to me and said, "You must be Don Hutson."

"Right," I said, thrusting out my hand.

"Hello, Don," he said. "I'm one of the branch managers with the company you're addressing this morning. I don't know if you're aware of it or not, but attendance at your session this morning is not mandatory. It's voluntary, and I'm not coming."

I was a little surprised. I said, "That's fine if you don't choose to come to the session, but you must have some reason for dropping in to see me this early in the morning. I'm curious to know what it is."

He said, "Don, I've only been in management two years, but I've got my act together in my branch. I have good people, I'm a competent manager, we're ahead of plan, things are going pretty well. I only have one problem in my entire sales organization, and I thought I'd come ask you this question, get your answer, and get out of here and still make my tennis date at 8:30."

I said, "I'll help you if I can. That's the business I'm in. What's your question?"

He said, "All I want to know is...how can I motivate my people?"

I said, "Oh, is *that* all you want to know? My answer is, you can't. Any other questions?"

Well, he was not ready for that answer. I wanted to be cordial, but I also wanted to be emphatic about where I was coming from. So I said, "We're going to spend two to three hours this morning talking about employee motivation. I can't give it to you in a sentence or two."

He elected to stay for the seminar. He was rather ill-attired, but that didn't keep him from listening, taking notes, and getting into the program. And what I told him, as well as the others in attendance, was this: In selling, you can't motivate anyone but yourself. A good salesperson or a good manager, however, will invariably equip himself or herself to create positive environments in which others are more likely to motivate themselves to the desired action. All motivation is ultimately *self-motivation!*

Motivation Through Personal Empowerment

You can't directly motivate your prospects to buy. Managers do not directly motivate salespeople to sell; it is an indirect process. Motivation has got to come from within. That's the good news: personal empowerment is a decision we make.

A few years ago my seatmate on an airliner said, after we had exchanged names and greetings, "Oh, you're Don Hutson, that motivational speaker." I said, "Yes, I suppose that's me." (I prefer the moniker "sales and management trainer.")

Then he said, "Well, I'll tell you what – I don't believe in motivation." When I asked why, he replied, "Because it doesn't last." That's when I said, "Well, a bath doesn't last either, but it's a good idea to take one once in a while!"

Motivation doesn't have to last forever to be of value. The longer it does last, the better. And the way we get personal motivation to last longer is to internalize it.

Though the *hype* we periodically experience is often temporary, the decisions we make while the hype is present can last a lifetime. I will debate anyone on the lasting benefits and results of quality motivation.

High performance salespeople do not wake up in the morning with one eye open and one eye closed and cobwebs in their head, moping around saying, "I wonder who's going to motivate me today?" They are not at the mercy of an external force of motivation. They create their own motivation!

High performers don't wait for the phone to ring. They don't wait for their ship to come in. They don't wait for the right prospect to come along. They don't wait until the weather's just right. High performers rev up their engines and make it happen themselves!

Put Yourself in Charge

My close friend, professional speaker Ty Boyd, says, "Everybody has more notes on their horn than they're playing." I agree. We all have lots of room to grow and excel beyond previous achievement levels, provided we tap into a more powerful source of motivation.

Two factors are involved in motivation: *direction* and *intensity*. Direction means which way you're headed. It can be toward your goal or away from it. It can be positive or negative. It can be well thought out or spontaneous. It can be right, or it can be wrong.

The intensity of motivation can be high or low. Energy and enthusiasm are characteristics of people with high intensity motivation. These are the people who really get with the program. You'll find people with low intensity sitting on the sidelines, complacently watching others take the lead, never making that one more call, reading that one more book, or stretching into one more advanced level of sales excellence.

There's another way of considering motivation. Your motivation will be either discipline-based or momentum-based. The foundation of both is skill. But with discipline-based motivation, you're in control and your direction is positive. You're calling your own shots.

With momentum-based motivation, you are largely at the mercy of the marketplace. Momentum-based motivation means that you are less in control of your life and your level of success. The peaks can be good when business is good, but when business is marginal, the valleys can be deep. Most high performance salespeople rely on discipline-based motivation rather than counting on momentum or some wonderful unanticipated event to inspire them to action.

All physiological and medical attributes being equal, your personal energy level will be the result of the motivational factors, premises, and actions you have internalized. Physical action comes principally from mental discipline and determination, and a lack of physical action is usually the result of laziness, apathy, and the lack of personal inspiration required to create a viable success plan. It is your creative thrust that keeps you alive and productive.

Your disciplined self-motivation, when properly internalized, is like a wound-up spring, driving you toward your goals. Disciplined self-motivation will give you the torque and irrepressible natural urge to get great things done.

Be a self-starter with and through self-motivation. Don't wait for someone else to set the pace. Be open to inspiration. Translate thought into action. Don't be immobilized with procrastination; don't be disheartened when something doesn't run smoothly.

An extraordinarily high intensity of motivation can, to some extent, compensate for lack of talent. But imagine what you can do when you have an abundance of both! Your disciplined self-motivation can become a springboard for accomplishment.

Successful Application 4

Featuring: Candace Welsh, Realtor and Vice President, John R. Wood & Associates; Naples, FL

Submitted By: John R. Wood, President, John R. Wood & Associates (and Past President of the National Association of Realtors); Naples, FL

A positive attitude isn't something that just happens for Candace Welsh. She works at staying "up." And working at being positive has paid off handsomely for Candace since she began her real estate career in 1983.

"I start every morning with my Affirmation Cards," said Candace. "These are positive, inspiring quotes and ideas that I've written down on index cards. Then, on my way into the office, I listen to motivational tapes. By the time I get to work, I'm enthusiastic and excited about the day ahead."

After working in real estate for only a few years, Candace Welsh is already a success. Starting with no clientele and on straight commission, Candace rose quickly in her field so that today she is vice president of her company, serves on the board of directors and is enjoying an impressive income. She attributes much of her success to the positive habits and time management ideas she has learned listening to motivational and sales skills tapes.

"I've heard that the average salesperson spends nearly 500 hours a year in their automobile," said Candace. "If I'm in my car 500 hours a year, I probably spend at least 50 percent of that time listening to tapes. The only time I'm not listening to tapes is when I have clients with me."

As part of her focus on time management, Candace keeps a daily planning book. Each day is divided into four columns, one each for Appointments, Day's Goals, Things To Do in Extra Time and a daily record of Events or Ideas Worth Remembering. "I never end a day without having the next day's appointments, goals and 'extra time' activities recorded in my planning book," she said.

Candace's positive outlook has even led her to see a past failure as a blessing.

"I was a professional tennis player and licensed teaching pro with the United States Professional Tennis Association until nine years ago," she said. "My husband is still a tennis pro. Back then, we owned our own tennis club. Real estate was just a hobby. We'd buy houses, fix them up and sell them. Then the tennis club went broke."

Experiencing business failure made Candace determined to learn the skills of real estate sales and become a success. Along with technical sales knowledge, Candace learned about the importance of a positive attitude and positive habits in selling.

"Having a positive attitude not only keeps me motivated and energized, but clients pick up on it too," Candace said. "They enjoy doing business with someone who's 'up' and excited. And your fellow workers also like to be around someone who is enthusiastic about their work every day."

The positive habits that bring her success in her work also go home with her every night now, Candace said. "I've learned that being positive can make every aspect of life better. I now practice goal setting, time management, and positive thinking in my work habits, in taking care of myself with good nutrition and exercise, and in my personal life. It's all tied into the balanced life concept. Being 'up' inspires you to learn new skills and make your life better too."

DON'S PARTING THOUGHT

The price one must pay for sales excellence is not a monetary one. It is a price we pay in the development of skills. The quest for success begins with mastery of the attitudinal process.

Skill #5

✦✦✦✦✦

Dealing with Rejection, Stress and Worry

❝There is no failure except in no longer trying. There is no defeat except from within, no really unsurmountable barrier save our own inherent weakness of purpose.❞

—ELBERT HUBBARD

We all know that every normal person loves the successes that the marketplace and life afford us. The big question is, how do you respond to the periodic failures that are part of the selling profession? I believe more potentially great sales careers have been destroyed by the poor handling of negative events and unsatisfying sales scenarios than practically any other cause.

High performance salespeople know exactly how to handle the rejection, the discouragement, and the worries that present themselves in selling. Do you? Let me give you an example of the kind of negative events I believe are the downfall of many salespeople.

One day you go out into the marketplace and make a call, giving a presentation in a one-on-one situation with a decision maker. The prospect is glad to see you. You are saying all the right things in all the right places, and your prospect is saying all the right things in the right places too. (Maybe you've noticed that *some* prospects don't know their lines!)

So you are ten minutes into the visit and you already have that gut-level feeling that you're going to make this sale. You've got your prospect totally involved. He's taking notes, he's asking questions. You identify his needs, you give an appropriate and professional presentation, and you ask him for his business. At which time he says, "This sounds terrific! My answer is yes."

You write it up and you're feeling great. You leave with check in hand, name on the dotted line. You walk back to your car on top of the world.

Then you drive off down the road saying things like, "Boy, was I good back there!" In sales training we refer to this as "positive self talk." And that's good. Positive affirmations are great for our self image.

So you keep passing along little compliments to yourself. Maybe you say, "Boy, I was so good back there that I think I will go out and unleash a bit more of this raw power and talent on some other unsuspecting prospect! I'm so fired up that I think it's time for me to make some good old cold calls."

How Could He Say No?!

Do you like to make cold calls on strangers? It can be a challenging and refreshing experience, but admittedly there is a higher probability of rejection here.

Well, you go out and make a cold call on a stranger. You get eyeball to eyeball and you turn on the same raw power and talent but…this prospect is not glad to see you. He stands there gaping at you like a tree full of owls. He keeps looking at his watch, treating you as an interruption. It's not going well, but you learned many years ago when you got into sales that we never pre-judge the quality of a prospect and the outcome of sales calls. When we are eyeball to eyeball with anyone, even if we're given only marginal response, it is our professional responsibility to never ever get psyched out. It's discipline, it's professionalism that calls on us to never compromise the quality of a presentation. We give it our best shot every single time.

So there you are, digging deep, a few beads of perspiration popping up on your forehead, you're working really hard…but he's not buying.

Then you say to yourself, "I'm not leaving here today without trying to close this individual. I've at least identified a few of his needs and I want to get some kind of a reading." And with that, you say to your prospect, "Well, tell me sir, do you think we might be able to do some business?"

Then this individual leans toward you, points his index finger about an inch from your right nostril and says, "NO!"

Have you ever experienced this phenomenon? It's known as rejection. Not nearly as much fun, is it? Now comes the big question – one of the biggest questions of your sales career – and that question is: How are you going to handle that "No"?

Rejection Response

High performance salespeople handle a "No" with great professionalism. Rejection for them is like water off the proverbial duck's back. They categorize that experience, classify it, plug it into their numbers so they always know where they are, but they never ever let it psyche them out. They promptly make their next call, carrying no negative emotional baggage with them.

There are some people (usually lower producers) who, when rejected, let the experience really get to them. They wear their hearts on their sleeves and take the negative response personally. They don't want to talk to anybody the rest of the day. Maybe for a week or two. A couple of careers, perhaps. They'll do anything to avoid an interaction with another human being. Why do you think movie theaters are open in the daytime? They're for salespeople who have just been rejected! I know, because I've been seeing them there for years. Well, not in recent years – I finally got over that.

All joking aside, rejection is a great test. How are you going to handle it? The high performance pro goes out and promptly gives another presentation, and that next presentation is as good as any he or she has ever given! High performers have a great handle on rejection. Poor producers invariably delay their next call and display only half-hearted conviction when they get there.

How do *you* react after rejection? You're driving away, headed down the road with the word "No" ringing in your ears. You're no longer fired up. In fact, you're down pretty low. Again you may be involved in a conversation with yourself, but this time it's what we call "*negative* self talk." Remember, *you* control your response and should never let it get you down.

Incidentally, negative self talk is very counter-productive, but we do it nevertheless. We say things like, "It must have been me." We take it personally when it is very seldom a negative directed at us personally. We have probably all participated in such behavior from time to time, but let's vow never to do it again.

It Was "His" Fault!

Or maybe you blame and impose guilt on the individual you talked to. Maybe you say to yourself something like, "That turkey was unbelievable. How can anybody have such a lack of respect for my professionalism, my product line, my ability through my company to provide great personal service and great value? That guy was *weird!*" Or maybe you weren't that generous in your description of him, right? Ever use any parental reference in your description of a non-buyer?

Let me give you a word of caution: Never take rejection personally. Take it professionally. Discouragement and the accompanying stress are heavy burdens to carry, so don't! High performance salespeople respond to a "No" with mature confidence, knowing that it doesn't mean "No" forever. It just means "No" for this moment. Sidney Harris says, "The major difference between winners and losers is that winners lose more than losers do!" Yes, rejection is very much a part of the success process.

Never Give Up!

If you are the type that folds his tent and goes away after the first "No," you might want to look at a less-threatening career path. Few people achieve great things by relying on their first attempt for success. Though I must admit that I was reminded of the rebuttal to this philosophy when recently I visited with my friend Brian Tracy, who said, "If at first you don't succeed, Skydiving is not for you!" (I've always wondered why anyone would want to jump out of a perfectly good airplane.)

You've probably heard the old adage that you aren't beaten until you give up. The late J. Douglas Edwards used to say that many top-producing salespeople make the majority of their sales after their fifth attempt to close. That means they experience at least four times more rejection than success in the sales process! Later in this book, I'll tell you how to make closing easier and more pleasant for all involved. Nevertheless, we can never hang our emotions and our feelings of well-being on any one prospect who chooses to say "No" at any one moment.

One of the things professionals have in common is a special brand of persistence. We're not talking about the simple "keep knocking on the door until it opens" kind of persistence. That's important too, but so is another kind of persistence.

A recent survey done by an association of sales executives concluded that 80 percent of the new sales in this country were made by 10 percent of the salespeople. And that survey shows the importance of the kind of persistence that top salespeople show when working on their own selling methods. This includes psychologically handling negative events without long-term negative results.

What "Not" To Do When You Are Rejected

When a prospect says "No," don't be mad at your prospect. That is irrational and counter-productive behavior. It will psyche you out of high performance on your next calls. My suggestion is to develop the discipline of blowing it off. Forget it.

One specific behavior I recommend after rejection is, when you return to your car, the airliner, etc., try closing your eyes, expressing thanks for the good things in your life, inhale deeply, and slowly imagine that the forthcoming slow exhale is your means of ridding yourself of the stress, negative feelings, and emotions associated with that non-buying prospect.

The next step is to make another call right away. Don't wallow around in the negative remembrance of that last call. Positive, confident activity is the antithesis and combatant of rejection and the self pity that often accompanies it.

Something Else Not To Do…

I once had a salesman who, whenever he missed a sale, would go read a sales book and try to figure out what he did wrong. Now you've gotta know that I'm in favor of *everyone* reading sales books, but not at 2 p.m. on Tuesday afternoon during valuable selling time! Reading and studying sales skills is for some time other than productive sales time. As Wesley Halliburton once told his son, the prolific writer Richard Halliburton, "By constant introspection, you can prove yourself a hopeless imbecile."

My recommendation is healthy introspection and skill-honed thought during your personal development periods. The value of the introspective process is largely determined by the timing and sincerity of its intent. Frankly, if I ever devoted time to in-depth introspection during selling time, the guilt and stress I would feel would overwhelm any potential for gain. Introspection can be valuable in reasonable doses; just remember that it is best suited for the non-selling hours.

Keeping Your Head On Straight

Do you know that all psychological problems tend to be derived from some form of self pity? Why don't you make a decision, right now, that you will never ever again participate in self pity. It is one of the most destructive human emotions you can feel. It can be a disastrous line of thought for salespeople, so avoid the temptation to gravitate into self pity when you lose a sale.

Sometimes there are positives, sometimes there are negatives in the marketplace. One problem is, we take a lot of the positives for granted, do we not? Learn to be thankful for the positive forces in the marketplace. Learn to recognize and count your blessings.

What, Me Worry?

The experts who have researched the topic of worry have determined that 95 percent of the things we worry about never happen. So don't drag yourself into needless despair. Mary Crowley used to say that worry is the misuse of imagination.

Let me share with you two ideas from experts about the avoidance of negative thoughts and worry. My friend Ed Foreman says, "Worry is nothing more than negative goal setting." We often reinforce negatives in our mind. Repeated visualization of a negative event can create the very disaster we would like to avoid.

The late Charlie Cullen used to say, "Don't use up vital selling time with worry. Every few weeks, appropriate an hour at the end of the day for 'worry time.' Don't dwell on it too long; just get all of the worrying and negative thinking out of your system so you can get back into a positive selling style."

To worry in an all-consuming manner uses up a tremendous amount of energy that we could direct positively. Worry seldom solves any problems. Henry Ward Beecher once said, "It's not work that kills men, it is worry. Work is healthy; it's hard to give a person more work than he can bear. Worry is rust upon the blade."

The Value of Negative Events

Orthopedic surgeons say that when a broken bone heals, often the mended bone is stronger than before it was broken. Maybe there is value in our experiencing negative events, provided we handle the experience properly. Yes, we grow stronger in the crucible of adversity. Learn and benefit from negative events, but don't surrender to them or dwell on them for too long a period.

Experiencing adversity, defeat and periodic rejection is the process by which individuals attain greatness. As Paul Harvey once told a group of salespeople at a convention where I was also a speaker, "Our ultimate success in selling is not determined by how much crow we can eloquently dish out. It's determined by how much crow we are willing and able to eat."

Remember that when Babe Ruth was the home-run king of baseball, he was also the strike-out king! What is the threshold for negative events in your career? I contend the greater your threshold for negatives, the more success you will ultimately enjoy.

Don't allow rejection, stress and worry to be a barrier to your success. Remember these inspiring words from Ross Mars: "Take away my capacity for pain, and you rob me of the possibility of joy. Take away my ability to fail, and I would not know the meaning of success. Let me be immune to rejection and heartbreak, and I would not know the glory of living."

Stress Management For The Sales Professional

Is stress something that *happens* to us? Or do we *cause* it to happen? I think the answer is a little of both.

Have you ever felt your blood begin to boil because the line you're in at the supermarket or the airport ticket counter turns out to be the slowest-moving line? Have you ever pushed the elevator button in rapid-fire fashion, even though you knew one push would do just as well?

Have you ever come out of a doctor's office with your blood pressure severely elevated because the long wait made you mad? Have you ever listened to a prospect's totally unrealistic demands or expectations – and wanted to choke him?!!

We all know stress is not good for us. It can affect our health. It can diminish our energy. And it can dilute our sales performance.

If you're suffering from stress, it can compound any other problems you may be experiencing in your sales career. A short fuse can make you lose sales and lose customers.

The building of trust and the experiencing of stress are often inversely proportional in the salesperson/prospect relationship. High performance salespeople know how to keep trust high and stress low. One way they do this is to always be sure that they are part of the client's solution, not one of his problems. High performance salespeople work to minimize their own stress level in order to facilitate their relationship with a client.

One way you can lessen stress is to concentrate on keeping things in perspective. When you start to feel tension and anger rising, ask yourself: Is this situation really worth losing my composure over or losing a sale over? Is it worth losing an hour to a headache? Worth ruining my day?

Winston Churchill amazed people with his ability to ignore certain matters and yet pay great attention to others. He appeared to be forgetful and disorganized until something significant arose. Then he was acutely attuned to the most minute detail. "Winny" knew how to control stress by putting things in perspective. Great salespeople do the same.

Pain But No Gain

Burnout is a different issue. I define burnout as negative feelings and emotions that result from expending considerable energy with a perceived low payoff. In other words, burnout is working hard over a period of time without gaining the expected rewards or gratification. This can become a burden that is difficult to carry.

Burnout occurs when people simply feel used up. It can happen in relationships with clients, co-workers, or family members. When you work hard for an extended period of time with only marginal results and without getting any "strokes," you're a candidate for burnout.

One solution for burnout within the selling profession is to look for creative ways to become more productive, simultaneously changing some of your standard procedures. Take a little time to research new innovations and sales approaches. Discover a new use for an existing product. Or a new prospect base. Try new or different selling skills.

Get creative and suggest a new product or service that your company could offer in response to growing or changing needs in the marketplace. Become an aggressive student of your industry or profession. Listen to good motivational tapes and/or training tapes. Read diligently. Jim Rohn says, "If you haven't read the 10 latest books on your industry or profession, you're taking your career too casually. And being casual causes casualties."

Complacency and repetition are incubators for hatching stress. Change your routine. Seek innovation in your job and your life. You'll feel your energy begin to flow again.

It's also true that the less a salesperson believes in the product or service he or she sells – or the less the salesperson believes in the mission and values of his company and its management – the easier it is for stress and burnout to set in. Conversely, the more enthusiasm a salesperson has about himself, his company and what he sells, the more energizing that enthusiasm becomes. The joy of success and high achievement usually chases away the blues of burnout.

Operate Out of Abundance, Not Scarcity

Bill Gove, an incredible platform talent who has been one of my role models and best friends for 25 years, reminds us to operate our daily lives out of abundance, not scarcity. He says we really have just about all we need to be great. We don't need to add much else. But we do need to subtract. Get rid of guilt, blame and unproductive habits. Then learn what you need to learn in your chosen field and go for it. Your expectations can become realities.

Some people withdraw and become vulnerable to every negative thought that comes their way. Don't let negatives take control. You call the shots. Feelings of scarcity can erode your confidence.

I find it interesting that so many people go through life trying to change the behavior of others and saying, "I can't help it" when asked about their own imperfect behaviors. I'm convinced that people would lead a happier, healthier life if they would quit trying to change the behavior of others and work on their own behavior.

It's a super feeling when you realize that you really can control much of the stress in your life. You can learn to put things in perspective. Maintain enthusiasm. Shut out guilt and blame. Once you become master over those emotions, stress and burnout aren't likely to come calling.

Productive Energy Inspires High Performance

My longtime friend Dr. Paul Green is an industrial psychologist with whom I've conducted more than 200 seminars. Paul has researched the

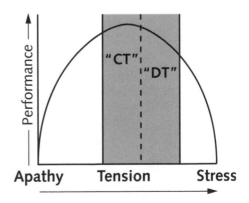

Productive Energy Curve

"CT" = Constructive Tension

"DT" = Destructive Tension

relationship between stress, burnout and high productivity for years. Paul and I put together a principle that might help you. We call it the Productive Energy Curve, and it focuses on apathy, tension and stress.

It's predictable what apathy will do to your productivity. Let apathy set in and sales will suffer. Apathy is on the same team with complacency; find either one and you'll find low performance.

Tension comes in two varieties: constructive tension and destructive tension. The constructive type is the tension you feel when you're standing in the outer office about to go in and see that prospective buyer that you've never met.

With constructive tension, you're aware that your creative juices are flowing, and that can be energizing. Constructive tension can help maximize performance, as the illustration reveals:

For a speaker like me, constructive tension is sitting there being introduced. I'm seldom nervous but I am thinking, "Boy, I want to be at my best today."

Destructive tension is not energizing. In fact, this is the early stage of stress. Performance is going to wane, and wane sadly.

I like the story about the guy who had a terrible morning. Flat tire on the way to the office. Secretary didn't show. His best client called at 9 a.m. to say he was taking his account elsewhere. Maybe you've had a disastrous day like that, too.

At noon the guy says, "You mean it's only lunchtime? I feel like I've been here 18 hours. I've got to change the scenery."

So he grabs a bite of lunch and heads for the golf course. You think the morning was bad; the afternoon got worse. In the water. In the sand. Every time he hit that golf ball, it went sideways. The tension just kept building and building. His jaws were clenched and his head was pounding.

Finally he plays the eighteenth hole and gets a 9 on a par 4. He looks around and there is no one nearby but his caddy. He throws his putter 30 feet into the air, looks at the caddy with fire in his eyes and bellows, "You are without a doubt the worst damn caddy in the world!"

But friends, the caddy was smooth. He had everything under control. "Oh, no sir," the caddy said. "That just couldn't be. Me, the worst caddy in the world? No sir, that would have been just too much of a coincidence!"

Who Is In Charge?

Bob Handly says that people who experience a minimum of stress are usually the same people who know how to control their lives. That's no coincidence, you can be sure. You can control stress by design.

Some people are more productive when tension is present. And whether high performance salespeople really thrive on tension or not, at least they've learned how to handle it. They make it work for them instead of against them. They use tension as a motivator to help them reach for excellence.

Remember, even constructive tension and moderate stress can enhance performance. We must train ourselves, when we feel stress or burnout coming on, to back off, re-think our position, and evaluate the thrust we'll need to put into a project. Few if any tasks are worth the sacrifice of our health and physical well-being.

You are probably familiar with Murphy's Law that says "If anything can go wrong, it will." Well, have you heard of O'Toole's Law? O'Toole's Law says, "Murphy was an optimist!"

Yes, things are going to go wrong. Stress and the possibility of burnout are going to hover on the periphery of your life as a high performer. Accept that some will be plagued by them, but vow that you won't be in that group. *You* control your behavior.

When To Lose Your Temper

Never. Any psychologist worth his salt will tell you that losing your temper is counter productive in any situation. There are some people who will say, "Well, I'm a lot better off after I blow off some steam!" But I believe it's better to stay under control.

When a person loses his temper, whether with a sales prospect, a family member, or a total stranger, it proves to be a negative situation practically every time. When you lose your temper, you are out of control – and when you are out of control, you will often say things that you later regret. Have you ever stopped to consider that it is impossible to un-say something? Remember, you are in control of you and, as much as you may hate to admit it, when you lose your temper, it's because you *chose* to lose your temper. Surely you're not letting someone else run your show!

Laughter, A Great Prescription

It is impossible to feel negative, over-burdened, or stressed out when you are laughing. Psychologist Dr. Herb True says that laughter releases biochemicals from your endocrine glands, which results in a reduction of pain as well as a relaxing of health-sapping tension. Laughter can do wonders for nurturing a positive attitude, even when the chips are down.

Negative feelings and emotions produce a depression that weakens the immune system, making the body less energized and more susceptible to illnesses. Positive feelings that come from humor and laughter, on the other hand, tend to strengthen the immune system.

Using humor whenever you can often results in people trusting you more. If they see that you can laugh at yourself, they believe that you won't laugh at them as readily. Laughter also tends to put people at ease, relaxing the normal stress that exists in tense negotiations and stressful situations.

My friend and fellow speaker Charlie "Tremendous" Jones has said this about laughter and its benefits: "Laughter is a therapy, a tonic, a release. It creates an atmosphere of hope, even in impossible situations. It makes good things better, it gives light to see more clearly. For growthful living, laughter is not an option."

Identify what or who makes you laugh and, during tough times, go to your laughter source to re-energize! Remember that customers like to laugh from time to time also, so be a refreshing resource to them. Share some sunshine with your customers, because they really don't want to know about your sorrows.

Successful Application 5

Featuring: Everett Jewell, President, Jewell Building Systems, Inc.; Dallas, NC
(Author Interview)

I didn't know it at the time, but I was an addict. And I was having withdrawal symptoms.

It was about 3:30 on a spring afternoon in 1983. I finished a meeting with my attorney and I told him, "I'm tired. I'm going home." I stretched out in my recliner, fell asleep in seconds, woke after midnight and staggered into bed. I opened my eyes at 10 the next morning. Then I fell back asleep until dinnertime.

This went on for another three months. Day after day I remained sluggish and unable to concentrate. I was the victim of a disease that strikes a lot of people like me. I had "burnout."

Now that I've learned more about burnout, I realize that I was the perfect candidate for the problem. After a successful sales career, I had started my own company and was putting in long hours. I was under extraordinary pressure. I wasn't a good delegator, and I felt guilty about spending much time away from the company. I was hard on myself, and I had been for years.

I was born "proud poor" in New Hampshire, the oldest of five children raised in a two-room house with a sleeping attic. When I was nine years old, I was washing dishes in a restaurant for 25 cents an hour. By the time I was 16, I was managing a Chevron service station and making $125 a week. When I was in the Navy, I sold encyclopedias on the side.

Back home, I got a job selling educational filmstrips. My territory was everything east of the Rockies. I worked hard, and I was good. Generally three Sundays a month, I would start by driving all night, pull into a territory Monday morning, work all day, drive all night to the next stop, work all day Tuesday and not see bed until Tuesday night.

By the early 1970's, I got into the mobile home industry, first as a salesman and then as regional vice president of a large mobile home manufacturer. My goals at the time were jet airplanes at my fingertips, Cadillacs, power. I told myself one of these days I'm going to walk down the street and people will say, "There goes Mr. Jewell."

The trouble is, I never walked down the street. I ran. I was still stuck in overdrive. My neglected marriage failed, and I fell into debt. I started selling insurance, burglar alarms and cemetery plots.

Finally, I found an opportunity to start my own company. In January of 1977, I started Jewell Building Systems with $30 to my name and some help from Atlantic Building Systems. I set up shop as a private-label distributor of pre-engineered steel buildings. Atlantic provided me with the structures and assisted with advertising and other matters. In my first year, I was modestly profitable, selling $1 million worth of small agricultural buildings.

I was always a good salesperson, but I never understood what it meant to be a manager. Even though I was now the head of my own small company, I was still working like a foot soldier, doing everything, even the smallest task. I was up at 5, at the plant at 6 or 6:30. Always the first one there and the last one to leave. My theme was this: I'll never ask a man to do what I won't do. And not only will I do it better than he will, I'll outwork him.

Like the founders of many small businesses, I experienced some problems. I let myself get talked into expanding into commercial buildings, and I went into debt. My bank reneged on a promised loan. A key employee left to start a competing company. What did I do when things looked dark? More of what had worked in the past: I relied on myself.

I rushed out and sold a few more buildings. I even helped build them myself. One night, a night with the temperature dipping below freezing, I found myself desperately trying to save a just-poured concrete slab. At that moment, Jewell Building Systems was sinking and the loss of that $5,000 slab would have been its tombstone. With bales of straw, a plastic cover and a heater, I managed to hang onto half of that slab – and the business.

I tried to build the company on sheer force, and finally it started to work. Things turned in the spring of 1983. For three months in a row we chalked up profits of $100,000 on sales of $350,000 to $400,000. I was on my way to my company's best fiscal year to date.

At last I was renegotiating purchase contracts without suppliers asking for my personal guarantee. I felt like I'd won the lottery. Then one day, at that very time, I felt really tired in the middle of the afternoon and went home. Burnout had stopped me dead in my tracks.

It was months later, after two doctors could find nothing wrong with me, after I'd finally regained my energy, that a third doctor startled me with a ready explanation.

It's simple, the doctor said. You went through adrenaline withdrawal. You were living on adrenaline. You had it going full blast all the time, and when the pressure eased, your body finally quit producing it. You had a three-month withdrawal as surely as anyone has withdrawal from cocaine or heroin.

With my burnout came self-reflection. Where was I going with my life? What price was I willing to pay to run my business? Having been conditioned all my life to working monstrous hours, having been rewarded for relying only on myself to perform all the important chores, it wasn't easy to change.

There was no dramatic answer to my problem. I had to fight it day by day. I hired some good people under me to manage the company's 60 employees. I learned to delegate more. I swore off working Saturdays. I began to take vacations. I began to work shorter hours, 50 hours a week, far fewer than before. I came to operate more like an executive who owns the company than an employee who does the detail work. The conclusion I finally came to is this:

Yesterday's gone. There's nothing I can do about it. I will do everything this day that I know how to do, but at the end of this day, I'm going home to see my wife and play with the kids.

DON'S PARTING THOUGHT

Don't stress yourself out and come unglued over the everyday hassles of life. Be thankful, work hard, work smart and save a little energy for the periodic catastrophes!

Skill #6

◆◆◆◆◆

Imagination and Creativity:
Go for the Big Ones

> ❝I have had a good life. I would not change much but, if anything, I think I would have gone for bigger deals.❞

—J. Paul Getty
(ON HIS DEATH BED)

If you want to become a high performance salesperson who makes the really big sales, you'll have to throw away your blinders and put on wide-angle lens. You'll need to be willing to try new, fresh, unusual, and unique approaches to each sales opportunity. You'll need to use imagination.

There are millions of conscientious people who put in long hours and do their jobs with diligence but never reach significant levels of achievement. One thing that may hold these people back is they don't *imagine* as hard as they work! They just keep repeating yesterday one more time.

Salespeople who get the big ticket sales usually do so with innovative approaches. They're the people who are engaged in an endless quest for more creative ways to get people to say "Yes!"

Teddy Roosevelt's go-for-it philosophy has always impressed me. He said, "Far better it is to dare mighty things, to win glorious triumphs even though checkered by failure, than to rank with those poor souls who neither enjoy nor suffer much because they live in that great twilight that knows neither victory nor defeat."

That's right – no risk, no glory!

In his audio tape album on "Possibility Thinking," Dr. Robert Schuller asks the question, "What would you try in your life if you knew you could not fail?" The undeniable answer for most would be *a significant goal*. But it's fear of failure that keeps many of us from trying great things and going for the big ones.

Anyone who is not periodically experiencing a failure or setback is probably not trying anything to test his or her potential or to stretch their vision and track record of achievement.

The Creativity Within You

When Thomas Edison was asked what was the greatest invention ever, he responded, "The mind of a child."

I subscribe to the belief that we come into this world with naturally flowing creativity, as Edison implied. How sad it is that most young people so quickly get their minds cluttered with demands, barriers and creativity-squelching instructions, often from mediocre minds who wield power over kids' imagination and spontaneity because of their power, position or adulthood.

Bill Gove says success for many people can mean a simple uncluttering process, tossing out limiting thoughts, previously-established barriers, and any other behaviors that tend to get in our way.

Mediocre salespeople often complain that they're just not creative. They seem to think that creativity is something you're born with. Well, that's not completely true. We can, to an extent, *learn* to be creative.

In his book *A Whack on the Side of the Head: How to Unlock Your Mind for Innovation,* Dr. Roger von Oech says there are 10 mental locks that keep people from being as creative as they could be. See if you've limited yourself with any of these mental locks:

1. That's not the right answer.
2. That's not logical.
3. That doesn't follow the rules.
4. That's not practical.
5. That's too ambiguous.
6. To err is wrong.
7. Play is frivolous.
8. That's not my area.
9. Don't be foolish. (Or, let's get serious.)
10. I'm just not creative.

Next time you're looking for a new way to make a sale, increase your prospect list, or solve a problem for a client, free yourself from all of those mental locks. If an idea comes to you, don't drop it just because it's not logical, not practical, doesn't follow the rules, etc. Creativity begins when you stop saying "It can't be done" and start saying "Why not?"

Have you ever heard someone say, "Boy, he has quite an imagination!" That's usually said in a critical way. But imagination is a positive trait, not a negative one. Imagination gives birth to creativity.

Let me tell you a story I heard from my close friend Ira Hayes about a man who never let comments like "That's not practical" or "That doesn't follow the rules" hold him back. He was a great salesman and a great leader. He was John H. Patterson, founder of NCR Corporation. Mr. Patterson, recognized by many as the father of professional selling, was a genius at creating visual aids and examples to convey a sales point or message.

Tear It Down?!

Sometime about the turn of the century, John Patterson invited his top salesmen to Dayton, Ohio for a meeting. One night they had a beautiful dinner party in one of the buildings that made up the NCR complex.

After dinner, Mr. Patterson said to his men, "This has been a fine evening, and now the carriages are waiting out front to take you downtown to your hotel. I look forward to seeing all of you back here in this dining room tomorrow morning for breakfast." The men said goodnight and departed.

What they didn't know was that Mr. Patterson had dozens of men standing by with horses, tools, shovels, sod and flowers. As the men drove away, Mr. Patterson had his work crew tear down the building, haul the pieces away, level the ground, lay the sod and plant flowers where the building had been.

The next morning the salesmen came in the carriages for breakfast. Mr. Patterson was standing nearby, watching their faces as they arrived. They were astonished. Dumbfounded. Where was the building?

Then John Patterson stepped forward and said to them, "I wanted some way to help you remember that you should get things done quickly and be dramatic in your presentations. I thought this might be a way to make my message memorable." Boy, was it ever!

Larry Wilson, author of the book *Changing the Game: A New Way to Sell*, shows us that we can use creativity and imagination to enhance our performance.

There are four steps to the creative process, Larry says. First, you must create the spark and envision what you want to happen. Second, take a detour from your traditional thinking process and allow your subconscious to create the vision and the solution. Third, repeat the vision again and again in your mind, adding detail until you know the script, the actors and the location by heart. And fourth, when the vision is clearly established, create reality out of that vision.

I like that process. It's consistent with Dr. Peter Drucker's line, "The best way to predict the future is to create it."

To Do Better, Think Harder

Can you remember the last time you exerted strong physical effort? Was it a part of your exercise program…an attempt to open a jar that wouldn't budge…lifting or carrying something that presented a challenge? These are fairly common occurrences, but when was the last time you *thought* hard?

Creative ideas don't come to shallow thinkers. To tap into your imagination and creative energy, you must think harder. To do this, get in a comfortable, uninterrupted environment with pencil and paper and let your ideas flow. If an off-the-wall idea comes to mind, that's fine; try to mold it into something useful. Think hard. Force your brain to dig deep for new ideas or alternate approaches.

One way to help stock the pool of ideas in which you can go fishing for concepts is to become a reader of stimulating books. The input you gain from reading thought-provoking, inspiring literature will cause creativity to flow more naturally. Books can be catalysts that awaken ingenuity in you. Read the works of writers who inspire you and cause you to think. Listening to the right tapes can be inspiring, even life-changing, as well.

At only 5 feet 4 inches in height, Danny Cox is one of the tallest men I know. He stands tall because of his attitude about growth and progress. He has more creative ideas of his own than most people, but he also diligently seeks to research and understand the great minds that have preceded us. While I have been an eager reader for years, I credit Danny, along with Charles "Tremendous" Jones, with my becoming a fanatical reader and, more recently, a collector of books. My life is better for it. (And books are easier to acquire and store than classic cars!)

I believe that people will do today pretty much what they did yesterday unless something intercedes to alter their habit structure. Great ideas from great books written by great thinkers can alter your thinking habits. Fresh ideas add measurably to your creativity quotient. Nothing is a more powerful intercessor to the status quo than a stimulating idea, one which captivates your imagination and inspires you to action. I feel sorry for those people who choose not to expose themselves to new and additional sources of power and growth.

Imagination Impresses Prospects

One way to make the biggest sale of your lifetime is to identify your prospect's biggest problem and come up with a creative solution to that problem. Find an answer that no one else has presented to him. It's likely that you will view the problem from an entirely different perspective than your prospect and therefore you may be able to show him solutions he hadn't considered.

Someone once asked Mark Twain, "How do you come up with those wonderful ideas and thoughts I've seen in your writing?" And Mark Twain replied, "The process is simple. You sit down with pen and paper and write them down as they occur to you. Writing them down is easy – it's the *occurring* that's so hard."

To think and plan how you will creatively make a big sale requires expending positive energy, limiting distractions, and focusing on the customer and his situation in a special way not previously considered. Depth of thought, without barriers or preconceptions, will help you achieve a positive intensity in this process.

Of course you will never consistently make the big sales without skill and knowledge. But Einstein once said, "Imagination is more important than knowledge; for centuries, thousands of good ideas have received tremendous criticism from mediocre minds." Einstein makes a good case for imagination outweighing knowledge, but I also believe we cannot perform beyond our knowledge base. Knowledge is the soil and imagination is the seed; both are necessary for creativity to flourish.

Embrace The No-Limit Assumption

A common characteristic of high performance salespeople is that they don't limit their vision. They have learned to extend themselves into the *no-limit* realm.

These people don't short-circuit their potential power with poor expectations and limiting beliefs. They decide what they wish to achieve, and then they find a way to achieve it. Don't tell these people it's never been done or can't be done. For the high performer, "never been done" is a challenge, not a deterrent.

One way to keep from negating the success you hope to enjoy in the future is to expect a lot of yourself. Success comes when we have high expectations followed by a realistic game plan or strategy for making our vision real. Most people who are sitting around just waiting for their ship to come in never sent a ship out!

Professional speaker Mike Williams says that manifesting your personal greatness means extending yourself to your limits. And since you don't know what your limits are, just assume you don't have any! That's an inspiring thought, isn't it? One of the principal ingredients in making the big sale is your expectation that you can. Remember the words of hockey great, Wayne Gretsky…"Every shot you don't take is a potential goal that you will never make!" None of us tend to exceed our expectations. If we do, it's usually accidental or some unanticipated catalytic agent enters the picture.

The high performance salesperson proactively and continuously works on his self image and expectations. He takes charge; mediocre salespeople tend to be reactive. They wait for things to happen and then respond in a very predictable manner.

What You See Is What You Get

Dr. Maxwell Maltz, the world-famous plastic surgeon who wrote *Psychocybernetics,* said in that best-selling book, "The human nervous system cannot tell the difference between an actual event and one imagined vividly and in detail." This fact is one reason I believe in the value of picturing or imagining ourselves in improved circumstances. Our future success will largely be a result of what we've imagined and expect of ourselves.

During his decades of practicing plastic surgery, Dr. Maltz said he found that when he changed a person's face, he often changed the person behind the face simultaneously. Many times people who had undergone plastic surgery reached impressive new heights of wealth, success and accomplishment. As a person's self-image was enhanced, his or her self-concept and expectations were also positively influenced. The power of the human mind and creative imagination are inestimable.

Dr. Maltz said his saddest experiences were when he changed a face for the better, but the person was chained to old, negative beliefs and an old image about himself or herself. In that case, the surgery was a success, but the patient seldom was.

I believe it's possible for us to experience a new surge of energy and enthusiasm without having to undergo plastic surgery. It can happen if we'll just learn to tap into the creativity that already exists within us and see the big picture.

How Does This Sound?

In his book *It Only Takes One: How To Create The Right Idea and Then Make It Happen,* advertising executive John Emmerling warns that success seldom happens the first time out.

Emmerling's book includes a revealing story about Mickey Schulhof, Vice Chairman of Sony USA. In the 1970's, Schulhof learned about digitally-reproduced sound, the concept behind today's compact discs. At a meeting in 1981, Schulhof excitedly presented the concept to others in his industry. When he hit a button, recording executives heard, for the first time, the sharp, clear music of the compact disc. Their reaction was lukewarm.

Schulhof was dismayed. After much consideration, he began to understand the problem. The heads of record companies are business people, with their ears more attuned to the sound of a cash register than sound quality. So Schulhof took a different route, arranging demonstrations for pop artists such as Stevie Wonder and Paul Simon. Three weeks after hearing the new sound, Stevie Wonder ordered $100,000 worth of equipment. Now that was a message recording executives could understand! Before much longer, the business people invited Schulhof to meet and discuss the new technology. Today compact discs are the foundation of a $25 billion dollar business. Sony has a big chunk of that business and they deserve it, thanks in part to the foresight of Mickey Schulhof.

Stifle the Stiflers!

To start your imagination and creativity flowing, you have to rid yourself of the things that stifle innovation. Here's a list of the Creativity Stiflers you need to overcome:

(1) *Negative Self-Talk.* Rid your vocabulary of phrases like "I've never done it that way" or "I couldn't do that" or "Nobody could accomplish that." This kind of talk is useless and damaging to your person-

al potential. Learn to replace those negatives with "I'm going to do it somehow, I've just got to find the how!" and similar positive responses.

(2) *Complacency.* When a salesperson gets wrapped up in routine, repetitive activities and procedures that offer little or no payoff, it's nearly impossible to be creative and develop innovative strategies for setting new records.

Do you go to the coffee shop at the same time every day, sit with the same people and talk about the same things? Do you always do your tasks in the same order? And exactly the same way? Did you establish for yourself some pattern that worked last year or two or three years ago, and so you figure "If it ain't broke, don't fix it?" If so, you've become complacent. Sometimes it's better to break things and start over!

Make a vow now that each year you will seek a new and better way to perform the tasks you did last year. Or maybe find better tasks to be working on! Just making yourself look at old routines and seek new approaches is likely to provide you with new ideas for success. Examine every aspect of your professional life and expand your horizons.

(3) *Fear of Failure.* Each morning, look at yourself in the mirror and repeat these words: "The only people who never fail are the ones who never try anything." Don't let yourself be counted among those who Teddy Roosevelt said "live in that great twilight that knows neither victory nor defeat" because they are afraid they may stumble along the way.

(4) *Giving Up.* Remember that you can never fail if you never give up. When you miss that big sale, say to yourself, "I didn't get it today, but I've got tomorrow to try again." And say that again and again and again, until you do succeed. High performance salespeople persevere.

(5) *Worrying What Others Might Think.* So often people go through life devoting endless hours wondering "What will they say if I...?" And then finally one day the person who was holding himself back realizes that "they" didn't really think much about him at all. Oh, they may have had some knee-jerk criticism or comment, but soon they forgot. Is it worth stifling your potential to win the approval of "they" (whoever they are)?

High Impact Imagination

When I was involved with the Positive Thinking Rallies tour back in the late 1970's, I was afforded the wonderful opportunity of getting to know the legendary W. Clement Stone. I always enjoyed studying this multimillionaire and truly unique man.

One day I found myself sharing a limousine with him from our hotel to the arena in San Diego. Stone was in his 70's, but he had lost none of his impressive powers. At the age of 32, I was not comfortable addressing him as "Clem," as some of his contemporaries did. So I said, "Mr. Stone, do you plan your retirement soon or do you still have some compelling goals to achieve?"

Stone looked at me with those dark, piercing eyes. He slowly and deliberately took his $4 Cuban cigar out of his mouth and said, "I still have one goal that I plan to achieve. It's simple. I want to change the world and make it a better place in which to live."

I was surprised…and impressed…and temporarily silenced. I remember that conversation as though it were yesterday. It had a profound effect on me and made me realize the value and importance of having a personal mission and thinking big. It also reminded me that age is little more than a state of mind.

Stone was and is a serious achiever. He progressed from skilled salesperson to manager to author to insurance company owner and entrepreneur. He also founded *SUCCESS* magazine, which is still a popular publication today. At the time of the incident in San Diego, the W. Clement and Jesse V. Stone Foundation had *given away* more than $770 million. Serious achiever, huh?

To complacently spend our days without a purpose that inspires or challenges us is to go through life without really living. Expect great things of yourself; tap into your creative energy!

Tap Into Your Uniqueness

Your individuality is one of your greatest assets. Ralph Waldo Emerson said this: "Insist on yourself; never imitate. Your own gift you can present every moment with the cumulative force of a whole life's cultivation. But of the adopted talent of another, you've only an extemporaneous half possession."

In other words, *do your own thing.* You can do things your way better than anyone else in the world. Don't worry if "they" laugh when you approach something creatively and imaginatively. When you land the really big sales, they won't be laughing anymore. They'll be taking notes!

See It Big!

We've discussed several ideas designed to enable you to focus on a bigger picture and gain greater results than you dreamed possible. Now I want to help you begin thinking with increased imagination and creativity about what you can do in the future. Here are five suggestions:

(1) *Begin to work harder on yourself than ever before.* By that, I mean work diligently to expand your self-image and expectations. Your sales skills, your personal goals and objectives, your personal image and level of professionalism – all of these are vital. Remember this: Until you work hard on *yourself,* any other hard work will not bring you as great a return.

(2) *Dramatically increase your focus toward your prospects, their needs and their desires.* You were probably doing a good job of this before you began reading this book. But now you need to give yourself a significant competitive edge by doing it even more. Focus on your prospects better and more consistently than your competition. See the big picture and work to find creative solutions to your prospects' big problems.

(3) *Never again be reactionary and narrow in your understanding of human behavior.* Respect the dignity and individuality of everyone you call on, and be dedicated to the process of developing individualized, targeted strategies. You will be handsomely rewarded for the creativity you devote to this effort.

(4) *Put yourself a cut above the rest of the marketplace with an extraordinary level of service.* Vow to maximize contact, and perfect your system of following up and following through. Give them attention and personal service beyond anything they have ever expected.

(5) *Within 48 hours of the time you finish reading these words, I challenge you to have in place one extraordinary sales goal!* The Roman poet Virgil, writing circa 20 B.C., said, "Fortune is for the bold." Keep in mind that your expectations influence your results.

Begin immediately on your achievement strategy, using the ideas we've discussed in this chapter. If you'll use imagination and creativity in the areas outlined, I predict your sales will skyrocket. Your self confidence will be at an all-time high, and nobody – *nobody!* – in your marketplace will intimidate you. You will be creatively going for and getting the big sales.

Successful Application 6

Featuring: Reese Palley, legendary Atlantic City, NJ shop owner and promotions wizard

Submitted by: Murray Raphel, Writer, Speaker and Consultant; Atlantic City, NJ

He is Atlantic City's self-proclaimed "Merchant to the Rich," the snobby phrase emblazoned on all the shopping bags from Reese Palley's posh Atlantic City Boardwalk art and gift shop.

His list of headline-gathering promotions is impressive, from a multi-million dollar sale of Boehm Birds to his fascinating scheme to fill Boardwalk hotels with private Palley Hoo-Ha Parties to his promotion in which the giant game of Monopoly was played out in the open on a board 32 feet square with bikini-clad young women as pawns.

You can see Reese Palley coming. At the top, a wild shock of crazy, messed-up white hair that looks like it is combed with an egg beater. Black horn-rimmed glasses on a grinning elfish face complete with small scruffy goatee. Black turtleneck shirt, black pants, black socks, black shoes, always with one splash of color: a western red bandana in his back pocket to wipe off his clients' kisses.

Reese Palley, ever ready to entertain, to fascinate. And always ready for the news media with quotable quotes. Among the sayings of the memorable Mr. Palley:

On Merchandising: "If a product doesn't sell, raise the price."

On Re-Merchandising: "If it sells fast, it's too cheap."

On Selling to the Wealthy: "Everybody wants to think and act rich. So we should charge VERY high prices to make them VERY happy."

On Pricing: Palley bought some made-in-Japan glass ash trays. Cheap. Brought out a dozen at $5.95. Sold the dozen in one day. "Ooops," he said, "wrong price, too low." Put out another dozen for $10.95. Sold six in one day. "Getting closer to the right price," he reasoned. Eventually sold them all at prices ranging up to $100 each. Then there was one left. Put a price tag on it for $295.00 with a note, "Last of its kind." Which it was, right? "The person who bought that," Palley said, "tells me to this day how everyone who comes into his home admires that marvelous rare Japanese ash tray. Now *that* was the right price!"

One of Palley's most memorable promotions was his Palley/Dali Paris Birthday Party.

"How can I celebrate my 50th birthday?" said the Merchant to himself. With that question, he proceeded to put together the most flamboyant of his nonsensical, never-never land schemes. The self-centered celebration made headlines from the Fiji Islands to Fairbanks, Alaska, from *The New York Times* to Paris *Match*, from the major TV networks in the USA to the Voice of America.

He borrowed the idea for the promotion from the cosmetic firms. They call it prize-with-purchase. You buy something, you get something free. Or at a ridiculously low price.

The basic ingredients were on hand. Palley wanted to celebrate his birthday. He was opening an art gallery in Paris featuring artists well known in the United States. The theme of his opening was "Bring something American home from Paris." He needed a hook, and soon he found it.

An agent of Salvador Dali happened to approach Palley with an art offer. It seems crafty Dali has done paintings of the face cards in a playing deck: the four jacks, queens, kings, aces and jokers. Dali would offer them as a limited edition of lithographs. One hundred seventy prints of each card. Total: 2,890 renditions. Voila!

Palley bought all 2,890 renditions. With an option, of course, to cancel if he found he could not sell them. How much did he pay for each lithograph? No one really knows except Palley. Some dealers say in this huge quantity he could have bought them for $50 each. Palley acts horrified at the thought. "Why, Dali lithographs sell *wholesale* for $180!" he proclaims.

He put together an inexpensive, quickly-done mailing piece. "Cost me about a nickel apiece," he admitted. The front page headline said, "This one you won't believe."

Inside, the copy explained that he wanted to spend his birthday in Paris opening his new gallery and he wanted his friends to travel there with him. He described the Dali lithographs and, as a kicker, offered a joker print to his customers for $650. Purchasing the Dali lithograph entitled each customer to a round trip passage to Paris for two for a four-day weekend including jet fare and hotel room. And he guaranteed to buy the lithograph back for the $650 at any future date.

Palley chartered a 747 with about 400 seats. He mailed the invitations and figured on sending out a follow-up. In four days, he was sold out. In ten days, he had sold out two 747s!

On the flight over he assembled a major art collection and there was a special offer. The price of each painting was less going over, but would be slightly *more* coming back.

Before the plane arrived, he had a couple of treats ready. To make sure everyone in the world knew he was giving a free trip, Palley preprinted postcards with Paris scenes, already postmarked, with the message ready to be sent back home to friends (who might want to come on future birthday jaunts!) The cards each said: "Free at last. Free at last. Reese Palley has given me something free at last..."

When the planes arrived, everyone was ready to head for customs. But wait! Now everyone was given a face-sized photographic mask with rubber-bands attached to hold the faces on. Whose face? Who else? The Benevolent One. Can you imagine the shock of the custom officials who looked up the corridor and saw, coming at them, 700 Reese Palleys?!

Settled in at the hotel, Palley held a press conference. He appeared dressed in costume as Napoleon. Then Palley set up temporary shop in the hotel lobby and took orders on Boehm plates. He sold four hundred sets at $300 each. And a few more Dalis. His customers who bought the jokers wanted jacks, queens, kings – complete sets.

To enliven the return plane trip, he announced his new organization called the National Association of Friends of Rare Porcelain. Dues were $5 a year and everyone joined on the trip home.

How much did Palley realize from this Dali-Palley-gaiety? His cost for the Dalis was probably around $50,000. Plus a hotel bill of $32,000. Plus the 747s for about $110,000. Throw in another $28,000 for expenses here and there. Total: about $220,000.

And his earnings? Well, for starters, there are the 700 lithographs at $650 each for $455,000. Plus a profit of about $60,000 for the Boehm plates. And the art he sold on the plane coming and going. If Palley didn't make a million from just the trip, he at least made a lot of friends all of whom are, of course, now members of the National Association of Friends of Rare Porcelain.

What will Reese Palley think of next? Only the headlines will tell. Few could plot the unchartered course of this man who loves sailing and has repeatedly sailed his 32-foot sloop "Unlikely" into the Bermuda Triangle. Which should come as no surprise to Palley watchers. Taking chances is simply the Reese Palley way of doing business.

DON'S PARTING THOUGHT

Stretch yourself! Make that big call you've hardly thought about until now. Use a bold, imaginative approach. Expect success and close the sale. Celebrate your success, then initiate plans for an even bigger sale. Remember, knowledge is the soil, imagination is the seed, and action is the water. Pour it on!

SECTION TWO

Sales Strategies
That Work...If You Do

SKILL 7: The Process of Building Trust

SKILL 8: Learning to Ask Questions and Listen

SKILL 9: Needs-Analysis Selling

SKILL 10: The Needs-Based Presentation

SKILL 11: Developing Business: From Suspect to Confidant

SKILL 12: Building Value Rather Than Cutting Price

SKILL 13: Understanding Human Behavior in Selling

SKILL 14: Selling With Adaptable Strategies

SKILL 15: Presenting Your Proposal

SKILL 16: Closing the Sale: Earning the Right

SKILL 17: Closing the Sale: Getting the "Yes"

Skill #7

✦✦✦✦✦

The Process of Building Trust

“The sale doesn't end when the customer says yes. That's when it really begins.”

—HENRY FORD

Do you have kids? Do you sometimes feel they must have come from another planet?

If your kids seem really weird, it's probably because there's a communication gap. Happens all the time between generations. Usually it's caused by a difference in value systems between parents and their children. Your goals aren't congruent.

Did you have stress with your parents years ago like you have with your kids today? Next question: Even though you have had problems with both, how come your kids and parents get along so well? It's been said that grandparents get along well with their grandchildren because they share a common enemy!

I've found that kids today are hungry for what is out there. But they may or may not want to work hard to get it. Maybe you have a competitor right there in your own marketplace who acts the same way, who behaves from time to time as if he would like to arrive without having made the trip. Doesn't work, does it?

The wider the gap between yours and your kids' value system – or yours and your customer's value system – the bigger the communication gap may be. And the harder you may have to work to establish effective communication.

I'll give you an example of how people are not coming from the same place. A while back I got home from a trip. The big news at home seemed to be that our daughter had just gotten all A's on her report card.

I wanted to congratulate her, so I walked back to her room. "Robin," I said, "I understand you got all A's this six weeks."

She said, "Yeah, I did!"

"That's terrific," I said. "I'll take you to dinner anywhere you want to go."

"Anywhere?" she said.

"You got it, anywhere," I said. I let her think just a minute and then I said, "Where do you think you might like to go?"

She said, "London."

Close the Communication Gap

Well, that's an example of a communication gap between family members. Now let's get out of the house and back into the business environment. If there is a communication gap between you and a customer, whose job is it to close that gap? It's your job, of course. The first task we face in creating goal consistency with customers is closing the communication gaps.

What's the next step in creating goal consistency? You can bet that the customer or prospect is endlessly asking himself this question: *What's in it for me? What will I get out of this relationship, this product, this presentation?* You need to let him know what's in it for him at the same time you must let him know that you care about his benefits and results.

Focus on the Customer's Goals

High performance salespeople concentrate on providing solutions, creating opportunities, and in general making customers feel good about the sale and the relationship, no matter what it takes. There have been some top professionals who actually refuse to take an order unless there is a definite match between their product or service and the customer's goals. Their focus on the customer goes well beyond lip service. This can be a powerful trust builder.

In contrast, average and below average salespeople never fully develop the skill. Instead, they seem more focused on *their* goals, even if those goals are reached at the expense of a customer. These people don't last in the profession of selling.

When I say goal consistency, consider the elipse below which represents your goals. Beside it is another elipse that represents the prospective buyer's goals. If they don't overlap at all, you have no goal congruence. Anything that you can do to move those elipses closer together in your sales presentation will increase your chances for a successful sale.

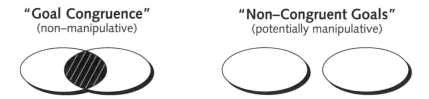

| "Goal Congruence" | "Non–Congruent Goals" |
| (non–manipulative) | (potentially manipulative) |

When you are able to make those elipses overlap, you are creating what we call *goal congruence or goal consistency.* It's a concept whereby you make the person feel so good and comfortable that they will look forward to the business experience with you. The greater the overlap of your goals and theirs, the greater the probability that you will close the sale in a win-win way.

It's salespeople who have goals that are totally foreign to or totally separate from the goals of the prospective buyer who don't even get to first base. Again, it's part of a learnable skill. Begin to think in terms of establishing goal consistency with all your prospects. When there is no overlap, a potentially manipulative or win-lose transaction can come into play.

Clarify the Customer's Goals

Now that we have outlined the importance and meaning of goal consistency, let's talk about how we can clarify the customer's goals for both parties.

You may begin by trying a question like this: "Mr. Prospect, my goal is to become a valuable resource to you and to be instrumental in helping you reach your goals. After eight years in the business, I think I've developed an ability to help customers reach their objectives. To accomplish this for you, I must first get a good idea of what your goals are." Then you can go on with some more specific questions to learn what's on that person's agenda.

Keep in mind that *customer goals* and *customer needs* are not the same. You may be able to ascertain what a customer needs in short order, but that customer's goals are more challenging to clarify. They will often be subjective, vague, emotionally driven, even irrational from time to time. But nevertheless, we need to identify them if we are going to establish the win-win relationship we seek.

How do we identify these goals? We ask our customers, we read between the lines as they talk, we reflect, we elaborate, we probe. Clarify and confirm major points often.

It is up to you to put in the hard labor to establish goal consistency with your customers. Remember, too, that the goals you discover today may be quite different from the same customer's goals tomorrow.

As you monitor a customer's goals, keep in mind that many factors can serve as the "change agent." There may be changes in personnel, unexpected successes and failures within the organization, changes in their industry or market structure, involvement in a merger or acquisition, new technology, changes in their competitive environment or other factors.

Remember also that when you don't focus on customer goals and align your presentation accordingly, the prospect simply doesn't have the confidence and belief in you that you need for the sale to be made. Goal consistency will be a major factor in the development of win-win relationships.

Building Rapport

In this chapter, I want to focus on ways to build a harmonious relationship and win the trust of customers. Whenever I think about trust, I am reminded of the story about the fellow who had become rather suspecting of his wife. In fact, he had become *totally* suspecting of this wife!

So the man decides to go home in the middle of the day and check on his wife. He goes into his apartment building, up the elevator, down the hall, turns the key in the door, walks inside and there stands his wife in her silky dressing gown at two o'clock in the afternoon. And a fresh, burning cigar is in the ashtray.

Well, the fellow knows instantly what must be happening here. So he begins looking around the apartment. He's looking under every bed, inside every closet but he can't find another man anywhere. And he's just certain that there's a guy hiding there somewhere. He's feeling really jealous now and he's burning with rage.

Suddenly the fellow gets a brainstorm. The balcony! He throws back the drapes, opens the sliding door and steps out onto the balcony.

Sure enough, nine floors below, he sees a guy down there on the sidewalk straightening his tie. He just knows that *has* to be the guy.

Well, this big powerful jealous husband runs back into the apartment, into the kitchen and grabs the refrigerator. Back through the apartment, out onto the balcony. He lines up very carefully and drops the refrigerator directly on top of the poor guy on the sidewalk. As you might imagine, it was instant death.

A short time later, St. Peter hears a knock at the pearly gates. St. Peter greets the new arrival and says, "What, may I ask, is your situation?" The guy replies, "St. Peter, I was walking down the sidewalk minding my own business, stopped to straighten my tie in a window and some turkey dropped a refrigerator on me and killed me."

St. Peter says, "That's a sad story, my good man. Come on in."

A few minutes pass and there is a second knock at the gate. St. Peter answers and says, "What, may I ask, is your situation?" The guy says, "Well, St. Peter, I had become suspecting of my wife. I went home in the middle of the afternoon to our apartment." And he proceeds to unfold the entire story.

He said, "St. Peter, after I dropped the refrigerator off that balcony, I was so physically and emotionally fatigued that I died instantly of a heart attack." St. Peter said, "That's a sad story, my good man. Come on in."

A few minutes later there's a third knock at the gates. St. Peter answers and says, "Yes, sir. What, may I ask, is your situation?"

Third guy said, "St. Pete, you ain't gonna believe this. I was sitting in this refrigerator…"

Well, that's my favorite humorous story about trust (or problems resulting from a lack of trust.) Now let's get more serious.

For any relationship to be long term and mutually gratifying, trust must be a key element. And like allegiance, trust must be earned. Both trust and allegiance can be earned more readily when we work hard to learn as much about our customers as possible.

But Do You Know His Dog's Name?

During Ted Jackson's tenure as vice president of sales of Nissan Forklifts (Ted is now president and CEO of Balkancar, N.A. in Chicago), I did a lot of training for his dealers as well as the Nissan corporate staff. Ted had built a great dealer organization. He knew every dealer well, and he knew what turned each of them on and off. He was a master at relationship selling.

At a sales meeting in Dallas, Ted's talk preceded mine. I was listening to him address his dealers and their salespeople when I heard him say, "You've got to know your customers so well that you not only know what their wants and needs are, you know all about them – their interests, their hobbies, their spouse's name, their kids' names. You should even know their dog's name!" Everybody laughed, but Ted was serious.

At the next regional meeting a week later in Reno, I walked up to Ted and said, "How are you, Ted?" After he answered, I said, "How's Sachiko (his wife)?" He answered and I said, "How's Max (his dog)?" Ted smiled and said, "Hutson, you're good!" I assured him that I only learn from the best. (My research on this was pretty easy, since my daughter Robin and Ted's daughter Jennifer went to school together.)

How much do you know about your best customers? Would more information be better? Probably so. Expanding your knowledge in the area of personal information about your customers and prospects will usually pay great dividends.

Unexpected But Never Forgotten

Insurance executive Ben Ward, C.L.U., a good friend of mine, sends a charitable contribution to the favorite charity of his agents when they make their first sales through his company. It's an unexpected gesture but one that's never forgotten. A good question to ask ourselves is, "What can I do that my competitors aren't doing that will enhance meaningful business relationships and do some sort of worldly good?" Bravo, Ben!

Earning Trust

If you haven't earned a prospective customer's trust, then when that customer has a definite need, he may choose to look beyond you for the solution to his problem. The best way to learn a prospect's dominant buying motive is to gain that customer's trust, then ask. If they trust you, they will tell you.

Trust is defined as *reliance on the integrity or justice of a person*. When you truly trust someone, there is an obvious sense of fair play which stimulates high quality communication and strengthens the business relationship.

To build trust, you must create a low stress environment. You cannot pressure somebody one minute and expect them to trust you implicitly the next. Fifteen years ago, a lot of sales techniques created high stress and low trust. Today's sales professional is a master at keeping stress low and trust high.

William James said, "The greatest craving inside the human being is for appreciation and recognition for the work he has done." Build trust and rapport by sincerely recognizing the efforts and work of the individual you are talking with. Show a genuine interest in him and his problem. William James also said, "One of the greatest courtesies we can extend to our fellow man is to listen to him and respond positively and pertinently to what we hear."

People who are skilled at developing rapport and winning trust use some of these positive strategies. But one thing they avoid using with customers is guilt.

Guilt Is Useless

Guilt is a useless emotion with no intrinsic value. If we could put ourselves or others into some kind of a rewind mode, or if we could relive an event, it might be useful. But we can't, so don't burn up energy on guilt.

You'll note that in their conversation, high performance salespeople stay on a high plane. It's been said that losers talk about others, average people talk about things, and winners talk about ideas and solutions. When you focus on win-win ideas and creatively pursue the desired results for that prospect or customer, you're on the right track.

Are we sometimes so vain that we can't see the talent, the creativity, the courage in others? If we are ever going to develop strong trust bonds, we must look beyond the mirror and into the hearts and minds of the people in our marketplace.

Needless to say, we can't build rapport and trust without vital elements like dependability, sincerity, and integrity. If all of these attributes are present, we have paved the way for long-term, trusting relationships.

Patience Yields A Fruitful Harvest

While we were visiting recently, my longtime friend and client Bennie Daniels, C.L.U. (Vice President, Associate Director of Marketing, Southern Farm Bureau Life Insurance Company), told me about Ron McCall, one of the company's top salespeople in the Vero Beach, FL agency. Ron's story of how he earned the trust of one of the nation's largest citrus wholesalers is an excellent example of the importance of patience in building a relationship. I subsequently interviewed Ron for this book, and here's the story he told me:

"Earning a customer's confidence and loyalty can be difficult. But it's even harder when you have to re-earn loyalty. I know because that's what I had to do with one of our top customers.

"The man was a hard-working vegetable and fruit wholesaler from New Jersey who moved to Vero Beach in the late 60's. I grew up playing with his kids, but I never realized that the family had money. That's not the kind of thing kids notice. I went through high school and college with some of his children, but it was only after I started in business that I learned what a prosperous citrus wholesaler he had become.

"After college I joined my father in his insurance agency, which specialized in the citrus industry and cattle operations in our area. The citrus wholesaler was a client of one of our former agents. We had his property account as well as some other business.

"In 1983, Florida Farm Bureau went through a major transition accompanied by some tough times. In an effort to maintain stability, local agencies had to cancel some accounts, including this gentleman's account. And he was the largest customer of Florida Farm Bureau at the time, which demonstrates the success he had earned.

"We assumed that every account we had to cancel would never come back. It was reasonable to presume that would be the last we'd ever see of the citrus wholesaler. But I wasn't willing to give up. After a while, I decided to try to recultivate our relationship and win back their loyalty.

"One of the man's stepsons that I had grown up with came back to town as corporate attorney for the company, and I kept in touch with him. I knew the company's CPA, and he helped me get to know other people in the company. Soon I was writing the personal insurance of all the company's managers. I worked hard to give each one of those individuals exceptional service.

"Eventually I introduced our health insurance program to the company and, after four or five years of being persistent and patient, we finally got their health insurance this year. That business was worth over $1 million in premiums. This year we'll also be writing their property and casualty insurance, which will be over $1.5 million.

"How did we earn back their business? Having a good product at a good price was a big factor. We offered a competitive advantage on health insurance that helped their company combat rising costs through managed care. We also offered a unique concept in self-insurance that enabled the company to assume some of the costs of managing their service.

"Just as important as the right product was our willingness to be patient, to take it one step at a time, to do a good job and demonstrate that we were worthy of their trust again. Fortunately, the company really didn't like to shop around and preferred long-term relationships. We did a good job, we stayed in touch, and they were impressed enough to give us a second chance. And this time, we expect to keep them as customers for life."

If You Say It, I Believe It!

Integrity is a vital issue for the selling profession. If we are going to make our prospective buyer feel comfortable, we've got to possess, believe in and display integrity as an internalized part of our modus operandi. Strong personal principles can in and of themselves be energizing.

In the past, the image of the *born salesman* was of one who would say or do anything to make a sale. That old image was of someone totally lacking in integrity. I've always had a problem with that stereotypical image. I see salespeople as the gas and oil of a free competitive enterprise, the men and women who make things happen. I applaud your participation in this worthy exercise! We who operate with integrity deserve better than the image that has been bestowed upon us. The good news is that this image is changing for the better.

Whenever I hear something to make me think of that old negative stereotype of salespeople, I am reminded of the story of an anything-for-the-sale real estate agent. He was showing this couple through a home when they came to the kitchen. The salesman got carried away and threw out a few lines that he knew would have high impact but were totally untrue.

Looking at the woman, the salesman said, "Madam, I'll have you know you are standing in the only kitchen in this state that has cabinets so well constructed that they are roach proof."

The woman looked at him with a leery eye and said, "Are you kidding me? Roach-proof cabinets? Why, I've never heard of such a thing!" She walked over, opened one of the cabinet doors and immediately she looked directly into the eyes of a big old cockroach that was just about to jump on her.

Well, that salesman may not have been factual, but he was fast. Quick as lightening, he said, "Yes, ma'm! Look at that, will you? We put that roach in this cabinet three weeks ago and he hasn't been able to get out yet!" Cute story but bad philosophy.

Even Better than "Lombardi" Time

My good friend and client Doug Cassidy, president of Dietary Products (an alliance of Baxter Health Care and Kraft Foodservice), told me recently about one of his company's top salespeople, Doug Danks, who has the *right* kind of philosophy about building trust among his customers. Doug Danks' goal – on each and every order – is not just to meet but to *exceed* the expectations of his customers.

"Earlier in my career," Doug explained, "when a customer asked when I could get an order to him, I'd say something like, 'By next Friday.' But now I always ask, 'When do you need it?' I let the customer feel in control by naming the date. I make sure, before I commit to the date named, that I can deliver by that date without fail. Then I make every effort possible to deliver the order before the time the customer expects it!"

In other words, Doug Danks makes a commitment to his customer on a delivery date, then he makes a commitment to himself to go the extra mile and give that customer more than necessary. This one technique – to always *exceed* the customer's expectations – has been the key to Doug Danks' impressive success.

Think Integrity First

Quick thinking is a desirable behavior in selling, but not at the expense of integrity. The absence of integrity and professional belief on the part of some salespeople is, in my opinion, the single greatest cause of the negative image I discussed earlier.

One of the best ways you can be successful and be a positive force for the selling profession is to think integrity first. With integrity, we have the foundation to achieve anything. Without integrity, we have nothing.

"Sales" is a dirty word to some people because for so long it was linked to images of manipulation and deceit. Let me share with you a couple of messages from the American College Dictionary:

MANIPULATE: To handle, manage, or use with skill in some process of treatment or performance. To adapt or change to suit one's purpose...

To me, that's a rather complimentary commentary on manipulation, a word which today has a very negative connotation. Now try this definition on for size:

SELL: To dispose of to a purchaser for a price. To cheat. Slang: a hoax.

Is that you? Is that me? I don't think so, and I resent the implication. But there are some salespeople who have both caused and perpetuated this stereotype by the way they've sold their customers. No wonder these methods turn people off!

Some sales training systems have actually encouraged manipulation and deceit by teaching salespeople tricks and techniques for getting the order in spite of what the customer really wants or needs. There are sales representatives today who still adhere to that approach. They believe that their job is to sell their products to as many people as possible, regardless of the circumstances, outcome or degree of customer satisfaction (or lack of it) that might exist.

In my research for this book, I read some material that really turned me off. Here are some examples of the topics mentioned in this material:

- "The Customer, Your Opponent"
- "How To Scheme"
- "Head Game Warfare"
- "How To Manipulate The Customer"
- "35 Tactics on Psychological Manipulation"
- "The Attack Plan"

What a turn-off! Fortunately, there is a trend in the training marketplace today toward the eradication of such shoddy approaches.

The high performance salesperson is not only a salesperson with personal and professional integrity, but one with a strong belief system. He or she believes in their products and services, and they believe in their ability to get the job done. We can't get the job done with tactics such as those just mentioned. It's not a win-win.

Today's high performance salesperson doesn't champion hidden agendas and secrecy. These sales pros are masters at creating and maintaining strong open lines of communication with customers. The more familiar with and focused they are on customer agendas, needs, thoughts and idiosyncrasies, the more of a competitive edge they gain.

These salespeople usually work for customer-driven firms. Their products and services come from market research of customer needs and wants, rather than from what executives need and want to sell. They believe in the value of the products and services they sell. Great salespeople have too much integrity to slyly sell something they don't believe in. By the way, if your lack of sales performance can be traced to a lack of belief in the product or service you offer, for goodness sake find something else to sell!

Another way these firms can usually be identified is that they are invariably believers and participants in sales skills training. These firms (and their salespeople) see those who make up their customer base as partners in progress, not as adversaries to be tricked and conquered.

The Principles of Accountability And Reliability

Today's high performance salesperson knows about, understands, and subscribes to the principle of accountability. Being personally accountable means understanding this basic truth of selling: We ultimately make exactly what we and our skills are worth. Accountability is a dimension of integrity selling. The essence of true accountability is asking this question: What kind of sales production am I going to require of myself?

The marginal producer's greatest skill is fault finding, and his lack of success is anyone's fault but his own. Just ask him!

Another attribute of today's high performance salesperson is reliability. High performance pros quite simply keep their promises and, as a result, they keep their customers. Many studies have indicated the number one cause of customer turnover is *perceived indifference of the salesperson*. Show high levels of interest, reliability and follow-up, and customers will love you for it.

Respect Uniqueness

Respect for the individuality of each customer is a trait I've noticed among high performers. They accept the individuality of everyone they talk to in the marketplace. High performance pros are true to their own goals and beliefs, rather than conforming to the value systems of others. This posture nurtures a mutual respect, which paves the way for long-term, win-win relationships.

High performers have character. You won't find many salespeople who endure for the long haul without it. What do I mean by "character"? I like this definition offered by Cavett Robert, the Chairman Emeritus of the National Speakers Association: "Character is the ability to carry out a resolution long after the mood in which it was made has left you." Strong resolve to do what you plan and say will set you apart from the masses. Strong producers seem to always be strong self-disciplinarians.

If you make integrity an integral part of your value system, not just for today but throughout your lifetime, you'll be on your way to becoming one of today's top professionals. Couple that with a strong belief in your product or service, in your company, and in yourself, and you are setting yourself up for high performance results.

Give Customers Reasons To Trust You

People sometimes withhold trust for self protection. Don't give your customers a reason to protect themselves. Give them reasons to trust you.

If people must always be on guard with you or constantly be suspicious of your motives, selling to them will be a long and tedious process. In fact, you may never get a sale from an uncomfortable prospect. People will open up to you only when they truly trust you. We will only reveal our true feelings to the extent that we can anticipate understanding.

High performance salespeople develop a win-win strategy based on mutual trust. The essence of this strategy recognizes an important and fundamental truth: *The best way for a sales professional to serve his own self interest is to make sure that the customer's self interest is served first.*

Success, the win-win strategist knows, depends on mutual satisfaction. We emphasize mutual satisfaction because manipulating the customer is only one way you can manage the sale. Another way is to allow yourself to lose so that the customer wins.

Some salespeople do this all the time, usually in the vain hope that doing their customers such favors will pay off in the future. Satisfying your customers at your own expense is, in the long term, just as bad as not satisfying them at all. A win-win approach to sales involves maintaining a delicate balance. It means keeping your customers happy without giving the store away. Total subservience and self-sacrifice do not have to be part of the formula.

So remember, authenticity is the order of the day. Authenticity pays off for both the customer and for you. How far are you willing to go in a relationship? How much energy are you willing to put in that relationship? Nothing worthwhile is easy to bring about.

Here are five trust and rapport factors for you to use in achieving the results you are looking for:

Factor One: Make the customer comfortable

A friendly, warm approach tends to break down barriers and set the stage for a good interaction. A pleasant smile and amicable approach is irreplaceable in this part of the process.

Factor Two: Treat the prospect with respect and dignity

Responding to the individuality and the personal dignity of others is admirable behavior. If you display respect for all people, it is an even more valuable skill. If you are observed treating others – regardless of who they are – with disrespect, you may create unsolvable problems for yourself.

Factor Three: Nurture openness

To do this, don't hedge; be positively straightforward. If you don't know something, admit it and offer to find out. This authenticity will be appreciated and admired.

Factor Four: Display a sense of fair play and dependability

Courteously deliver all that you promise and never promise more than you can deliver. I've found that when these qualities are displayed in the marketplace, they are returned in kind with few exceptions.

Factor Five: Stay in touch

I have never heard of a salesperson who went too far in terms of staying in touch with prospects and customers. Maximize your written communications; send them notes, pertinent articles, etc. Everytime they get something from you, they think positively of you and feel good that you were thinking of them. This is an excellent trust builder, which not only improves customer relationships but also shortens sales cycles.

Go 50-50?

Maybe you've heard it said, whether it is in selling, business in general, or in relationships at home, that all good relationships must be 50-50. This is erroneous information. It's bad data. And the reason it is erroneous is that 50-50 is not good enough in high quality relationships.

Are you familiar with how the ancient Chinese built a bridge? The ancient Chinese method of building bridges illustrates an extremely valuable concept for us.

When these people wanted to build a bridge over a river, they would get a big tree on one side of the river and strip all the limbs off the tree. Then they would stretch the tree out across the river. They'd get another big tree on the other side of the river, strip away the limbs and stretch that tree out across the river. Then they would lash the two trees together and from the bound trees, they'd hang a bridge.

Would you agree that the greater the overlap of those two trees as they are lashed together, the stronger the structure? Certainly.

Suppose, in one instance, the ancient Chinese decided to build a bridge by getting a spindly little tree on one side of the river and stretching it out half way across the river, then getting a spindly tree on the other side and engineering it so each tree was about 50 percent across and the tips of the trees just touched. If they could figure out a way to lash these two spindly trees together and hang a bridge from it, would you want to cross the river on that bridge? Not interested, right?

The fact is, the 50-50 process – going halfway – is not good enough. It doesn't work in building Chinese bridges, and it doesn't work in human relationships.

What about an overlap of 75-75? Even better, how about 90-90? Sometimes people will say to me, "Well, Don, you know 90-90 would be wonderful. Even 75-75 would be good. But when I'm out calling on prospects, sometimes they don't want to go 50-50; they don't want to go even half of the way."

Have you ever had a prospect that didn't want to go their portion of the way? Well, guess what: You're going to have *more* of them!

What if you have a prospect who's only willing to go 30 percent of the way? You're going to have to go about 80 percent so that you can create some overlap to tie that relationship together.

Remember, it is our responsibility to close communication gaps. We cannot control the behavior of other people, but we know we can control our own behavior. If we sincerely want to build trust, we need to do this gladly, realizing it is part of a high performance salesperson's job.

Successful Application 7

Featuring: James E. Jewett, Ph.D., Founder and Vice President, Telco Research Corporation; Nashville, TN

Submitted By: Bill Gove, Professional Speaker; Atlantis, FL

One morning five years ago, Federal Express delivered a totally unexpected package to us. It contained 15 pounds of famous Buffalo Chicken Wings, sent directly from a bank in Buffalo to our offices at Telco Research in Nashville.

Those chicken wings tasted deliciously good to me, not because I'm especially fond of chicken but because they'd been sent by a customer whose respect and trust we had earned the *hard way.*

The gift reminded me of a central lesson I'd learned working with that client: that to really make customers happy, you have to treat them as *partners.* This attitude has proved to be the key to satisfying our clients, and ultimately to the prosperity and growth of our young company.

Necessity first motivated us to think of our customers as partners. I started Telco Research in 1975 with zero capital. In building our software development and consulting firm from scratch, we invested "sweat equity" in place of the financial kind. We worked very long hours, took very low salaries, and reinvested any profits right back into the company. We didn't have any outside funding to invest in R&D or for any fancy advertising and promotion. We had to substitute creative selling for cash!

In those early months and years, we had to make a new customer's experience with us so extraordinarily superior from their experiences with other vendors that our customers would become our R&D partners and our best sales force. The depth of this type of relationship had to be built on trust.

So we chose our first customers as carefully as a small, struggling firm could afford to. We looked at their needs to see how good a match there would be with our products. We actually "interviewed" potential customers in an informal way, watching them in trade show situations, determining whether they had the respect of their peers, deciding if they would make good advocates for us.

We needed customers who would be more than quietly happy with what we'd developed for them. We wanted people who would shout and stomp their feet in excitement when we delivered what they wanted. We wanted customers so delighted they would practically kill for us and enjoy doing it!

We found them, but only because we made a conscious effort to seek out the best available "buyers" and then make them active partners in the R&D process. That's what happened with the Buffalo bank.

I had originally traveled to Buffalo to discuss with the bank the capabilities of a proposed product we were planning to sell for $6,000. As I met with them, I discovered to my chagrin that the software package we were proposing didn't really meet their needs. However, rather than folding my briefcase and catching the next plane back to Nashville, I kept asking them to talk about what they *did* need in a product that would capture and charge back all the calls made by bank employees. As I listened, I thought of several changes in our product that would make it extremely useful to them.

So, at that point, I asked, "If we could deliver a highly-reliable PC-based software product with the features you've described, how valuable would it be to you?"

To my amazement, they said it would be worth over $100,000. The major competing product at that time sold for about $80,000. After much redesigning and added sophistication to the product, I proposed selling our new product to them for $60,000! And they answered with an enthusiastic "Yes!" When you respond to people's needs and enjoy high trust in client relationships, great things happen.

We were off and running, working hand in hand with the banking staff to create a better product than we had originally envisioned. The bank was so delighted with the result that they enthusiastically recommended our product to other banks and companies throughout the country.

That product's success fueled our ability to grow at 65 percent a year, become a national leader in our industry, and earn us the unusual distinction of being named to *INC.* magazine's list of the 500 fastest-growing companies for three years in a row.

Ironically, our relationship with the Buffalo bank almost evaporated at one point. In the sales profession, you can't take anybody or anything for granted just because things were rosy last week! You must earn trust continuously.

I had negotiated a contract with the telecommunications department and, when I arrived at the bank a few weeks later to sign the contract, I was met by a vice president of purchasing (a new person in the decision loop) who wanted to disregard our contract and start all over, using his standard vendor contract.

I refused, calling this unethical. He was unbending. I finally stood and walked to the door. Just as my hand touched the door knob, the vice president relented. We then signed the contract I'd brought with me. That contract was saved by a hair's breath of difference. The difference came, I'm convinced, because of what he had heard from his associates about the degree to which we could be trusted to follow through professionally.

I think my impulse to walk away from that situation was correct. The customer isn't always right. The customer is simply and always a *partner*. That's why those chicken wings tasted so good to me. We'd established a long-term, mutually-beneficial relationship. We'd opened a new market niche for the product that our customer/partner helped us re-design. We'd both taken risks, and we'd both won.

Those wings didn't taste like chicken. They tasted like success!

DON'S PARTING THOUGHT

During challenging times, in tough periods of negotiation, and even in good times, never give your customers reason to doubt your integrity or your genuine interest in them and their problems.

Skill #8

✦✦✦✦✦

Learning to Ask Questions and Listen

❝God gave us two ears and one mouth for an excellent statistical reason. Many salespeople behave as if they have two mouths and one ear!❞

—ANONYMOUS

To become accomplished at asking questions is one of the greatest skills salespeople can develop. It's a skill that will make your prospects appreciate you more, and it's a skill that can have great impact on your ultimate sales performance.

Fred Herman was one of America's greatest sales trainers and a real master at asking questions. One time years ago he appeared on the Mike Douglas Show and that show's host gave Fred an opportunity to demonstrate great salesmanship at work.

Mike Douglas said to him, "Fred, it's a real honor to have you here. You know, there's a lot about selling today that has an impact on everyone's life, and we want to find out what selling is all about. We'd also like to know what a great sales trainer does, how he gets persuasive techniques to work for him, and how he get results."

After they'd talked a few minutes, Mike said, "Fred, if you're so great, sell me the ashtray on that table there." Fred Herman looked over at the ashtray and he looked back at Mike and very casually said, "Mike, why do you suppose you'd want this ashtray?"

Mike answered, "We have guests who sometimes smoke. That particular ashtray was sent to me as a very meaningful gift from a friend, and it looks nice on the table."

Then Fred said, "Mike, tell me, what do you suppose you'd give for that ashtray?" Mike Douglas mentioned a figure and Fred Herman said, "OK, I guess I'll let you have it."

Fred was smooth and effective, and all he did was ask questions. The audience loved it! It doesn't always go that easily, but the more we ask questions in a skilled manner, the better results we'll gain.

Asking the right questions in the right way is more important now than ever. The thrust of high performance selling today is responding to needs and tailoring a solution to meet those needs. Faulty information-gathering procedures can short circuit the entire sales process, so it's vital that it be done correctly.

Asking Sensitive Questions

Your questions about sensitive or personal issues may go unanswered unless you first assure your customer that you'll keep this information in confidence. You might say something like, "Mr. Prospect, in order to do the best job possible for you, I need to ask some questions. Some of the questions will be simple and routine, and some may touch on some in-depth or rather confidential areas.

"I want to say two things to you here. One is that any questions you would rather not answer, just tell me. No problem. Second, please be assured that the information you share with me will not be available to anyone else unless I first run it by you, which I would do in the event that an opportunity to share the information would serve you better."

In effect, you are simultaneously doing three valuable things:

1. You're asking his permission to ask him questions.
2. You're letting him know that this is a necessary part of the process for best serving him.
3. You're assuring him that his information will be kept in confidence.

This process should reduce any defensiveness or apprehension the prospect may have toward you, and it should make him more comfortable with you.

Now let's talk about some guidelines for asking questions. First, what do we want to learn?

Ask Questions To Help You Learn

Ask questions that will reveal the prospect's mind-set or position on the topical area. Something as general as "How do you feel about thus and so?" will usually work well. But assuming that we know how a customer feels about an issue can get us in trouble. Remember that *reality is a viewpoint,* and his viewpoint may be very different from ours.

Ask questions necessary to inform you of what the client wants to accomplish in the subject area. For example: "Mr. Prospect, would you tell me about your goals in this area?"

Next, why are we asking questions? The answer is, to carry out the information-gathering process in a professional manner and let the prospect know that it is his needs you'll be addressing. Also, to eventually be in a position to make the highest quality recommendation to him.

I think you'll agree that the toughest person to sell is the one who never says anything. The best solution to this dilemma is to get the prospect talking by asking questions of him or her. The better we are at asking questions, the higher the quality of the interaction and the more involved we will be with the prospect.

So, how do you go about asking questions? Ask an appropriate quantity of questions for openers. Don't overdo it, but be thorough enough to be professional. Simply asking the prospect his opinions can be extremely effective.

Get Them Talking – And Take Notes!

Don't ask questions which tend to induce feelings of guilt or inadequacy. Always justify asking questions which may touch on those sensitive areas mentioned. A relaxed, low-key style is conducive to gaining more in-depth answers. When you ask questions that are difficult to answer, you create tension on the part of the prospect. This can only work against you.

Always take a lot of notes. You will retain more. A secondary benefit of taking thorough notes is that it's a nonverbal way of showing your interest in the prospect.

When do you ask certain questions? Timing is important. Be sure the prospect is comfortable with you and that you've established a good communications flow. As a rule of thumb, ask the more basic questions first, then the more personal and in-depth ones a bit later.

To whom will you direct your questions? If you're selling an individual or couple, *who* is an easy question to answer. But in a corporate or industrial setting, the situation becomes more complex. You need to do some creative research to identify the principal decision makers and the decision influencers. Try to talk to everybody who is in the decision loop, if possible.

If you do your primary questioning with someone who is giving you data inconsistent with the priorities of the principal decision makers, you're obviously setting yourself up for frustration and potentially a lost sale. I'm comfortable making this broad recommendation: Question all of the decision influencers you can, but plan your eventual presentation proposal around the input gained from individuals you think have the most influence on the ultimate decision.

Types of Questions

Questions come in all forms and weights. First there are *results-oriented questions*. An example of a results-oriented question would be, "Are you looking for ways to increase net profit *and* sales, Mr. Prospect?" His answer should give you his desired result.

Then there are *open-ended questions*. This is also known as the indirect probe. It might go something like, "How do you feel about our terms, Mr. Prospect?"

Next we have *closed questions*, known as the direct probe by some. An example of the closed question would be this: "When will a decision be made on this, Mr. Prospect?" That's a direct question requiring a direct answer.

Another type is *relationship-enhancing questions*. This is any question you can ask that will give your prospect the idea that you're working for him and that the relationship is important. If he sees you as a professional and valuable resource rather than a self-serving type, you are on your way to a shorter sales cycle and a greater probability of getting a "Yes." Here's a possible example: "I learned ten years ago that I could never present solutions that would serve my customers' best interests until I thoroughly understand their project mission, Mr. Prospect. So may I ask you the priorities of the goals you've shared with me?"

There are also *confirmation questions*, which are very useful in avoiding misunderstandings. An example would be this: "Let's see if I understand your greatest need. You want this training to ultimately decrease salesperson turnover and increase average size of order, correct?" Another good one is this: "In terms of priority, which of these do you and your fellow executives want to work on first?" Restating answers can be very effective. Let your restatement follow the words, "Let me see if I understand correctly…"

It's important that your questions be non-threatening and easy to answer. We want this to be a pleasurable, informative experience for both parties, not frustrating for your prospect.

Asking questions in the selling process is considered an art by many. To ask the right questions, at the right time, in the right way, is a true skill that requires diligent practice and pays great dividends. I'm convinced that the vast majority of true high performance salespeople today have mastered this skill and continue to cultivate it in an attempt to perfect it even further.

The Fine Art of Listening

Mastering the art of asking questions won't do you much good if you neglect the art that's the Siamese twin of asking good questions, and that's good listening.

Do you know people who ask good questions, then don't pay any attention to the answers? Their problem is usually a lack of attention to detail. I've had that problem from time to time myself. And when it happens to me, I'm reminded of the story about Fritz.

During World War II, the French general got all his infantrymen together and said, "Men, we must defeat the Germans, and I've decided how we can do it. We will use creative battle strategy.

"Most of the German soldiers are named Fritz, " he said. "What we'll do is get down on the front lines and we'll holler, 'Hey Fritz!' Fritz will stand up and say 'Ya!', and POW! We shoot him down."

The infantrymen cheered. They thought the plan would work. And it did! For days they are wiping out Germans right and left.

Well, one smart German general figured out the French general's game plan. He called all the German infantrymen together and said, "Men, we must defeat the Frenchmen, and we are going to beat them at their own game.

"Most of the Frenchmen are named Pierre," he said. "We will get down on the front lines and we holler, 'Hey, Pierre!' Pierre will stand up and say, 'Oui!' and then POW! We shoot him down."

The German infantrymen thought this was great, right? The first old German gets down on the front lines. He said, "Hey, Pierre."

Pierre said, "Is that you Fritz?"

And then Fritz stands up and says "Ya…"

Well, you know what happened. Failure to listen can be disastrous. It was for Fritz. And it can be disastrous for your career. Unless you develop good listening skills, even the most effective questions will be useless.

It's OK Don – The Richest Man in America Is Laughing

When I addressed the annual sales meeting of Foster and Kleiser Outdoor Advertising at the Anatole Hotel in Dallas, I was amused to learn at the end of my talk that financier and multi-billionaire John Kluge was in the audience. John has been recognized by *Forbes* magazine on their

"400 Richest Americans" list as Number One (the richest) for several different years. His Metromedia, Inc. owned Foster and Kleiser.

John Kluge loved the talk and laughed as hard as anyone at the Pierre-Fritz story, even though he is of German descent. John Kluge is a gracious man with a philanthropic spirit. He paid for the life-saving brain surgery on Craig Shergold of England, the young man who earned the *Guinness Book of World Records* for receiving more get well cards than anyone, ever. Isn't it amazing what happens when you set a goal and ask for help from people who care?!

Murphy Is Always With You

Here's a story to show what a mistake you can make by not asking the right questions. A salesman approached an old man in a rocking chair on his front porch. A dog was resting beside the man. The salesman thought he'd break the ice, so he began by asking, "Does your dog bite?"

"No," the old man said. So the salesman reached out to pet the dog, and the dog tried to take the man's arm off at the elbow! The salesman looked with amazement at the old man and said, "I thought you told me that your dog doesn't bite?"

"He doesn't," the old man said. "But that's not my dog."

Well, the cost can be high for failing to ask good questions, listen, and evaluate what you hear. It can cost you time, money, productivity, relationships, opportunities, sales, and, in some cases, an arm or a leg!

A Neglected Skill

Have you ever missed a luncheon appointment by going to the wrong restaurant? Or missed meeting someone at the airport because you had the wrong flight information? I have a friend who flew in for a meeting to find he was a day late, and others who found themselves in Hot Springs, Virginia when they were supposed to be in Hot Springs, Arkansas!

What's the central problem behind these scenarios? That's right: poor listening skills. It's been said that we receive twelve to fourteen years of training in writing, eight to ten years in reading, six weeks to a year in learning about speaking. But how much training have any of us ever received in listening? Not much, in most cases.

If you're like most of us, you have very little if any instruction in how to listen. And yet, studies say that when you look at the breakdown of how we communicate, you'll find that we spend 9 percent of our time communicating by writing, 16 percent by reading, 30 percent by talking, and 45 percent of our communication takes place by listening. This means you have the least amount of training for the way you communicate most often!

Without good listening skills, we don't understand or remember what was said. I'm told that on the average, we forget 64 percent of what we hear in 24 hours and 96 percent after 15 days.

I'm persuaded that high performance salespeople possess above- average listening skills because they work at it. It's one of the reasons for their outstanding productivity. They absorb, then reflect and respond.

The Price We Pay

Poor listening can be the cause of internal conflict, accidents, production breakdowns, lost customers, personality clashes, family stress, poor morale, and bad communication. Many of these dilemmas are avoidable with good listening skills.

One of the reasons some people are poor listeners is that they don't pay attention to the speaker. They fail to hear because their minds are undisciplined. They think about today's lunch or last night's game, anything but what's going on. Often the poor listener is self-centered and considers what the speaker is saying less important than other concerns.

Good listeners, on the other hand, are oriented toward the speaker. They focus on what's being said, and they come away with the right information. Good listeners hear what other people say. They are involved in external reality. External reality is a concern for not only what the other person is saying, but the meaning behind those words.

Poor listeners are usually involved in *internal* reality. Internal reality is concern for yourself and your inner thoughts while being oblivious to what is being said by the other person. Remember this: If you miss an important buying motive or a special need because of poor listening, nobody wins but the competition.

One reason people fail to hear is that they think faster than others speak. I'm sure you've had those times when you've been in a conversation wondering, "When will this person get to the point?" This difference creates a vacuum that needs to be filled, a vacuum called psychological slack.

One Cause Of Listener Distraction

To illustrate psychological slack, assume that the typical listener can comprehend at a rate of 600 words per minute. And that the typical speaker talks at the speed of approximately 150 words per minute. The difference is slack. And that's the time when our minds wander to everything but the matter at hand.

Psychological slack can become a trap of mental tangents unrelated to what's being communicated. You've heard of people getting off on a tangent. We all do it periodically, I suppose, in speaking and listening. Just remember that it detracts from quality communication when we allow it to happen. Discipline is our ally in good listening. It helps us direct attention to the subject at hand.

I believe there are certain factors that can make a real difference in your ability to listen well, and there are certain steps you can take to be a better listener. You see, good listening is not an accidental happening but a skill.

Six Steps To Becoming A Good Listener

First, good listeners *absorb*. Poor listeners impatiently wait their turn to speak, thinking about what they'll say next. The best way a salesperson can absorb is to go into an interview with a pre-determined resolve to concentrate on what the prospect says.

Secondly, good listeners *reflect*. They reflect what's just been said to acknowledge and ensure their inner thoughts. Or they reflect outwardly or verbally. An example of verbal reflection would be when you say something like, "Mr. Prospect, am I understanding correctly that your senior vice president has mandated securing higher quality components?"

In other words, we rephrase and clarify important points to improve understanding as well as general listening skills. Poor listeners jump in often with a poor bridge to the speaker's previous comments. Instead of reflecting what has just been said, poor listeners turn the focus on themselves.

Third, good listeners *respond* to what has been said. A general or simple comment in agreement with the speaker's premise is all it takes. Poor listeners often respond with an off-target statement. If this has happened to you, you know how frustrating it can be. Off-target statements really turn prospective buyers off.

Fourth, *pay total attention.* Concentrate on your prospect's remarks and try to read between the lines to ascertain full meaning. Don't just pretend you're listening to appease your prospect; try to learn more than your competitor would in the same scenario.

Fifth, *be a student of non-verbal skills.* People don't always say exactly what they think or feel. Observe gestures, expressions, voice inflections, and special emphasis on key points. Remember, too, that you can usually increase a person's inclination to talk with good eye contact, nods, positive responses, etc., and decrease their verbalizations with a lack of these behaviors.

Sixth, *enable venting* when the prospect feels the need. Sometimes a prospect gets emotional and must speak out about the strong feelings they have. Let them! Don't interrupt or take issue. Let them get it all out, and then sensitively say something like, "I can understand how you feel…"

Quality Listening Makes People Feel Important

Prospects want to feel understood; they want to feel important and acknowledged. I have a feeling that you do, too. Now if that's the way I want to feel as one member of the conversation, how do the other participants want to feel? My bet is they want to feel the same way.

People don't care how smart you are, how creative you are, how entertaining you are or what you're selling until they know how you feel about them and their needs. And how you listen to them is one of the big indicators of your feelings towards them.

The degree to which we participate in quality listening is, in my opinion, determined by two things. One is the *interest level* of the listener in the person speaking (very difficult to hide, incidentally) and the subject matter being discussed. Two is the *degree* to which the listener has developed disciplined listening skills.

Say What?

Long-time friend and Mannington (the flooring professionals) executive Frank Hearst was recently telling me about one of the company's best dealers, a man who has achieved consistent extraordinary results in a tough, competitive market because of great communications skills. He is Al Keppler, general manager of LFO Linoleum & Carpet in Springfield, NJ. Al says quality listening has helped him earn business for years.

On one occasion a woman came into Al's store to choose new kitchen flooring. Al immediately established rapport with her, then began asking some key questions. He listened carefully to her responses and took notes.

When Al went to the woman's home to measure the kitchen, she made several phone calls from the kitchen where he was working. Without intentionally eavesdropping, Al happened to overhear the woman talking about buying carpet for several hotels she owned. It was just too promising to neglect, so Al made his move.

"I can't remember if I mentioned it to you in the store the other day," Al said, "but I wanted you to know that we do institutional carpeting also – schools, hotels, those kinds of projects."

"Funny you should mention that," the woman said. "I'm in the market for some hotel carpeting. I've already selected what I want, and would you take a look at it and give me your professional opinion?"

She showed Al her choices for the rooms, and he told her it was nice but she would undoubtedly get better service and longer life from something a little heavier. Her selection for the stairs was a burber-texture carpet, and Al suggested something a little less casual to work better with the hotel's more formal interior decorating scheme. He gave his honest opinion without being pushy.

Before the week was over, the woman was back in Al's showroom looking at *his* carpet. Al eventually was able to sell the woman carpeting for several hotels. And the sale happened because Al kept his ears as well as his eyes open for opportunity.

Remembering Names Pays Dividends

Case in point: How many times have you heard someone say, "Well, I can remember faces, but I just can't remember names"? Have *you* ever said that? Do you know why people can't remember names? Usually it's because they never caught the name in the first place!

If you get that name within the first 30 seconds of meeting someone, you have increased tenfold your chances of remembering it. When you hear it, repeat it immediately to the person you're meeting by using it in a sentence. Write it down at your first opportunity if you must, but get it in your mind early on. If you get the name, you can use it to preface an important question. The prospect will listen to you with greater interest after hearing his or her name used.

Don't forget to clarify pronunciation also. Picture the spelling and put effort and concentration into the process. Remembering names is more a function of listening than a function of memory.

All of these variables and activities fit under the umbrella of "the art of listening." If we're going to be quality listeners, we must put quality effort into the process.

My friend Dr. Manny Steil has spent a great deal of time researching the topic of listening. "The ability to listen well, if ardently pursued, will reap enormous benefits," Manny Steil says. I'm convinced that effective listening will pay great dividends in every salesperson's future.

The listening errors that cost money, ruin relationships, and even result in the loss of life can be dramatically reduced. Beyond this, cultivating the ability and desire to listen well will allow us to maximize our potential. Listening is surely essential to any genuine meeting of minds and hearts. And we both know that if minds and hearts fail to meet, few sales are made.

Successful Application 8

Featuring: Scott Reid, Sales Representative, Smith & Nephew Richards Distributor; Dallas, TX office

Submitted by: George Howard, Senior Vice President, Sales and Marketing, Smith & Nephew Richards Orthopedic Division; Memphis, TN (A unit of Smith and Nephew, London, England)

My rookie year as a salesman was 1991, and I learned plenty during that first 12 months. One of the most important lessons I learned was that reading your *customer* means as much as – maybe more than – reading all the product literature and technological journals. It's essential for a salesperson to have in-depth product knowledge, but you've got to know your customers in-depth too.

The best way to get to know the customer is to ask a lot of key questions and then really listen to what the customer says. By listening, I mean not just hearing the words but reading between the lines – eye contact, body language, what the customer *doesn't* say.

There were two things I did after talking with a customer that I think made a difference in my effectiveness as a salesperson. One, I'd keep a detailed record of what the customer had communicated to me about his or her needs, problems, goals, interests, or whatever. I have a little microcassette recorder that I keep in the car and, after every call I made, I'd record what was said and done at the meeting. I included all the specifics on anything the customer had asked me to do. Then I'd make notes from the recording and plan my next call on that customer, based on my notes.

The second thing was that, when I met with the customer again, I'd always bring them something that was exactly what they had requested when we last talked. I'd remind them of our conversation and what it was they had indicated an interest in. This impressed customers because they knew I had listened carefully and worked hard to meet their needs. Once I started doing this, customers were glad to see me when I came in.

Doing your homework is important to all salespeople, but it's even more urgent when you're calling on doctors because they are always rushed and have little time for chit-chat. You may have only a minute, maybe 30 seconds with the doctor, so every word and phrase counts. If you don't get their interest immediately, you'll miss a lot of opportunities and sales.

Before every call, I'd review my notes and know exactly what I would say the minute I had the doctor's attention. I'd practice three or four different ways to say my message, based on the situation. I would then decide which of these rehearsed approaches would have the greatest positive impact and practice it further. This process enabled me to maximize my effectiveness on every call. It all begins with asking quality questions, then listening carefully.

Today everyone in my industry (orthopedic medical supplies) has products that are similar, so product differential seldom determines whether you get the sale or your competitor does. Service is everything, and I'm talking about high-powered, highly-personalized service. You learn to read your people, to really understand what they are telling you, and then you start servicing them before they know what hit them! That's my philosophy, and it's one reason I won recognition *in my rookie year* as "General Surgery Representative of the Year" out of 225 salespeople in my company.

Don's Parting Thought

Converse with as many decision influencers as possible. Ask quality questions with great skill. Listen attentively and care about the answers. Take diligent notes. Probe further for detail, depth of feelings, and opinions. Clarify and confirm often to avoid misunderstandings. Never forget the reason you have two ears and one mouth!

Skill #9

✦✦✦✦✦

Needs Analysis Selling

"In selling, as in medicine, prescription
before diagnosis is malpractice."

—JIM CATHCART

In the profession of selling today, the diagnosis stage is the process of performing an in-depth Needs Analysis. Today the Needs Analysis is a more important step in the selling process than ever before.

You can do a better job for your customers, your company and yourself if you'll perform a Needs Analysis with each sales effort. All other things being equal, the salesperson who can competently perform a Needs Analysis will enjoy a significantly higher closing percentage than salespeople who cannot or do not. The salesperson today who makes a presentation on his product, service, or idea without first performing this Needs Analysis is simply stacking the cards against himself and shooting himself in the foot.

Many years ago, the selling process often evolved into a debate. The salesperson who had more answers than the prospect had objections often made the sale. A win-win attitude is favored today and, as time goes by, will become even more important. Confrontational, debate-oriented sales approaches are a thing of the past. They are not conducive to making a sale today or developing relationships for making future sales.

Objection-Free Selling?

When salespeople are involved in Needs Analysis selling that is done properly, they experience something that often amazes them. The number of sales objections they experience will customarily drop dramatically.

One reason this occurs is that you have uncovered the prospect's true feelings – their apprehensions, desires, needs, and expectations – so well that negative input in the selling cycle is less likely.

Another reason Needs Analysis selling is so valuable is that it not only puts you in a position of making higher quality recommendations and thus doing a superior job for your customer, but it also shows your customer that you are genuinely interested in him and the results he gains. The customer is far more comfortable with this approach because he sees you as a professional problem solver who is a valuable resource to him, rather than a shallow persuader who wants to get into his pocket.

Give yourself a competitive edge. Vow today to become one of the best in your field at Needs Analysis selling.

"Needs Analysis" Defined

What is "Needs Analysis" selling? It's a process of information-gathering performed to help you discover customers' needs and desires, followed by in-depth examination of all factors that have impact on the buying decision.

Your goals in performing a Needs Analysis should be:

1. To create initial positive prospect involvement (a means of winning the prospect over early)

2. For you and the prospect to become keenly aware of, and begin to focus on, existing needs and desires

3. For you to gain a clear assessment and understanding of those needs as the prospect sees them. If there are multiple needs, attempt to ascertain client priority.

4. For you to establish genuine trust and rapport with the decision makers and the decision influencers as you gain an authentic understanding of their feelings and desires

5. To gain sufficient high-quality input so that you are postured for an affirmative decision when you make your recommendations

Let's Get Started

Now let's get into the process. First a question: Did you ever hear of a salesperson who gave an absolutely magnificent sales presentation to someone who could not make a decision? I bet we've all done that at some juncture in our selling career.

Work diligently to try to talk with every person whose opinion will impact on the ultimate decision. That might well include not only principal decision makers, but also users of the product or service or people on the periphery who might well be decision influencers. Even if your interaction with these people is brief, remember this: The more people whose opinion you ask, the more you will learn and the more allies you will have in that organization. This will facilitate your attempt to make the sale, and it will be very helpful in subsequent sales calls on that organization. People enjoy being given opportunities for *authorship!*

In a good Needs Analysis setting, you should do 20 percent or less of the talking and your prospect or prospects should do 80 percent or more. Remember, the Needs Analysis is an information-gathering process and you should take in-depth notes. When I perform a Needs Analysis, I'm usually writing as fast as I can, gaining page after page of valuable data.

The Palest Ink...

I'm sure you've heard it said that "the palest ink is better than the greatest memory." One thing that impresses prospective buyers is for you to reference specific details, quotes, facts, etc., that you learned from him in a previous visit. It shows him that you are a pro, a good record keeper, a person concerned about the details related to his needs, someone who is concerned about helping him make quality decisions based on thorough information gathering. It also serves to remind him that no interaction with you is a waste of time.

As I stated earlier, memory experts say we forget 64 percent of what we hear within 24 hours, and 96 percent of what we hear within 15 days. Based on the interim period between sales calls, if we don't take diligent notes, we can turn prospective buyers off with our inability to capture, store and reference important data from previous appointments.

One good reason for taking lots of notes is the high-impact, positive impression it makes on the prospect. People love to see you write down what they say; it's ego nurturing and will represent a behavior your prospects relish. The prospect will be impressed when you say, "Mr. Martin, you may recall that on November 2 you told me that your loss-claim ratio was approximately two percent...is that still the case?" Don't rely on your memory; take notes and save that mental energy for amassing new and additional closing skills.

Incidentally, if you are talking to a group of people in a Needs Analysis setting or interviewing numerous people individually, I suggest you put the initials of the individual in front of the notes you take so you will know later who said what. This can be very important to you later when evaluating all the information gathered and the source of it.

Gathering Information From The Masses

Many times you will find that several people will be involved in the Needs Analysis process. I think this is good.

Most people would agree that all of us are smarter than one of us. And many times a great synergism can be created. Just remember that high performance salespeople always assess needs before selling products and services. That's another code you should never violate. A good guideline is to assess needs first, then present solutions.

The length of time spent on a Needs Analysis can vary widely. If you sell a high-ticket item, the Needs Analysis might require several visits with numerous people over an extended period of time. On the other hand, if you're selling a low ticket item or product, you might make a call, do a brief Needs Analysis, and give your presentation and recommendations in one call.

I'm convinced that in any selling scenario, the Needs Analysis, even if brief, will contribute greatly to your sales results. Following are some helpful guidelines that I think you can use in performing your Needs Analysis:

1. Do more listening and writing than talking.

2. Try to get pertinent in-depth information. Get below the surface issues if you can. You may need to assure your prospect that the information will be kept confidential.

3. Ascertain what kind of solution they have used in the past for similar problems and needs, since the best predictor of future behavior is past behavior. This will help you know your prospect better, his company's *buying behavior,* and perhaps influence your recommendations.

4. Learn their company philosophy, goals and mission when you can, and learn who the key players are. That will normally be very helpful later.

5. Always end your Needs Analysis with a general question. Try something like: "Based on what you know about me and our company, in what area do you feel we can be most valuable to you?" This is general, but it usually ends the Needs Analysis session on a high note with a good interaction.

The 34,000-Foot Needs Analysis

Meeting a stranger on an airplane and ultimately selling him my service is a gratifying experience. I've done this on numerous occasions through the years after conversing with an interesting executive at a high altitude.

A few years ago on a non-stop flight from Memphis to San Francisco I met Charles Sebastian, a distinguished executive and President and CEO of Aerojet Tactical Corporation. This was my first (and only!) encounter with someone in the business of manufacturing rockets.

We exchanged pleasantries, began talking, and soon he had invited me to call him "Chuck." As we continued to talk, I sensed some frustration on his part, despite his upbeat professional style.

More evidence of Chuck's frustration came to the surface as he began explaining that he had been with Aerojet for about 20 years but president for only six months. The company's dozen or so senior vice presidents were doing a good job, he went on to say, but several of them were disappointed that they did not get the nod for the presidency. (Chuck had been an Aerojet senior vice president himself before being named president.)

As he elaborated, I learned that the morale in the upper ranks of this organization was not up to par, despite Chuck's diligent efforts as the company's new leader to win the senior vice presidents over after the transition. After discussing some of the problematical aspects of this situation in depth, Chuck turned to me and asked, "What business are you in?" I replied, "I am a speaker and consultant to corporations."

"You are? Well perhaps you would have some ideas on how I can deal with this dilemma," he said.

"Chuck," I replied, "I do have some ideas on it, but if we are going to look into your situation in greater depth, I would like to do it right."

With that, I got my briefcase out from under the airline seat, pulled a legal pad from it, and proceeded to begin my Needs Analysis process. "Let's start from the beginning," I said.

At those words, Chuck eagerly jumped in and began providing detailed information for me as I furiously took notes. Remembering that in a good Needs Analysis session the salesperson should do less than 15 percent of the talking, I made my questions brief and direct. In the best case scenario, the customer or prospect will take the lead and start giving in-depth responses. Fortunately, that's what Chuck did.

He relished seeing me taking notes. In fact, he looked over my shoulder quite often to observe what I was writing down. In one case, he even leaned over closer and pointed to the pad, saying, "You misspelled that name right there." He was really into it! An hour and forty-five minutes – and several pages of handwritten notes – later, the bell sounded that signaled our descent into San Francisco.

I decided it was time for a trial close, so I said, "Chuck, as I understand it, what you would like for me to do is consider this information and put together a proposal that would reflect my perspective of the best solution to the problem from a training point of view."

"That's right," he said. "If you could get something to me in a couple of weeks, that would be great."

I said that would be fine but, I added, "If it's okay with you, Chuck, I may need to call you back on a couple of occasions to gather more information and perhaps to talk with some of your senior vice presidents. Would that be OK?" Chuck eagerly agreed.

I sent him my promotional kit, references he had requested, etc. upon my return to Memphis, and by then I was into *program structure*.

Chuck and I talked on the telephone on two or three occasions during the following week to discuss minor details of the training assignment. I also had conversations with some of his key people. I then put together and sent by Federal Express a comprehensive proposal representing a substantial corporate training package for Aerojet. Chuck liked what he saw and he bought it.

I am convinced that Chuck signed that contract, not because I was a great salesperson, but because I did an excellent job of gathering information and then presented to him a solution *which he helped create.*

Successful Application 9

Featuring: John Schumacher, Director of Regional Sales, National Linen Service, a division of National Service Industries, Inc.; Atlanta, GA
(Author Interview)

While employed as national sales manager for an Illinois-based manufacturing company, I received a chilling phone call one day from our top salesman. He informed me that our relationship with a major health care buying group was in serious jeopardy. This account was not only our number one commercial customer but also represented over $100,000 in annual commissions to our representative.

We were in the final quarter of our second consecutive three year (sole source) contract, and our most powerful managerial allies had been promoted to operational vice presidents in different divisions. Unfortunately for us, their replacements had well-known preferences for our biggest competitor. It appeared that we no longer had the inside track.

As anticipated, we were instructed to appear before a newly-established purchasing committee of seven, whose purpose was to evaluate the primary manufacturers in our market. Further, we were required to submit samples and a contract proposal for three years.

During an emergency strategy session, our company agreed that we would maintain the integrity of our national account pricing, even though we were certain that at least two competitors would attempt to "buy the business." We resolved that we would use uniqueness coupled with creativity in our sales negotiation. We were determined not to be "out professionalized"!

This is the approach we adopted:

I. We developed a telephone survey that would:
   - Evaluate our six-year reputation as to user satisfaction, product performance, and service
   - Identify any current system malfunctions so that we could take corrective action
   - Invite candid critique of our equipment, our installers, and our company

II. Within the health care buying group, we surveyed 100 percent of all users of our equipment. A total of 187 surveys were completed.

III. We provided each committee member with a three-ring binder containing information about the survey. Included in the binder were:

- Copies of all 187 completed surveys for review by committee members
- Details on those individuals interviewed, their department and the geographic location of their facility
- An analysis/summary of the survey, which revealed 95 percent customer satisfaction. According to the survey, only 23 systems had required service and 97 percent of those serviced rated our product good or very good
- One sheet of positive comments and one sheet of criticisms
- Final section for conclusions and recommendations
- Testimonial letters from members of their health care group

IV. We created a two-part video in which our company president discussed the importance of this customer's account and expressed appreciation for their patronage. In the video, our company's director of research and development told viewers how two suggestions from the survey had resulted in new product modifications. We decided to show samples of the two product improvements along with our other samples.

V. Our proposal and contract were presented in a leather-bound book with the name of the buying group and the corporate logo hot-stamped on the cover.

Our investment figures were the highest of the companies that were interviewed by the committee. But after the committee had completed its interviews and discussions, our company was awarded a *five year exclusive contract!* I believe the special effort we put forth in examining the needs of our customer, conducting the survey, and preparing an impressive presentation contributed greatly to our triumph.

DON'S PARTING THOUGHT

If you proficiently perform the Needs Analysis, you are preparing yourself to ultimately deliver a presentation that your prospects helped design . Do this and you'll sell more, faster than ever before.

Skill #10

◆◆◆◆◆

The Needs–Based Presentation

"There are very few problems in business that more sales won't solve."

—ELMER WHEELER

Have you ever known a salesperson who had "I" trouble? That's a person who goes into a presentation armed only with "I" words: "Let me tell you about what I...me...we..." This is a salesperson asking for disappointment. Prospects consider such conversations extraordinarily boring.

High performance salespeople don't have "I" trouble. They go into a presentation focusing on the prospect they want to serve. They use "I" to ask, "What can I do for *you?*"

When you focus your conversation and energies not on yourself but your prospects, when you get into the prospect's head and identify his needs and dominant buying motives and human behaviors, guess what happens? You give a higher-quality presentation than ever. One reason this happens is that you are using a skill which virtually ensures that you will keep his attention.

Eliminate The Probability of Failure

No matter how great your product is, if you let yourself get preoccupied with what you want to sell instead of directing your focus on the needs that have already been articulated by your prospective buyer, your presentation will normally not be good enough to get a "Yes." You will compromise your closing percentage with that approach.

Your presentation to each prospect should be designed based on your knowledge of what your product can do for the prospect. But even more importantly, you need to focus on what you've identified and agreed on as the *customer's need.*

If you have a professional needs-based sales approach that focuses on what you learned in your information-gathering process, giving the presentation that your prospect helped design will seem like a smart approach. I promise you, this approach will dramatically increase your chances of getting a "Yes."

You need to be so aware of the needs and desired results of your prospects that you never ask them to do anything that is inconsistent with those needs and desires. Can you see where the development of that skill could be of immense value?

To make a presentation based on your prospect's needs, you must be very aware of your prospect's agenda. Such a presentation, one that focuses so strongly on a client's need, is the beginning of the end of the old canned sales pitch of years ago – the verbatim sales talk in which a salesman would have to start all over again if he was interrupted in the middle. By the way, today we don't give "pitches." The word is presentation. The viability of the use of certain words, phrases and presentation components in your business may be undeniable, but your personal presentation of that information is what makes the difference.

During today's needs-based presentation, you must work diligently to tie in the customer's needs. You will have discovered those needs through the information-gathering process just discussed. You'll feed back the data prospects have given you, using a creative win-win strategy to maximize the presentation's impact.

For example, you might say, "Mr. Prospect, you mentioned last week that you get frustrated with people who sacrifice substantial quality for slightly lower price, so I have factored into this proposal a high quality component I think will give you far greater value."

Third Party Impact

Next idea: Share your past successes, either verbally or in print, in a tasteful, low-key manner. Provide information on the great job that you've done for others. Printed referral pages and letters can be helpful in giving your prospects the confidence they need to take action. The more those references relate to their problems and needs, the higher the impact they'll have.

In their excellent book *Strategic Selling*, Miller and Heiman said, "Having a guru or an R&D expert tell a prospective buyer that your company is at the cutting edge of a certain technology may be a much more effective way of getting your message across than your saying, 'We have the best stuff on the market.' " This is a great way to demonstrate your abilities from concept to application.

The "Inside Influence"

Let's discuss the "inside influence" and the trial presentation. The inside influence is an individual with whom you have a special relationship and a special communications link. I have enjoyed several such relationships through the years. These were people who really wanted the company to buy my training and were willing to help any way they could to assist me in closing the boss.

Your inside influence will tell you more than others within the organization might tell you. He or she will be very frank as to what people want and need and what others are thinking about your proposal. The inside influence can be extremely valuable to you in the process of putting together your offer to an organization.

I recommend that you make a trial presentation to your inside influence. This presentation should be informal, confidential, no visuals, just verbal. Run it by them before you give your formal presentation. Ask for specific feedback. Say something like, "Sue, let me give you a rough idea of what my presentation will contain and see how you feel about it before I formally present it to the committee." Even with your inside influence, it is risky to go into the numbers. Talk concept, not price.

Present the material to your inside influence in an informal fashion. Get and evaluate his or her response. Also ask how she or he thinks others on the committee will respond. What are the individual feelings that might be expected as a result of that presentation and the concepts being presented? Ask about any "hot buttons" you may be overlooking.

Incidentally, if this person reveals your offer to other key people before your formal presentation, this idea could backfire. It could take the wind out of your sails, so be careful. You may want to withhold some facts or numbers in the trial run before your inside influence.

Have A Consensus Audience

I also suggest that you do yourself a big favor and attempt to have every decision maker and decision influencer present for your formal presentation. A presentation without them is often foolhardy, not unlike an airline sending a 747 non-stop across the ocean with two passengers on board. What a waste. Remember, too, that there are some people who can say "No" but don't have the authority to say "Yes."

Sometimes you're better off to just come out and ask, "Mr. Prospect, are you the decision maker in this area, or are there others we'll need to get feedback from?" Be careful not to come across as pushy or offensive here; just try to find out. Often you can learn who the decision maker is by asking a knowledgeable third party.

Another idea is to present yourself (and/or your firm) as one which does some consulting. Tell your contact that there is no charge for Needs Analysis research, information gathering, and program (or presentation) creation; the only thing you request is that all decision makers and influencers be on hand for your presentation. This is a reasonable request and may give you positioning for a presentation to some key people who might otherwise be unavailable to you.

You Tell Me, I'll Tell Them

This is a bad deal! The prospect you are talking with wants you to do a lot of work but won't let you present to the decision makers. This is not a win-win situation.

In a number of instances, I have declined to do the initial research under these conditions. Think about and evaluate your position carefully when a similar situation arises, because that prospect cannot and will not effectively present your product or service for you (even if they promise to do so!)

Project A Positive Team Image

Next idea: Don't ever refer to your boss, your company, or its executives with the word "they." This has a negative connotation, and it implies a lack of commitment as well as the absence of a team spirit at your firm. It can take the punch out of your presentation. Always say something positive and favorable about your company and about your immediate superiors within the organization. Why is that good? It creates the image of teamwork and a cohesive unit.

I know that some of you will have to look a little harder than others to say something positive about your boss. Bill Gove used to have some great lines on this topic. He'd tell about the salesman who said, "You know, it's a good thing you're buying from me instead of the guy I work for. Boy, what a turkey! I'll tell you how bad he is: If I ever need a heart transplant, I want my boss's heart because it's never been used."

We improve our chances of a sale when we study a prospect's needs. Develop a presentation strategy in advance and use all of the many simple things discussed in this book to deliver a high impact presentation pertinent to your prospect at the time.

Presentation Uniqueness

Try to make every presentation unique. The observant salesperson should be able to make each presentation a one-of-a-kind experience because each individual prospect's problems and priorities are unique. Encourage that prospective customer to participate in the design of the recommended actions. You can do so by simply asking a prospect's opinions and monitoring their responses throughout the interview.

In a sales situation, you're not involved in an attempt to dominate and control. You should be involved in a free-flowing exchange of information, feelings, and opinions. The result of such an exchange should be that the prospect's trust in you is high and, because of that, he'll seldom reject you. The customer will openly advise you of what's getting in the way of a positive decision so you can address any problems in a win-win environment. I'm convinced that the sales presentation which focuses on solution development can be a unique opportunity for you to set yourself apart from your competition.

There's a certain feeling, a special camaraderie that develops when you present your ideas in a manner that specifically and creatively addresses a prospect's needs. Make some references in your presentation that are so specifically and perfectly directed at your prospect's company that he'll know for sure you have designed this for him.

Remember, the way in which you develop and deliver your presentation needs to be exceptional or you'll be *just another salesperson* in the eyes of the prospect.

Assess Motives

You presumably have done a professional job at this point of identifying and clarifying your prospect's needs in the development of a sales presentation. Be sure, too, that you've always done a thorough job of identifying the buying motives of each of the decision makers and decision influencers.

A motive is defined as *an emotional impulse which causes one to take action.* Nothing is more frustrating than giving what you perceive to be a great presentation, only to get an indifferent response. When this happens, it's usually because the presentation missed the mark and didn't focus on the client's dominant buying motive. By the way, it is possible to address *need* without addressing *motive,* so be very careful here. Anytime you can, address both. You're positioned perfectly for getting the "Yes" when you do.

Remember, the I…me…we…focused salesperson will undoubtedly experience a higher level of rejection. It's possible that the most valuable idea you will gain from this book is the art of giving a focused, needs-based presentation.

In conclusion, let's keep in mind that the presentation process should not only focus on client need and motive, but also follow a logical, high-impact sequence. Ask yourself these questions

1. Have I established rapport and trust?

2. Are all of the decision makers present?

3. Have I clarified the decision-making criteria?

4. Am I benefit- and solution-oriented in what I'm about to propose?

If you answer "Yes" to all four questions, I'm convinced you'll be hearing many more "Yes" answers from your prospects . I hope you get firm, positive decisions at the time of your presentations, but sometimes it doesn't all come together. This brings us to another important component in the success formula, Follow- Up.

The Art of Following Up

Have you ever bought something from a salesperson you never heard from again? I think you'll agree that's a depressing experience. High performance salespeople understand the importance of follow-up with prospects as well as existing customers.

Let me give you my definition of follow-up. First, there is *pre-sale follow-up.* This is staying in touch to track the prospect's interest level in your product. It lets your prospect know that he and his ultimate buying decision are important to you.

Secondly, there is *after-the-sale follow-up*. This is staying in touch to track the progress of product use as well as customer satisfaction. Following up after the sale ensures higher customer satisfaction and also keeps the communications channel open and active. I'm convinced that poor follow-up has been instrumental in many lost sales and business relationships that deteriorated.

A recent survey revealed that the number one reason a company did not buy again from a salesperson after the first sale was *indifference*. Today some sales organizations are taking follow-up so seriously that they have paid tens of thousands of dollars for computer software packages designed to meet their needs in the follow-up process. These companies understand the necessity of staying in touch with customers, tracking their needs, monitoring their satisfaction levels, and doing everything possible to serve those customers better than ever.

Still The Best Idea

One simple yet powerful technique many high performance salespeople use is what I call the PHN – the Personally Handwritten Note. These little personal notes are worth their weight in gold. A simple hand-written note on folded card stock is ideal. I believe so strongly in the value of writing personal notes that at one time years ago I developed a full one-hour talk on how to write and send such notes for maximum impact.

I had a gratifying experience last year when I was approached by an audience member following an after-dinner speech in Las Vegas. He said, "Don, I came up to thank you." I said, "I'm glad you enjoyed the speech."

He said, "Don, I'm not thanking you for your remarks tonight. I'm thanking you for the idea you gave me 20 years ago when I heard you in Cincinnati." He went on to say that he had heard my talk about the personally handwritten note. He still sent out handwritten notes religiously, and he estimated that idea had earned him at least $100,000, maybe far more, in commissions during the 20-year period. (Comments like this tend to offset the hassle of endless travel in the speaking/training business.)

Let me give you a couple of guidelines for the PHN's most effective use. It is strongest as a pre-sale follow-up strategy after your initial contact. It sets you apart from other salespeople. Yes, I know all others know about it, but they don't do it. Believe me, 999 people out of 1,000 simply don't do it. And remember this: Our success is not based on what we know, but on what we *do* with what we know.

In terms of guidelines for the effective use of the PHN, I recommend:

1. Keep it brief and relatively non-commercial.

2. Make it personal and write it yourself. (If you are a sloppy writer, try harder.)

3. Use wording that assures the prospect he will get unparalleled attention and service from you. You might say:

Dear Mr. Matthews,

   This is just a note to let you know that I enjoyed meeting you today and look forward to our next visit on May 18. If I can be of any service to you in the meantime, please feel free to call me at the office, 795-4444, or at my home, 797-4444.

Enthusiastically,
Don Hutson

4. Mail the letter promptly after the contact, the same day if possible. It will have a stronger impact that way. You may want to use a commemorative stamp on it. Don't enclose a brochure or any literature with sales copy on it in your PHN.

5. Keep your stamped envelopes, note cards, address book, and anything else you'll need with you when you make calls. Carry them either in your briefcase, car, or wherever they'll be readily available. This isn't a direct sales strategy. It's an indirect means of building your customer base, and at the same time, building their confidence in you.

6. Send PHN's to people other than customers who could have an impact on your sales success – people such as receptionists, your shipping supervisor, or a decision influencer in any area. Also, send a PHN to anyone who gives you leads. A good policy is to always thank people who positively impact your livelihood.

If you like this idea, and I hope you do, plug it into your system for success. Make it a part of your disciplined code of success, a code you simply don't violate. The majority of those who receive your note won't even mention it, but don't let this discourage you. They know you sent it, and they appreciate it.

Codes of Excellence

Would you agree that in professional selling there are some things that represent codes of excellence? I'll give you an example.

Let's take a little trip in our imaginations. You are going to board a flight in Boston and fly non-stop to London. You'll probably be in a jumbo jet regardless which airline it is, and as you walk aboard that aircraft, you may look toward the cockpit and see a captain there. He has gray hair, looks experienced, and makes you feel comfortable.

Maybe you know it will be 20 or 30 minutes before push back, so you think, "I've never been in the cockpit of a jumbo jet. I think I'll say hello to the captain."

And with that you walk up, glance in and say, "How are you doing, captain?" And he says, "Fine. How are you?" You establish rapport, look around, and then you say, "Boy, this is some piece of machinery. It looks like an incredible, state-of-the-art aircraft."

Then you feel compelled to ask him a couple of questions and you say to him, "Tell me captain, how many years have you been flying airplanes?"

And he says something like, "Oh, I guess about 40 years now. I started when I was a kid." You say, "How many hours of flying time do you have?" The captain might look at you and think a second and say, "Oh, probably upwards of 23,000 hours now."

And then you might say to him, "All those years, those hours of experience, that's incredible. By the way captain, you don't still fool with the checklist with all that experience you have, do you?"

I predict that the smile might leave that captain's face, and he might look at you in total seriousness and say something like, "There are some things in your professional code that you never, never violate. For a pilot, the rule to never violate is '*Always use the checklist.*' Not most of the time – always."

You see, no matter how many years of experience or thousands upon thousands of dollars of income they may have, professionals simply don't violate the codes of excellence!

Never Violate Selling's Professional Codes

We have codes in the profession of selling also, and we have a responsibility to adhere to them. The codes of aviation may seem a little bit more critical because those people have lives right there in their hands. On final approach into London, you don't want your pilot to remember to lower that landing gear nine times out of ten. You want that sucker to go down *every time* and lock in place!

We have obvious codes almost as vital that we must live by in selling – codes of integrity…criteria of excellence…education and training standards…etc. Never violate the code; it is a dimension of professionalism.

Successful Application 10

Featuring: Flavil Q. Van Dyke, Management and Communications Consultant, Flavil Q. Van Dyke & Associates; Franklin Lakes, NJ

Submitted By: Christopher Hegarty, Author, Speaker and Consultant; Tiburon, CA

As a young IBM sales representative, I had one product in my line that was very difficult to sell: dictation equipment. Even changing the name to "input processing equipment" didn't help much.

The product was probably over-engineered. I could tell potential clients about gold contact points, triple-plated jeweler's chrome, and a cycolac microphone that would withstand an elephant's weight. I could talk about a piece of equipment that would seemingly last until the year 3000. The problem was that all this quality gave my product a price tag that was two to three times more than that of my competitors. On a couple of occasions, I created a very favorable buying atmosphere, only to have my competitor pull the rug out from under me with price.

My principle account was a major university, and the purchasing department delighted in presumed "savings." Continuing to develop accounts for my competitor was foolhardy; I needed to do something different. I needed more user commitment in addition to product acceptance.

I found a university source willing to give me information regarding faculty promotions and new hires. Even before they settled into their new offices, I moved quickly to set up my equipment on their desks. When they arrived, I'd return to introduce myself, ask questions and further identify their needs as well as give thorough instructions to that person and the secretary. I offered the use of the equipment for a period of time and my personal instruction session as a service so that the potential user could focus on the substance of their new position and not the process.

The people almost always began to use my product right away. After all, it didn't cost them anything. And once you used it, you became hooked. It was truly an exceptional product. Through use, one came to appreciate its intrinsic value. That fact – plus my intense focus on developing good, supportive relationships with my prospects, including a special focus on their individual skills – gave me a tremendous edge over my competition.

I dropped in periodically to see how things were going, to do a little coaching, and to increase my personal visibility. We appreciate your thoughtfulness, people told me. I always tried to remind the user of some benefit he or she received from my equipment, a benefit that I knew my competitor could not offer. I always inquired about special needs or applications they were experiencing in order to be sure that I and my product would be of maximum benefit to them. Purchasing (and my competitors) were strangers to this service that I was rendering to potential customers.

After two to three weeks, when the user had developed a symbiotic association with my product, I gently suggested that we "officialize" the ownership. I had prepared a sample requisition form that made ordering almost automatic. Price was rarely challenged, and the user typically became personally willing to take on the purchasing department if necessary. More often that not, this "routine" processing of a requisition emerged as a purchase order without my competitors ever getting into the act. When they did, the user was already well sold and often adamant about which product he or she wanted.

I found this process worked great. If at anytime I had pushed hard and attempted to close the sale prematurely, it would not have worked. It would have short-circuited the presentation process I had perfected. My approach was the antithesis of the canned presentation followed by the hard close. Instead, my presentation was built on the identification of customer needs coupled with my sincere desire to find solutions to my customers' problems.

This non-traditional type of presentation turned around a negative situation. As a result, a dormant account became one of my base accounts, and I became a national sales leader for IBM.

DON'S PARTING THOUGHT

Identify *customer needs* better than your competition does. Gather information from as many of the decision influencers as you can. Deliver a needs-based presentation that the customer helped you design to the people who have the power to make the decision. Get the commitment, then follow up. Become so valuable a resource to your customers that your competition won't know what hit them!

Skill #11

✦✦✦✦✦

Developing Business: From Suspect to Confidant

❝Man sit in chair with mouth open for very long time waiting for roast duck to fly in.❞

—CONFUCIUS

Confucius was right! If we sit around waiting on things to happen, the only thing that's likely to happen is that our competitors will prosper.

In addition to nurturing existing accounts, we need to have a minimum acceptable number of new calls to make and new accounts to gain each week. This is Step One in building tomorrow's business.

In 1980 the average cost of a sales call, including everything from travel expenses to sample costs, was $137 per call. In 1990, it was over $250 – and it's still climbing. When you consider that expense, any salesperson who isn't working an account for all it is worth is doing his company and himself an injustice.

Brain Damage?

I always enjoy asking sales audiences, "How many of you love to make cold calls on total strangers?" I invariably get a few (but *very* few) hands. It usually gets a roaring laugh when I follow up by asking one of those responding, "How long have you had this brain damage?!" Making cold calls takes courage and intestinal fortitude, but the payoff can be great because you'll have little competition. Most salespeople simply don't like to make cold calls, and I genuinely admire those who do.

It has always been a great challenge to all types of businesses and industries to prospect and develop new business. It must be done or predictable customer turnover will eventually destroy the customer base. Few companies or salespeople have so much business flowing in over the transom that they can afford to neglect the quest for new business.

If companies didn't constantly need new customers, there wouldn't be the need for nearly as many salespeople. Companies in today's sophisticated marketplace need salespeople who are willing to make calls and who are willing and able to develop long-term business relationships.

The Loyalty Ladder

In this chapter, I want to give you six categories of people on what is called the "Loyalty Ladder," which is illustrated on page 144. I was introduced to this idea by my friend Murray Raphel who, along with Ray Considine, developed and researched the concept years ago. I have altered it a bit by adding another rung to the ladder.

I hope you will learn the attributes and definitions of each step on the Loyalty Ladder. Remember that the endless goal of salespeople is to sell more by developing bigger and stronger personal and company followings. Such followings can be developed by clearly understanding the six categories, beginning with the one on the ladder's bottom rung.

Rung 1: The Suspect

The individual at the bottom of the Loyalty Ladder is the one we call the Suspect. A Suspect is an individual or organization who may or may not know about you or your company and may or may not be qualified to buy.

There are usually lots of Suspects, and you'll have to work hard to find out which Suspects can be moved into the second category on the scale. Normally the only way you can find out is to make calls and talk to people.

Rung 2: The Prospect

The second rung on the ladder is the Prospect. A *qualified* Prospect often knows of you or at least your company and, in your opinion, has the ability to buy. This person should be cultivated.

As you work on these Prospects, you'll face the true challenge of selling. This is the crucial point when you are critically compared with your competition and indiscriminately evaluated. You'd better be at your best if you're going to move Prospects into the third category, that of Customers.

Rung 3: The Customer

A Customer is someone who has bought from you or your company at least once. That's a simple enough definition, but many salespeople never grasp the fact that often the easiest sale is one to an existing customer. It can frequently be our best source of additional business.

You probably have lots of Customers to whom you could or should be selling more than you are, either in terms of volume or items in your line. Think about it and I'll bet you'll find some immediate business within your existing customer base. Customers become better profit centers when they become Clients.

Rung 4: The Client

The fourth category is the one into which we want to move the Customer, the category of Client.

A Client is someone who trusts and respects your judgment and accepts your advice. Professional salespeople have Clients. Average salespeople develop very few. They seldom get beyond the Customer category.

The high performance salesperson is a master at developing maximum levels of business from his Prospect and Customer base. Clients are great and should never be taken for granted, but you should try to turn those clients into Advocates, our fifth category.

Rung 5: The Advocate

An Advocate is someone who believes so strongly in you and your products and services that he not only eagerly buys from you everything you have to sell that fits his needs, but also sends you unsolicited business. An ability to develop relationships to the Advocate level is the reason high performance salespeople make strong sales performance look easy. In a very selective way, you may try to move Advocates into our final category on the scale, that of Confidant.

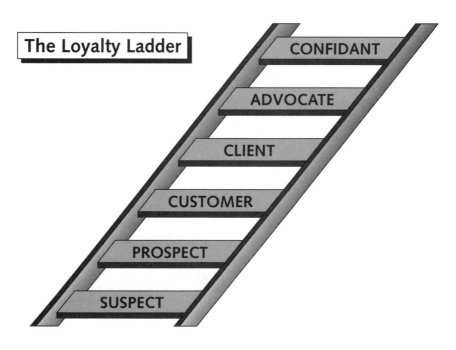

The Loyalty Ladder

CONFIDANT
ADVOCATE
CLIENT
CUSTOMER
PROSPECT
SUSPECT

Rung 6: The Confidant

The Confidant stands at the top rung of the Loyalty Ladder. This is someone with whom you have a special and very close relationship. The Confidant freely and unselfishly gives and takes private advice, with your best interests and friendship being a prime consideration. This relationship requires a great deal of time and commitment to develop and maintain.

Some people may go a lifetime and never have a Confidant. Some may have several. A Confidant buys from you with an unspoken, natural, flowing commitment that often includes all of their business. This relationship is the ultimate in terms of in-depth, authentic communication. You should treasure it.

Manufacturing Good Luck

Perhaps you have seen a salesperson who succeeded magnificently and everyone says, "Oh sure, he's got the such-and-such account. He's had it for years. I'd be making big bucks too if I had that account. He's simply lucky."

Well, critics usually have no idea of the energy, effort and unselfish commitment that goes into such a relationship. In that situation, the successful salesperson is usually selling either to an Advocate or Confidant. As you work on relationships in your territory or marketing area, try to continually upgrade each person's status relative to the six categories we have just discussed. It's an opportunity to manufacture your own *good luck!*

To move people up the Loyalty Ladder, I recommend you follow a specific procedure. First, perform an analysis and profile of your current business base. By that, I mean you should put each account in one of the categories just defined. Next, establish percentage of the total in each category. Then target those accounts you feel can be moved to the next plateau within the next 90 days.

If you're not making progress, you need to work diligently on relationship skills and focus more intently on customer goals and needs. The higher you move a customer up the Loyalty Ladder, the shorter your selling cycle will become and the less competition will be an issue. Speaker and trainer Don Thoren says, "All relationships and their accompanying

145

psychological contracts are being continuously renegotiated, whether we acknowledge it or not." Always maintain respect for those you deal with, and continuously ask yourself, "How can I be more valuable to them?"

Keep Adding To The Pipeline

One other vital component of the equation is that, in addition to moving people up the ladder, we must be adding new accounts to the pipeline.

Adding new accounts will normally require an organized process of making cold calls. Keep in mind that making cold calls can contribute significantly to our growth process and ultimate level of success. You really don't have anything to lose by making the call, and you might realize substantial gain. If you don't consistently make some cold calls, you just may wake up one day and find yourself with no one to talk to.

Many salespeople are reluctant to make that first cold call. There are two simple reasons for this. Number one is that the salesperson feels rather negative about calling on Suspects or marginal Prospects because of the time that it normally takes to get an order from them. That type of call has the longest selling cycle. And number two is that salespeople know that the farther down the scale a prospect is located, the greater the probability of rejection. As discussed earlier, many salespeople handle rejection poorly and don't want to risk it. There's one sure way to avoid it. Quit making calls.

Remember, when you call on Customers, Clients, Advocates and Confidants, your selling cycle becomes progressively shorter. My advice to you is to erase any inhibitions you have about people in any of these categories and go to work hard and fast now.

Set Yourself Apart From Your Competition

Sometimes the non-traditional and creatively-different approach to something will draw new interest levels and a unique following. The need to create a "following" among clients is more than apparent. Before you laugh at what appears to be an off-the-wall approach to achieving your goal, look behind you to see if anyone is following you to hear what you have to say!

Have you developed a creative approach to capturing the intrigue of others, or are you among those in need of a charisma transplant? Set yourself apart with a noble cause that others will become aware of and be impressed by. It can be as captivating as the establishment of a new charitable institution or as basic as a sales idea or customer service technique that is admired by all.

Stanley Mills, one of the most successful real estate sales professionals I know, once heard that a primary reason for the erosion of a client base is that salespeople do not adequately stay in touch with their clients and prospects. Stanley not only sends his clients birthday and Christmas cards, but he also calls each man in his data base three days before his anniversary to remind him of the upcoming event. You won't be surprised to learn that it's the only such call they get that day!

Where Did All My Competitors Go?

Almost every business and industry operating today is becoming more competitive. But, on a personal level, I'm convinced we can largely eradicate our competition. How? By being so relationship-focused and personally proficient at moving our customers to the higher levels of the Loyalty Ladder that the majority of our business is on the top three rungs!

On the bottom three rungs, you are dealing with people who will cut your throat for a hundred dollar bill! (Well, almost.) The competition is fierce down there, and you are just one more member of the masses. Get your customers to the higher rungs on the ladder, and you will be one of the elite big hitters who devotes his time and energies to substantive client issues and problems, rather than groveling with every competitor in town for a single trifling piece of business. Remember, the higher the rung on the ladder you are operating on, the less vulnerable you are to the competition!

Successful Application 11

Featuring: Randy Talaski, Sales Consultant, Healthco International; Tampa, FL

Submitted by: Gerry Mundy, Southern Region Manager, Healthco International; Charlotte, NC

When people talk about developing new business, I think the key word in this phrase is "develop." To me that means cultivating and nurturing a relationship over time, not overnight.

When I started selling for Healthco, I was given what we called a "Yellow Pages" territory. What that meant was that you went into a city and your client list was – you guessed it – the Yellow Pages! Cold calls on dentists. Knock on doors. Lots of us started that way, right?

The way I approached a cold call was to go in with my product and ask the prospect if he was happy with the product he was using now. If the prospect said "No" or hesitated on the way to an affirmative answer, I'd take my product out of my bag and do my best to sell it. But if the prospect was happy, I didn't try to change his mind. At the end of every call, I'd always ask, "Is there any other way I might be able to help you?"

One day early in my career, after I'd asked that question, this prospect who knew I had a service background before becoming a professional salesman began telling me about a piece of equipment he was having problems with. "If you'll give me a few minutes, I'll take a look at it," I told him. "I think I can take care of it and you won't have to call a service technician." That was music to his ears. I went in, repaired it, and didn't charge him. Then before I left, I said, "I want to be a resource to you. Anything I can help you with – products, technical information, even repairs – I want to help. And in the future, when you're thinking of ordering something, I hope you'll remember me."

I didn't get an order that day, but the next time I went in, I got a nice order. And the orders got bigger as time went on. One day that customer told me, "What really impressed me was that you were willing to give of your time and not necessarily expect something in return. It was like you were planting acorns and giving them time to grow."

In my opinion, that's a good description of how you develop business. You plant the seed, cultivate the prospect, nourish the relationship, take good care of the prospect with attention and service and, in most cases, your percentage of that prospect's business will grow. Those early calls, then, are acorn planting.

There's another technique I use in developing my business that may not be for everyone, but it has worked for me. In recent years, I've started to focus in on the clients I want to do business with. Every year I weed out the lowest five percent of the people and companies I call on. I just offer them to a fellow salesperson. That's after I have gone to the company and told them my goals and objectives.

I say, "I'm trying to develop my business so I give my time to the customers who really need me. I've been calling on you for five years, we still aren't doing much business together, and these calls really aren't cost-efficient for me. Am I doing something you aren't satisfied with? What keeps you from giving me a large portion of your business?" That direct approach either turns them into a committed customer or clarifies for both of us that I probably won't be back.

By weeding out smaller accounts that take up an inordinate amount of my time, I'm able to give my larger accounts extraordinary service. These people know that I'm going to be there for them, and they rely on me very heavily. Now my average business per account is larger than that of most salespeople in our company, and I can feel good about the service I'm providing every customer I call on.

DON'S PARTING THOUGHT

Patiently nurture customer relationships with greater creativity and sensitivity than your competitors and you will earn unparalleled allegiance. Your competitors will be calling each other, quizzically trying to figure out what you are doing that is destroying their market share!

Skill #12

✦✦✦✦✦

Building Value Rather Than Cutting Price

❝It's easier to explain price once than
to apologize for quality forever.❞

—ZIG ZIGLAR

High performance salespeople not only sell higher volumes of goods, but they often sell those goods at higher prices. How do they do it? I believe it's because they understand what I call The Value/Price Perspective.

Anytime anyone makes a decision, they consider principally two factors. They consider the perceived value of that product, service or idea. They also have a mental image or perception of the price which they should pay.

The more skill a salesperson possesses, the less likely it is that he or she will be at the mercy of price. In this chapter, I want to share with you some techniques and skills that will help you build a prospect's image of value to the point that price becomes a less significant issue.

The Prospect's Perception

In many situations, people will have a mental image of a price that's greater than their mental image of value. When that happens, is that a sale or no sale? Usually, no sale. That's because people who are normal psychologically usually won't allow themselves to make an affirmative decision if price appears greater than value.

This will happen from time to time to all salespeople. If you are selling products of high quality, there are going to be times when a premium price is involved. You never want to apologize for that. What high performance pros do in this situation is build value. A prospect's perception of value is subjective and, therefore, subject to influence. The good news is that people are more willing to pay for quality and value today than they have ever been!

Keep in mind that a prospect's mental image of value will vary, based on their needs and their perspective regarding price. Every successful salesperson knows that you don't sell everybody the same product the same way. We must consider needs and applications for each prospective buyer.

Perceptions of price involve more than a dollar sign or a specific amount of money. Other factors that impact on a prospect's perceptions include fear of the unknown and the possibility of an undesirable outcome. Convenience, reliability and timing also may be influential.

We can better illustrate the relationship between value and price with this Value/Price Perspective chart:

VALUE/PRICE PERSPECTIVE

Items impacting on one's mental image of VALUE:	*Items impacting on one's mental image of PRICE:*
• Visual appeal of tangible product or visualized appeal of intangible product (and results they offer)	• The "hard cost" of product
• Their perception of your service, your expertise, and your follow-up	• Associated risks
• The sensitivity you display in managing relationships and in offering convenient responses	• The degree to which one perceives others approving or disapproving his/her decision
• The degree to which you focus on the customer's needs and present appropriate product applications to meet those needs	• The probability that one could obtain essentially the same product and/or service elsewhere for less

The best way I know to build value in the prospect's mind is to talk benefits. People say to me, "Don, that sounds fine, but what kind of benefits are you talking about?" Needs-based benefits, based on what *that prospect* needs *at that time.*

In our earlier chapter on Needs Analysis, we learned how to ascertain what people are truly looking for. We build value by showing how our product, service or idea can satisfy those needs. Our value-based presentation should feed back to the customer needs-related data that was gained in the Needs Analysis.

If you don't know how to build value, you'll be faced too often with the alternative of cutting price. And I've been told by sales executives throughout the free world that cutting the price is a less desirable alternative!

My Old Kentucky Home

The best example I've ever experienced of building value came after I'd had the opportunity to address the annual meeting of Jockey International. You know, the underwear people. Don't snicker. In a group of 100 business people, Jockey products will invariably be very well represented!

I did an after-dinner speech to about 700 people for Jockey in Chicago. They were a fabulous audience, positive and responsive. A few weeks later I got a phone call from a man who said, "Don, I heard you speak at the Jockey meeting, and you were terrific."

"Thanks!" I said. "You must be with Jockey."

"As a matter of fact, I'm not," he said. "I was a guest at that meeting. Actually I'm president of a firm that's one of Jockey's suppliers. The chairman of the board of our company and I heard you, and we want you to come give that same talk to our people at our annual meeting three weeks from Saturday. Can you make it?"

Now I love to sell dates on a calendar as much as you love to sell your products or services. But when I looked on my calendar at the date he mentioned, I knew there was going to be a problem.

I saw that Saturday came at the end of a week in which I had six speaking appearances scheduled in six cities in five days. I was to leave town at 5:30 on Sunday afternoon and not get home until 11:15 p.m. on Friday night – a grueling week. So I can tell you that, at that point, my mental image of the value of earning one more speaking fee that week was pretty low, and my mental image of the price I would have to pay was very high.

I had made a pledge to my kids years ago that anytime I was out of town all week long, I'd try to be with them on the weekends. It looked as if the price I might have to pay was greater than my perceived value of the speaking engagement.

So I said to the man, "You're gracious to invite me, but I don't see any way I could make that date. However, I have a lot of friends in the business, so why don't you let me get you another speaker this year and use me next year?"

He said, "Don, let's not give up so easily. Didn't you say in your talk the other night that your wife is into horses?"

"You've got a great memory," I told him. In my talk I had said that years ago, my wife and my secretary got into the Tennessee Walking Horse business. For me, it was about like supporting a heroin habit! He remembered the line.

"Don," he said, "would it intrigue you to learn that we are having our meeting this year at the 5,000-acre horse farm outside of Lexington, Kentucky that belongs to our chairman of the board?"

What is he doing to me here? Well, he's building my mental image of value, is he not?

I said, "5,000 acres? That sounds incredible, and I know it's got to be a beautiful layout. But it's my wife who is into horses. She doesn't normally travel with me. And the truth is, I'm allergic to horses."

Did this slow him down? Not in the least.

"Don," he said, "as I understand it, the problem is that on that Saturday, you need to be with your family. Is that the problem?"

"That is indeed the problem," I told him.

"Well, let me try this one on you for size," he said.

Oh, was he adaptable! Oh, was he ever *smoooth!*

"Tell you what," he continued. "At 10 o'clock on that Saturday morning, if you and your wife and your kids will be at Memphis Aero at the Memphis International Airport, we will send our company Lear jet down to pick you up."

He continued, "It's only a 40 minute flight in the Lear jet from Memphis to Lexington. Then we'll get you and your family off the jet and put you on our Jet Ranger helicopter.

"Now Don," he said, "here's the question I want to ask you, and you ask your wife the same thing. Have you ever experienced a cool, crisp early autumn morning in central Kentucky? When you get into the Jet Ranger helicopter, you climb about 100 feet and you look out and all you see is a hint of fog on the horizon. But then you climb up 200, 300, 400 feet and the fog miraculously dissipates. And as you look across the horizon, you begin to see those rolling bluegrass hills…white fences…prancing race-horses out on their morning run. Have you ever seen that from 400 feet in a Jet Ranger helicopter, Don?" he said.

"Not lately," I said weakly. (You must know that his value-building exercise was working like crazy with me.)

"Don," he continued, "we'll get you over to the meeting to give your talk. After your talk, you can stick around for our social activities if you're so inclined. When you are ready, we'll put you back on the chopper. You, your wife and your kids will be back to the Lexington airport in short order, back on the Lear jet and back in Memphis by 4:00 that afternoon!"

I felt like saying, "Let's book the program. Forget the fee!" Of course I didn't say that. Never cut price when value is there, right?!

One of the best ways to initiate the value-building process is to find out what turns somebody on and give it to them! When the price seemed high to me, the man made the value seem higher. That's what selling is all about: Getting inside people's heads, giving them what they need and what they want, focusing on value and presenting it with good strategy. That gets people turned on. Incidentally, it was a tremendous trip!

Value Is A Viewpoint

Remember that when a person says no or gives you negative feedback, all they are really saying is this: "Based on what you have told me so far, the value of your product, service or idea does not seem great enough to cause me to take positive action when compared to the price."

Keep in mind that even though the value/price perspective is not sufficient to get a "Yes" at this point, as long as your potential client is willing to continue listening, your opportunity to make a sale is still alive.

Remember, too, the premise set forth earlier: You never lose a sale until you give up!

To be a high performance salesperson, you must increase that perceived value by talking needs-based benefits. Learn to keep building value and you will have acquired one of the most valuable skills a salesperson can possess.

The Price of Price–Cutting

Price cutting is a far more expensive exercise than most people realize. For example, if your company is offering for $1,000 a product which has a 40 percent gross profit in it ($400), and if a salesperson gives the customer a 10 percent ($100) discount, that represents a 25 percent decrease in profit! A little bit of discounting goes a long way.

One alternative to discounting in this scenario would be to add value by explaining product superiority or unique benefits that would accrue to the buyer when he selects this product.

Another alternative to the price-cutting process would be to include a premium item. For example, in the earlier scenario, rather than discounting the $1,000 product by 10 percent, you might offer the customer as a premium a whiz-bang widget valued at $149 (your cost – $40) at no additional charge. You would thereby increase his perception of overall value, but it would cost you or your company $40 rather than $100. This way, you have sacrificed only 10 percent of your gross profit rather than 25 percent.

All salespeople should understand margins, the impact of price-cutting, and the creative alternatives that will protect our sacred margins. Without "margin protection," the future viability of our enterprise is questionable!

Don't give away your margin, give away your heart. Give your heart away through extraordinary service and simple caring. Your heart will only get bigger when you give it away. Give away your margin, and you will be mortgaging your future.

Successful Application 12

Featuring: Will Shulte, sales representative of
Chromcraft Furniture; Senatobia, MS
Submitted by: Martin Michael, President, Chromcraft
Division (Senatobia, MS) of Chromcraft Revington, Inc., Delphi, IN

Several years ago one of our successful sales professionals, Will Shulte, called on the national headquarters of a rental company to present our office seating line. We wanted to become the primary supplier for the company's rentals to businesses.

Will already knew that our seating was priced at least 20 percent higher than the product the rental company was carrying. His approach was to build his presentation on the quality and performance of the Chromcraft product in order to justify the additional cost.

At his first meeting with the company, Will realized that this sale was not going to be easy. Price, as he had anticipated, continued to be the primary objection. But even after several unsuccessful calls on the buyer, Will persisted in looking for the right button. Finally he found a way to let facts and figures do the selling for him.

Will did an analysis based on the rental company's records of replacement costs, repair costs, and life of the chairs they were using (our competitor's product). He compared these figures with records on our chairs used in specific large industrial installations.

When this analysis was laid out in front of the decision makers, Will Shulte made his sale. He showed the rental company that, even though they were paying less for our competitor's chairs, they were really paying more! With Chromcraft, they would pay less in returns and repairs and enjoy a longer rental life. And the real icing on the cake came later for the company, when the resale of the Chromcraft chairs after several years of rental turned out to be higher than the company was experiencing before.

Within a short time, Will turned that company into one of the largest purchasers of Chromcraft seating in the United States. And he did it with a quiet, simple and very effective technique: he dazzled them with the details and showed them what real value was.

DON'S PARTING THOUGHT

We can all learn something from Will Shulte. Price is not a singular, obvious number; price can be very complex. There is price as it appears on the surface, and there is actual price. What is your product's *actual price* after considering every aspect of savings and benefit? I suggest you become knowledgeable about your competition's actual price as well. Remember, your boss could hire hobos from Harlem at minimum wage to go into your marketplace and cut prices. He chose you instead! So go forth and talk value with great conviction.

Skill #13

✦✦✦✦✦

Understanding Human Behavior in Selling

❝Everybody's weird once you get to know'em.❞

—'BROTHER DAVE' GARDNER

Human behavior is not totally predictable. When we're dealing with people, things don't always go as expected. Even people we know will sometimes surprise us. But generally, I do believe that the best predictor of future behavior is past behavior.

Back when computers first started showing up and many of us were still awed by those amazing machines with blinking screens, a fellow was walking through an airport lobby and saw a computer over on the sidelines. Above the computer was this message: "Ask the computer any question. Only 25 cents."

"Well," the guy thought, "this will be a great opportunity for me to learn of the destiny of my late father!" Wondering whether his father had gone to heaven or hell, he walked over to the computer, got his quarter out, and wrote down this question on the piece of paper: "Where is my father?"

He programmed the question into the computer and put his quarter in. Lights started flashing, blinkers blinking and buzzers buzzing. Momentarily the answer came out the other side. The message read: "Your father is off Nova Scotia fishing."

The fellow was surprised and puzzled. That's a strange answer, he thought. Then he decided that maybe the computer didn't understand what it was he wanted to know. So he decided to try again, and this time he rephrased the question and asked, "Where is my mother's husband?"

He programmed the new question into the computer and slipped in his quarter. Again the lights flashed, blinkers blinked, buzzers buzzed and momentarily the new answer popped out the other side.

This time the card read, "Your mother's husband is in Glory Land, but your father is still off Nova Scotia fishing!"

This fictitious story underscores my point – that people will surprise us sometimes. That's why we say that the study of human behavior is a soft science, imperfect at best.

Hard Science vs. Soft Science

Let me give you an illustration to differentiate between the proverbial *hard science* and a *soft science.* I am holding a pen in my right hand and I'm about to drop it. Do you think you could accurately predict what is going to happen when I let go of this pen? Of course. It's totally predictable.

162

You know this pen is going to fall straight down until it hits something. It's not going to go up or sideways or float around. That's because the pen will follow the law of gravity, which is an irrefutable law. It works every time. So we're dealing here with a hard science.

It's more difficult to make irrefutable statements about human behavior, but we have learned a great deal about how humans typically behave. And now behavioral scientists can, in most instances, predict how certain types of individuals will behave in certain situations.

Human Behavioral Research

We're going to approach the behavioral side of selling in a manner that will enable us to take advantage of the many years of research that have been done.

Dr. Carl Jung formulated much of the early research in the behavioral sciences. More recently, renowned psychologist Dr. David Merrill as well as psychologists Marson, Lefton, and Guyer have had great impact on the development of the behavioral style models that are so helpful to high performance salespeople today.

Larry Wilson, Tony Alessandra, Jim Cathcart, Don Thoren and I (though not psychologists) have burned the midnight oil as well, studying human behavior. Don and I have discussed behavioral styles hundreds of hours in our research efforts. His in-depth knowledge in strategy development has helped me be a better trainer.

I first researched the behavioral styles concept of Dr. David Merrill. Merrill wrote the book entitled *Personal Styles and Effective Performance,* along with Roger Reid. This is an excellent book for understanding human behavior in the business environment. I recommend you buy it, study it, then study it some more.

Sell Different People Differently

If you want to become and maintain your status as a high performance salesperson, you simply cannot fall into the trap of trying to sell all prospects the same way. Wouldn't it be great if all prospects behaved in exactly the same manner? If they did, sales training and the development of persuasive skills would be easy.

High performance salespeople have recognized that it isn't that simple. Do you remember in an earlier skill the example of a salesperson who made a call on a prospect with whom he was totally comfortable? He easily made the sale. Then he made a call on someone with whom he was totally uncomfortable, and he missed the sale. He left frustrated, accusing the prospect of being "weird." Let's discuss this incident in greater depth.

What's a good, one word definition of "weird"? Odd, strange, different – all of these are good. We'll go with the word *different.*

Here's the premise: *The more ways people are different from each other, the more effort will be required to communicate and to achieve a mutually acceptable outcome from the interpersonal relationship.* That's a rather formal behavioral/psychological way of saying that the weirder someone is, the tougher it's going to be to sell him!

Even Weirdos Buy

Now I'm going to share with you some information that should make you some money. I promise you this information will be helpful to you if you never forget it. I'd suggest you get your pen and paper and write down this tip so it will be indelibly burned in your memory.

We're talking about weird prospects, right? The tip I want you to remember is this: Who cares if he's weird if his checks clear?

Now I don't want you to think that line, whether it's uttered by me or anybody else, makes someone sound like a money grubber. That's not where I'm coming from. The point is that customers aren't all alike. They won't all think or behave like you do. And that's OK.

What the sales profession is about is writing business, not looking for people like ourselves. The fact that a customer's behavioral style is different from yours shouldn't matter if the customer needs, wants, and can buy your product or service. You must learn to understand and deal with behavioral differences in order to achieve your goal of closing the sale. We should not be judgmental about other people's behavior; we should be observant of other's behavior so we can learn from it.

Behavioral Dimensions

To get a solid handle on human behavior in selling, let's look at the three basic dimensions of human behavior customarily measured to establish one's behavioral style. They are Assertiveness, Responsiveness, and Adaptability.

To get a clear understanding of Assertiveness and Responsiveness, we should examine these characteristics more carefully. As we do, remember a very key point: Assertiveness and Responsiveness are *quantitative* but not *qualitative*.

Let's define "assertiveness" first by considering the following model outlining characteristics:

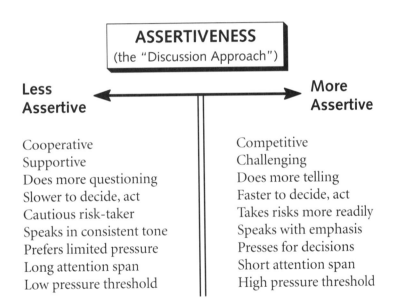

Cooperative	Competitive
Supportive	Challenging
Does more questioning	Does more telling
Slower to decide, act	Faster to decide, act
Cautious risk-taker	Takes risks more readily
Speaks in consistent tone	Speaks with emphasis
Prefers limited pressure	Presses for decisions
Long attention span	Short attention span
Low pressure threshold	High pressure threshold

Definition of Assertiveness: The predictable technique for exchanging information and influencing others

NOTE: Both More Assertive and Less Assertive types have active approaches to controlling conversations and influencing others' points of view. While these approaches are different, they can both be very effective in selling, managing, parenting, etc.

I recommend that you study (even memorize!) the outline of assertiveness characteristics. If you learn these and evaluate your prospective buyers according to which extreme their observable behavior tends to lean toward, you will be on your way to understanding prospective buyers better than ever.

The next important dimension of human behavior to study and thoroughly understand is Responsiveness.

RESPONSIVENESS
(the "Emotional Content")

Less Responsive

Low display of emotion
Appears cool and distant
Poker-faced
Responds to facts and logic
Calm, reserved behavior
Shares information
Uses few gestures
More serious

High display of emotion
Appears warm and friendly
Lots of smiles and frowns
Expresses opinions, feelings
Excitable, emotional behavior
Shares personal reactions
Uses many gestures
More playful

More Responsive

Responsiveness is defined as the extent to which a person reacts, shows feelings and displays emotions.

While heredity and environment both influence current behavior, the people with whom we grew up and the behavior they demonstrated, expected, or praised have contributed to the emotion we have developed the habit of displaying. Verbal and nonverbal responsiveness clues are easy to observe if we pay attention. This information should assist you greatly in developing and utilizing an effective strategy for selling different people differently.

The third principal dimension of human behavior, adaptability, is covered in detail in the next chapter.

Observing Human Behavior

It's obvious to anyone with just the slightest knowledge of the behavioral sciences that people are psychologically coming from different places. I hope the foundation we established earlier in this chapter has helped you gain some perspective on these differences.

Now let's look at the bigger picture and discuss how we can profit from paying concentrated attention to the behavior of those people we deal with everyday.

We tend not to observe human behavior to the degree that we should. We observe people as a habit, but most of us have not developed *observing* into a skill. We *react* instead. We observe in terms of like or dislike, accept or reject, etc. Reactions of that type aren't productive to us as salespeople. We need to be less reactive and more observant.

Whenever I conduct a training session, I know that within two minutes after I'm introduced, people are reacting to me – my style, my content, my voice and accent, my mannerisms. Maybe the reaction of some leans toward the positive side of the scale. With others, it may lean toward the negative side. I have to win them over like you do in a sales presentation.

That kind of immediate reaction to another person is normal. But while it is normal, it's not the appropriate response if you intend to become a high performance salesperson. High performance salespeople don't react, they observe.

When I say we must learn to observe human behavior, I mean that we must keep our eyes and ears open. We must tune in to the behavior of others, and we must learn from what we observe.

To really learn, it is not enough to just watch and listen. We'll need to take written notes, remember things, categorize, read between the lines, and really study the behavior we have observed. That's how we'll be able to achieve the other step that's necessary to make observing human behavior productive, and that is to be able to strategize from what we've learned.

Human behavior is observable and verifiable. It's not totally 100 percent black and white; there's always a little gray area. But it's definite enough that we can indeed learn and strategize from it to be more effective with people.

Four Behavioral Styles

Merrill and Reid developed the original "social style" model at Tracom. They defined "social style" as a particular pattern of actions others observe and agree upon for describing a person's usual behavior.

Merrill and Reid's social style model was later adopted by Wilson Learning , and today it has not only received wide acclaim and high visibility but has influenced many researchers studying behavioral styles. I have used a variation of these concepts for years now in my sales and management training activities. I credit Dave Merrill with much positive influence on the strategic sales skills I developed in the late 1970's and early 1980's. (It was a pleasure working with and learning from Dave Merrill in those days as a member of the Professional Associates Network.)

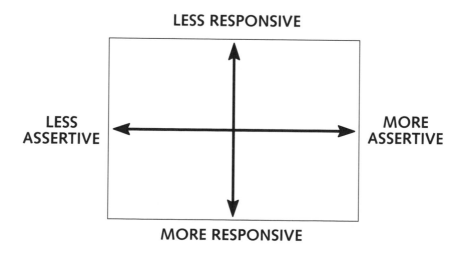

The previous illustration should help you understand the concept of the four behavioral styles. If you combine the horizontal Assertiveness line and the vertical Responsiveness line into the creation of a grid framework, you will find it much easier to quantify and categorize the behavioral styles of your prospects.

Four different combinations of these two behavioral dimensions reveal four distinctly different behavioral styles. Now let's discuss the four resulting behavioral styles.

ANALYTICALS *also known as* *Technician or Thinker* **Less Assertive, Less Responsive**	**DRIVERS** *also known as* *Dominant or Director* **More Assertive, Less Responsive**
AMIABLES *also known as* *Relater or Supporter* **Less Assertive, More Responsive**	**EXPRESSIVES** *also known as* *Socializer or Influencer* **More Assertive, More Responsive**

1. DRIVERS

The Driver is the more assertive, less responsive individual, which means that Drivers come on strong with a low display of emotion. At their best, Drivers are task-oriented and achievement-focused. Their short attention span is a motivator to get a lot done in a short period of time, which is another strength. One of the weaknesses of Drivers is that, if they are not careful, they will appear to some as cold, calloused, and unsentimental. They are disciplined about time and reject inaction. A Driver is also known as the Director, the Dominant, or the Reserved Teller.

2. EXPRESSIVES

The Expressive is the more assertive, more responsive type person who comes on strong with a high display of emotion. A strength of Expressives is that they are stimulating, dramatic and goal-focused. At their worst, Expressives may appear to some as loud and disorganized. Expressives like an exciting environment and tend to reject boring, detail-oriented meetings and data. The Expressive is also known as the Socializer, the Influencer, or the Emotional Teller.

3. ANALYTICALS

The Analytical is the less assertive, less responsive type who is laid back and has a low display of emotion. Among the strengths of Analyticals is they are precise and exacting, and they tend to be excellent on detail. At their worst, they will appear to some as boring, picky and dull. The Analytical tends to focus on historical facts and data as their foundation for understanding, and they reject the tendency to shoot from the hip. The Analytical is also known as the Thinker, the Technician, or the Reserved Questioner.

4. AMIABLES

The Amiable is the less assertive, more responsive type who is somewhat laid back but has a high display of emotion.

At their best, Amiables are relationship-oriented and will say or do just about anything within reason, short of compromising their integrity, to minimize conflict and get along well with others. At their worst, they come across to some as rather wishy-washy due primarily to their tendency to move slowly on decisions until they understand how everybody feels. The Amiable tends to be an excellent team player and rejects decisive behavior that is insensitive to the feelings of others. The Amiable is also known as the Relater, the Supporter, or the Emotional Questioner.

Which Is Best, Which Is Worse?

There is no best or worse quadrant in this model, since we all have strengths and we all have weaknesses. It is my opinion that the most successful people in selling and, for that matter, practically any other endeavor, are the men and women who identify their personal strengths and build on them as their foundation for success. They simultaneously identify their human weaknesses, eliminate the ones they can, and at least minimize or manage those they can't totally eliminate. A combination of these strategies increases an individual's effectiveness and performance in dealing with others. Don't fall into the trap of being one who fails because of a functional blindness to your own defects. Equally as important, don't be oblivious to your greatest assets.

So, which of these styles make for the best salesperson? The answer is all of them at one time or another.

Years ago the proverbial "born salesman" was a stereotype comparable to the Expressive style, which was thought to be the best behavioral style for selling. Later, as technology and sophistication grew in all areas, the Analytical's tendency toward accuracy and precision gained favor. This is the stereotype of those often called "Sales Engineers."

Then, when the business world got on a productivity kick a few years ago, Drivers were considered to be among the most successful salespeople. It was thought their result-oriented thrust would bring in more orders. Most recently, with the relationship orientation of business and industry and the high interest in customer service, the Amiable's skills are in the spotlight.

In my opinion, today it's possible for all of us to be high performance salespeople, regardless of how we're labeled. One of the things I like most about this subject matter is that there's an underlying respect for individuality. You don't have to be just like anyone else. You can learn to be the best you are capable of being by implementing whatever moderate and well-thought-out behavior modifications are needed for maximum effectiveness. A big issue here is your ability to identify the style of your prospect, adapt to that style, and develop a strategy that works best with each prospect.

Regardless of which description you key in on when formulating your high performance sales strategies, it's important to keep the behavioral styles in mind. Salespeople who try to sell everyone the same way will simply suffer unnecessary stress and a low closing percentage.

Successful Application 13

Featuring: Jim Cathcart, Speaker and Author; La Jolla, CA
(Author Interview)

Having made more than a thousand professional presentations worldwide and having been exposed to some very smart and creative individuals and teams, I'm pretty hard to impress. But that day in Denver was a classic.

My assignment was to teach team-building skills to a 90-person sales organization while teaching sales psychology at the same time. I had assessed everyone's behavioral style in advance of the program, using six different evaluations of each person. During the session, I presented the results of the evaluations and explained how each participant could learn from his or her evaluations. But these salespeople needed an experience to drive the ideas home.

I divided the participants into groups according to behavioral styles. (They were unaware of how I had selected the groups.) Each group was sent to a separate room, and I told each of them, "Your group is at a business convention in a foreign country, and you've just been captured by terrorists. You know nothing about them, including their intentions. They've put you in a room and told you that they will be back in one hour. Take this time to get your act together and determine what to do."

With those instructions, I left them to their own devices. What ensued was a classic textbook example of how each behavioral style deals with a situation. With only one hour to prepare for the impending return of the terrorists, here is how each group behaved:

In the Relaters' (Amiables') room, the first strategy was to befriend their captors. One of them wrote on the chalkboard "Viva La Revolucion!" The group's spokesperson told me, "By convincing the terrorists that we are no threat to them, they will be more cooperative and lenient toward us."

The Directors (Drivers) made a very quick decision to lay in wait for the captors and, upon their return, to jump them, take their weapons and gain control. A spokesperson for the Drivers told me, "Look, they started this – and we're going to finish it!"

What do you think the Thinkers (Analyticals) did? Their room was very quiet during the strategy-planning time. In a calm and logical discussion, they had established a chain of command among themselves and agreed their number one priority was not to lose their composure. At the last minute of the hour, one of the group laid a gun on the table. Really! She said, "If it comes right down to it and our plan doesn't work, I'll handle it." Whew! Their group devised a series of systematic fall-back positions and strategies for each contingency, but ultimately they ran out of time to complete their agenda.

You could hear the Socializers (Expressives) all the way down the hall. They had left their door open and were loudly brainstorming the creation of an elaborate play in which each of them had a role. Their strategy was to create a diversion that allowed someone to escape and go for help. This meeting sounded more like a party than a planning session!

The four different groups came up with four different strategies: befriend them, control them, out-think them, or charm them. Any one of the four strategies could have worked. But since each group knew nothing about their captors, any approach was as good as the other. That's no way to assure your survival – nor is it a good way to make a sale!

When the four groups reassembled into one body of 90 people to discuss their experiences, everyone had a big laugh at themselves. Their behavior was so stereotypical of their behavioral styles that they immediately saw how unprepared they had been to assure a good outcome.

After discussing the results of this exercise, the group as a whole decided that, whether you are selling a product or an idea to an individual or a group, the best strategy would be to recognize the four different approaches that could be used and use the one best suited to your prospect.

In the real world of selling, the only way to assure success is to let your prospect show you how to deal with them. You do this by observing your prospect's behavioral style and then adapting to it.

DON'S PARTING THOUGHT

People are different. We all have behavioral idiosyncrasies, but we each have a predictable behavioral style. The salesperson's job is not to be judgmental but to get orders from all types. Respect a prospect's individuality and figure out where they are coming from psychologically before trying to sell them. Who cares if they're weird if their checks clear?!!

Skill #14

✦✦✦✦✦

Selling With Adaptable Strategies

❝Do unto others as they like to be done unto.❞

—"THE PLATINUM RULE"

I hope you feel good about the obvious respect that experts have for each of the behavioral styles we discussed in the last chapter. Remember, anyone from any of the four styles – the Driver, the Expressive, the Analytical, or the Amiable – can be a high performance salesperson if they develop the appropriate skills for adapting to others.

In this chapter, we'll deal principally with our willingness and ability to adapt to the styles of our customers. In my opinion, no skill is more important for the high performance salesperson than adaptability. I believe adaptability is strategic for two reasons: one, you will sell more, and two, it is simply the right thing for people who respect others to do.

We must adapt to our prospect's style, to their level of understanding, and to the subject matter and areas of focus in which they have the greatest interest and need. Being versatile and flexible and interacting with people can make all the difference in getting results.

Defining Adaptability

Adaptability is an effort to please more people while keeping your objectives intact. It's being resourceful in varying your methods to be understood and accepted. It's balancing your concern for self, others, and the task at hand with a willingness to step out of your own comfort zone. Synonyms for adaptability are flexibility and versatility. Since we are all creatures of habit, this can be a challenge to learn. But there is *good* news, too.

Adaptability is a learnable skill, and it's a skill high performance salespeople have often perfected, whether knowingly or unknowingly. They've internalized it, and it works for them. For many high performance salespeople, it's a natural and spontaneous thing. They've learned how to get to where they need to be in their behavioral mode in order to get on target with the other person.

You've heard about stimulus response, right? You are the stimulus, and you will evoke a positive response if you are the appropriate stimulus. High performance salespeople in an adaptable mode prove to be a positive stimulus. Salespeople who are not very adaptable are simply a negative stimulus and usually have a low closing percentage.

Follow The Rules

People who are highly adaptable in the selling process are the men and the women who are knowledgeable about, adhere to, and practice what is known as the Platinum Rule.

We all know the Golden Rule is, "Do unto others as you'd have them do unto you." You can't refute that. That's like apple pie and motherhood; that's good stuff!

The Platinum Rule is a beautifully simple, valuable concept that says "*Do unto others as they like to be done unto.*" That's good stuff too! I recommend to you the Platinum Rule, not *instead* of the Golden Rule but *in addition to* the Golden Rule. Following the Platinum Rule will enable you to increase your closing percentage, to intensify and improve relationships, and to become more attuned to the goals of your prospective buyer.

Low adaptability people lack the skill of being interpersonally versatile. They are individuals who are oriented to "Me". The focus in their sales presentation is me... me, I... I, us... us. "Look what *I've* got; see what *we've* got," they will say. Their "Me" focus turns prospective buyers off.

Low performance salespeople are seldom skilled communicators; they are the Archie Bunkers of the sales world. Picture Archie Bunker's style of communications: "Here's what I think, here's where *I'm* coming from, and what you think and where you're coming from doesn't even matter!" Salespeople with this attitude and behavior typically fail.

High performance salespeople focus on the prospective buyer. They are highly adaptable and versatile people who are "you" oriented. These are the people who will have the highest closing percentages.

My friend and fellow professional speaker Charlie "Tremendous" Jones says, "Selling is identification. If I can identify with you, we can interact for only a few minutes and have a meaningful exchange. If I can't identify with you, we can talk all day and won't say anything to each other."

If you think that becoming highly adaptable takes a lot of work, you're right. The thing that will work in your favor is that you can start *now*, using the experience and the skills you already have. Work to become more adaptable, and you'll see results quickly.

Adapting to Behavioral Styles

We all have at least a little bit of each of the four behavioral quadrants in us. But there is a place which represents *your* usual behavior. For example, my home base is Expressive. But I get into each of the other modes occasionally.

I think my family members would probably tell you I have my Amiable moments. I think my secretary would probably tell you I have my Driving moments. Would you believe me if I told you I even have my Analytical moments? I do! When do you think that would be? It's when I'm flying my airplane. If I'm flying at 20,000 feet, 220 miles an hour, that's a time, I want you to know, when I'm into detail. (If not, I may do something that will screw up my whole day!)

Components of Adaptability

There are four components of adaptability that we need to understand if we're going to make this skill a natural reflex. If you will study these components and review them frequently, asking how you can apply them to your sales approach or, even better, to specific prospective buyers, I believe you will enjoy positive results. Let's look at each of the components more closely:

- IMAGE. An individual's or an organization's image is not a constant; it's an ever-changing variable. Image is made up of five things: how you look, what you say, how you say it, what you do, and how you do it.

- PRESENTATION. Presentation, in this case, means how you tell your story. Key questions should be answered here: Is your presentation targeted? Is it appropriate in every way? Does it reflect your knowledge of their needs? And, most importantly, is it preceded by a Needs Analysis?

- COMPETENCE. Competence relates to knowledge of the subject at hand and how to deal with it. I learned many years ago that your breadth of competence will either turn people on or turn them off in short order. In today's competitive marketplace, people want to do business with a pro. They are intolerant of uninformed salespeople and simply won't waste their time on them. Expand your knowledge and competence far beyond your competitor's and you will enjoy a refreshing competitive edge.

- FEEDBACK. Your willingness and ability to constructively and positively give and receive feedback is a vital part of your communications expertise. Be eager to gain ideas from prospects and clients on how to be better. Ask them for feedback, and listen carefully to their response. When giving feedback to others, do so constructively and sensitively, not critically.

Selling Strategically

To give an effective, adaptable and results-oriented presentation, you need to think in terms of keeping tension and pushiness low, and keeping trust and credibility high. This will enhance your prospect's comfort level.

A first step toward making your prospect comfortable is to identify his or her behavioral style. If you can then master the skill of selling people the way they like to be sold, your production will skyrocket. There are some specific strategies that can help you accomplish that.

I. With the DRIVER, be *to the point...* Remember that the Driver tends to be the "come on strong" type with a low display of emotion. Drivers reject inaction and respond to an efficient, to-the-point presentation.

II. With an EXPRESSIVE, *get excited.* The Expressive will get excited with you if you appeal to their visions and goals in a stimulating manner. A preponderance of paperwork, complex forms, etc. will be counterproductive with Expressives.

III. With an ANALYTICAL, be *detailed and specific.* If you aren't accurate with an Analytical, you will destroy your credibility. The Analytical wants back-up in the form of spec sheets, computer print-outs, etc. Get overly enthusiastic with an Analytical, deprive them of the data they require, and you'll never sell them. Trying to close an Analytical too early in the selling process is like knocking on the turtle's shell to get him to stick his head out. It just won't work.

IV. With AMIABLES, be *warm and sensitive.* Keep the peace with the Amiable; don't try to close too hard or fast. Create a good relationship before you ask an Amiable to buy. Take time to earn his or her trust and you will increase the probability of enjoying a long-term, mutually-beneficial relationship with an Amiable.

With every prospect, we must use a sensitive, effective strategy to get and keep his attention. And that means we need to try to understand his behavioral style, where he's coming from and how he feels.

It seems that for decades the traditional image of selling was to find a prospect, tell him your story, handle objections, close him quickly and go on down the road to find another prospect! In other words, give a canned presentation… have more answers than the prospect has objections… hammer the prospect into a decision *now*… then go find someone else who will allow you to do the same thing to him. That kind of high-stress, low-trust relationship is history, friends. The new world of high performance selling requires spending more time with qualified prospects, building influence within their firms and trust with each person in the decision loop. Sell them in a manner they feel comfortable with and you will get their order in the short term and earn their allegiance in the long term.

The Adaptable Salesperson Gains Allegiance

I'd like to make a prediction for your future in professional selling. Here it is: *You will never again be in a position to take for granted the allegiance of your prospects or customers. Never. Not at any time in your entire sales career.*

That's true for every salesperson. It's a lesson everybody learns at sometime. I learned it the hard way.

I worked my way through Memphis State University selling. That was in the 1960's, and back in those days, most of us took classes in the morning and worked in the afternoons or evenings. I was selling real estate, and the only training I had received was some early courses in "the school of hard knocks." It was during this time that I learned to never presume the allegiance of prospects or customers. Here's the story of my learning experience.

During those years, a group of us usually got together for lunch in the student center. One of the students in our group was a nice guy named Tom, whom I got to know fairly well. Over a period of a few months I guess I shared the lunch table with Tom maybe two or three days every week.

One day Tom wasn't there and someone in the group mentioned that he was probably busy. "I understand Tom and his wife just bought a home," my lunch companion said.

The Unsolicited Stress Injection

My ears perked up…probably turned red, too, like my face. Here I am, a young, hard-working real estate agent, supposedly aggressive. I've been looking for prospects, and they tell me Tom has just bought a house – and I knew nothing about it! This was frustrating for me, as you can imagine.

Well, I did a little research and found out that Tom and his wife bought a home from a competitor of mine in the part of town I specialized in. And they could have bought that same house from me! I must tell you that I experienced what would be known today as *STRESS*. Here I am, having lunch two or three days a week with the guy. I thought we had become pretty good friends, and he buys from someone else. Unbelievable!

For a couple of weeks, I didn't say anything about it. Finally one day, Tom and I were sitting at lunch once again, and I mustered the courage to mention the situation. I didn't want to seem angry or upset. I just wanted to find out what went on inside this guy's head that he would go out and buy from my competitor.

I said, "Tom, I understand you bought a new home recently." Well, he got excited and started telling me all about his new home. I had tremendous difficulty sharing his enthusiasm. But I managed to smile through his descriptions. "It sounds like a great place, Tom," I said. "By the way, I know the builder who built your new house. In fact, I know the house. You're going to like it there, and I'm really happy for you."

Then I said, "But you know, Tom, I've got to tell you that I'm a little frustrated. I am in the real estate business. I sell homes. In fact, I specialize in that particular part of town where you bought. I could have sold you that very same home."

I will never forget as long as I live the response I got. Tom looked at me a few seconds, snapped his fingers, pointed squarely at me with a surprised but serious look on his face and said, "That's right, Hutson! You *are* in the real estate business, aren't you?" It seems he had temporarily forgotten.

That happened over 25 years ago, and I remember it just like it was yesterday. I didn't make that sale, and I didn't deserve to. Why? I hadn't told Tom, or I hadn't told him enough, or I hadn't told him in the right way, that when he was ready to look for or buy a home, I was ready to help him. I had done nothing to nurture the professional side of the relationship. I hadn't earned the allegiance or the right to sell him.

That was a great lesson for a young salesperson like me to learn at that time. You can never, ever take allegiance for granted. It doesn't matter if you have lunch with someone every day. It doesn't matter the degree of the relationship. If you're taking allegiance for granted, you're going to get blindsided.

Earning and Re-Earning Customer Allegiance

The other day I saw a salesman in a phone booth talking on the telephone. I couldn't help but overhear. I walked by and noticed he was crying. I looked closer and he had tears rolling down his face. He was under tremendous stress.

What's going on here? I ask myself. So I turned my ear toward the phone booth and I heard him say, "But I just can't believe that you bought from my competitor. How could you do this to me… Mom!!"

No, that didn't really happen to me – but it *could* have. We can't assume allegiance with *anyone.*

One of the things we must do from the outset is create an awareness in every prospect, not only of the business we are in, but that we are on the leading edge in terms of service and professionalism. Once awareness is a given, we must earn that prospect's allegiance and their business.

How do you earn allegiance? By gaining trust, having a sharp focus on what is important to the customer, and projecting a pleasant image of professionalism.

The moment you succeed in gaining a new account is the time to start thinking about the next thing you can do for that customer. Repeat business from established customers should be worked for and worked for *hard.* It's often the best kind of sale to go after because you don't have to track down these customers, prove your reputation, and start from scratch. Established customers have already shown at least once that what you provide is what they need. The true test of the professional high performance salesperson is not that they can make a sale, but that they can maintain repeat business.

Any person, given enough latitude – price reductions, increased benefits, etc. – can make one sale. The real question is: Can you gain their allegiance and get other sales from that customer under normal competitive conditions?

Remember, if we are going to provide proper customer service, the kind of service that earns repeat business, we *must* know what is important to our customers. We must look at products and services from their point of view. Only then can we be sure that we can provide the level of satisfaction that will cause them to consider us a valuable resource, a resource worthy of allegiance. The higher the level of satisfaction they feel, the more allegiance we can expect.

Once you've sold someone, the best way to maintain allegiance is to give that person service beyond the call of duty. We must keep every promise we make to them. We must give them more than they deserve, more than they expect from us. As Tom Peters, author of *In Search of Excellence,* said, "To assure highest levels of commitment and allegiance from your customers and clients, get in their face and serve them to death." That says it well.

Remember, too, to stay in close touch with your customers at appropriate intervals. Don't contact them only when you want to sell them something. Professionally service their needs and the relationship. Contacting customers frequently (but not to the point of bothering them) may be the thing that keeps you from losing a customer to the competition.

If a problem arises in a relationship with a customer, solve it fast. Don't let it fester and grow. If you do, it might well become the principal reason why they choose not to continue their relationship with you.

A recent survey revealed that anytime a customer is pleased with your product and service, they will tell three people about it over a period of time. If they are displeased with your product or service, however, that same customer will tell eleven people of their displeasure!

Things We All Love

People want to be understood. People love to be right; proving them wrong strains the relationship. People love service, especially more and better service than they have gotten in the past. People love to trust others, when reluctance has been washed away through an understanding relationship. People love a deal, but most love quality and reliability even more. So…

If you will master and put to work the skills regarding human behavioral styles that you've learned in these chapters, I'm convinced that your transactions will become much larger than with the old traditional approach to selling. I think you'll also find yourself receiving more unsolicited referrals than ever before, and you'll build a clientele greater than you've ever experienced.

Sell people the way they like to be sold and *everybody* wins!

Successful Application 14

Featuring: Jim Stone, Salesperson, Oakwood Mobile Homes; Ashland, VA office

Submitted by: Nick St. George – President, Oakwood Mobile Homes; Greensboro, NC

Talk about desperate!

It was the last day of the year, and while others were getting in a good mood and readying to celebrate the arrival of the New Year, I was frantically searching for one more sale.

I was completing my first year with Oakwood Mobile Homes, having moved to the Ashland, Virginia, sales center from a depressed area. Sales were better in Ashland, so my quota was raised. But I was starting from scratch and had no prospecting base in an area new to me.

As the end of the year approached, I was one sale short of quota. If I made quota in dollar volume as well as in numbers, I'd have a nice bonus of several thousand dollars waiting for me when the New Year rolled in.

But I had worked every potential buyer hard during the past month. I had talked with people in person, made telephone calls, and followed up by mail. I had looked in every corner and under every rock for one more sale, but it seemed there was no sale to be found.

Finally, on that December 31, I went back over my record of calls one by one. I racked my brain, trying to think of someone, anyone, who would be a quick close.

Halfway down the list I came to the name of a woman I had talked with months ago. A quick close? Not a chance. She was an Amiable type with tendencies toward analyzing as well. She was financially capable of making the purchase, and she wanted to buy, but she just couldn't decide if it was the right thing to do. She was a renter, and buying was like diving off the high board for her. She couldn't decide to take the plunge.

OK, I said to myself, so she won't be a quick sale. I've got all day, so I'll take it slow and easy. She's a long shot, but looks like she's my only shot.

I telephoned and asked if she could come back to the sales office. The winter sky seemed to brighten a little when she said yes. Once she arrived, I made her comfortable and spent a good bit of time re-establishing rapport. I again presented her with the facts, benefits, and quality of our product. I assure you I covered every single benefit any Oakwood Mobile Homes salesperson had ever thought of!

Just as before, she was indecisive. She just couldn't get herself to make the commitment.

Maybe it was because I had exhausted my voice reciting all those benefits, but I decided then and there to let her do the talking for awhile. I wanted to let her express all her objections. I figured if I could get her to enlighten me about her reservations, I'd know exactly what I had to overcome to make the sale.

Well, she began by letting out all her doubts. Then she just kept talking! She poured out her whole life story in detail. The more she told me, the more morose her story became but, at the same time, the more confidence she seemed to have in me. I took notes and listened attentively.

As she talked, I could hear her slowly turning all the negatives she had felt into positives. We sat there for about two hours. By the time we had finished, she had almost closed the sale herself.

Normally I'm an assertive salesperson. It took a lot of patience for me to sit there for so long and let someone else do all the talking. But it was worth it, because I learned an important lesson that day. Sometimes you simply have to *listen* to hear the sound of money!

DON'S PARTING THOUGHT

People love to be sold – *if* the salesperson does it right!

Skill #15

✦✦✦✦✦

Presenting Sales Proposals

❝The ability to speak effectively is an acquirement rather than a gift.❞

—WILLIAM JENNINGS BRYAN

The skills discussed in Chapters 9 and 10 – "Needs Analysis Selling" and "Delivering The Needs-Based Presentation" respectively – created the foundation for the skill of presenting sales proposals. As with the strategies discussed earlier, the success of the sales skills covered in this chapter is highly dependent upon a quality information-gathering process.

Pitfall Avoidance

One major deterrent to gaining positive response in a timely manner is that many salespeople simply *give* their quotation or proposal to their primary contact and leave; their plan is to await a decision that is to be made at some future point.

High performance salespeople figure out creative ways to keep the sales cycle short. One way is to do everything in your power to be present when the decision is made. You can quell doubts, remind those in the decision loop of important value-building benefits, and keep enthusiasm high regarding your product and the service your prospect will get with it. You can also offer input that justifies urgency and thus a timely decision. If you are at the mercy of some vague group made up of people you haven't even met, you are an accident looking for a place to happen.

I know some salespeople who tell buyers or prospects going in, "I'll work very hard for you, investing my energy and expertise over whatever period of time is necessary to best serve your needs. My only request is that I have the opportunity to interview the decision influencers and be present at your decision-making meeting."

This sounds gutsy to some people, but a lot of sales professionals have found that access to the decision makers and the opportunity to win them over is not difficult if you ask. If you don't ask, you don't get the access! This is one simple interim closing technique that will help you get orders.

Buy My Grass, It's Great!

The presenting of a proposal can be as easy as a one-minute verbalization or as complex as a 300-page dissertation. Here's an example of the verbalized version:

A Vice President of Monsanto was sitting in the Astrodome skybox in a premier seat. He turned to Judge Roy Hoffines and prepared to ask the closing question. Hoffines had spent the last 45 minutes casually examining the turf sample that Monsanto felt would be perfect for Houston's Astrodome.

After spending some time elaborating on the versatility and benefits of the product, the Monsanto executive said, "Judge, we can install this turf in the Astrodome for you for only $350,000." The judge, with lightning quick reflexes, turned to the Monsanto executive and said, "$350,000? What a coincidence! That's the exact figure I had in mind charging you for the right to call this product *Astroturf.*"

So it is, thousands (if not millions) of times a day, people try to persuade others to buy their product, service, or idea. Most of the world's populus engaging in this persuasive rhetoric are not called salespeople, but they're selling just the same. They are not born with this skill; in my opinion, they learn and develop it over a period of time so that they can get what they want out of life.

As you might have guessed, Hoffine's Astrodome got a beautiful *Astroturf* floor, and Monsanto got the right to use that great name. So who won? Both, of course.

The Effective Sales Proposal

There's a special class of sales techniques that can be instrumental in helping you close many new sales. I'd like to share with you some suggestions on how to make those techniques work for you. The following are some of my ideas on how you can make your sales proposals strong and effective.

Suggestion One: Avoid mailing your proposal

Always try to present your sales proposal in person. A good guideline to follow is this: The higher the dollar figure of your proposal, the more important it is that you make the proposal in person.

There are a number of reasons why mailing a sales proposal works against you. If you are physically on the scene, there are many things you can do to create an environment for getting the "Yes" you desire. The best written proposal ever created can't compete with a good salesperson's ability to explain, inform, promote, and sell the proposal when it's being presented in person.

If you are not there, you and your proposal are at the mercy of the prospect company's *administrative flow*. When there's a lot at stake with your proposal, you can't afford to let it be shelved for days and weeks.

A salesperson for a client firm recently told me that his closing percentage was well over 50 percent when he presented proposals in person and was on hand to discuss the details with the key players. When it was mailed, his closing percentage plummeted to less than 20 percent. He said that there was always some confusion or question that needed answering, so mailing the proposal tended to eat up time rather than save it.

Suggestion Two: Customize each proposal for each prospect

Make sure your proposal doesn't appear to be boiler plate. Make each proposal as personalized and targeted as possible. It's very important to remember and use the rules of Needs Analysis in each proposal you prepare. Customization should refer to "Information gathered from Msrs. Brady, Shaw and Stevens on July 19," for example. The more you have given decision influencers authorship, the greater the probability of your getting an affirmative response.

Suggestion Three: Don't distribute your full proposal in advance

When you are making a presentation, don't pass out your proposal in total to the group you are addressing. In a worse-case scenario, they will all turn to the last page, read the numbers, and get up and leave in unison. You'll be left standing alone, wondering what happened.

To maintain control of your proposal and the presentation process, I suggest you distribute the proposal one page at a time. If you have a six-page proposal to present to three decision makers, go into a meeting with six manila folders, one for each page of the proposal. Take extra copies in case others sit in on the meeting.

Begin by passing out page one to each person in attendance. Discuss the first page thoroughly, then field questions and comments. Next, distribute page two. Repeat the process with each remaining page.

It's vital that you don't short-circuit your own presentation by giving your prospects the entire proposal *at once,* allowing them to flip through the pages without following you. Control the proposal presentation and your chances of success will be enhanced.

Suggestion Four: In organizing your proposal, consider sequence and structure

A proposal can be a powerful means of presenting your ideas and gaining the buyer's commitment if it employs the right structure and is presented in the most appropriate sequence.

Ron Willingham, an author, speaker and friend, has devised a simple, well-thought-out structure designed to lead smoothly into an affirmative decision from your prospect. He suggests we call our presentation a "Proposed Action Plan" rather than a proposal. Organize the Proposed Action Plan into three sections. The first section would be entitled "Client Profile" and would have three subtopics, as follows:

I. Client Profile

    A. Type of firm

    B. Size and makeup of firm

    C. Previous and current experience
       (in your area or product category)

For me, the "previous and current experience" would concern training. For a widget salesperson, it would be widget procurement history and so forth. In this area, you would feed back the information you gained in your Needs Analysis. The more detailed and accurate this section, the better. However, you should try to make the information succinct. I've found that the more complex and lengthy a proposal, the more cumbersome the decision-making process becomes.

The second section in your Proposed Action Plan would be "Client Needs." Add the appropriate number of subtopics according to the needs you determine. It's best if you can condense and categorize the needs into six subsections or less, so that this section fits on one page.

II. Client Needs

    A.

    B.

    C.

Again, you are feeding back the data you gained in the information-gathering process and adding your specific recommendations as well. Try to make the wording of the various "Client Needs" match as closely as possible the wording and thrust your prospect used when you talked with him or her. If you perceive a need he or she didn't know about and you want to list it, that's fine – but don't make it first. Add it further down the list.

The third section will be the "solutions and applications" section designed to address the needs outlined in Section II. This is where you can articulate your recommendations. Make your recommendations as specific and benefit-oriented as possible. Don't be apprehensive about including information on the unique and valuable aspects of your products. Your prospects probably need to be reminded, and there may be people present who did not know of some particular benefits.

III. Solutions/ Applications

    A.

    B.

    C.

You may want to follow up with the A, B, and C in your "Solutions" section corresponding directly to the A, B, and C in your "Needs" section, but sometimes this is difficult. You may have spotted five needs but will recommend only three solutions, due to overlapping positive results with certain solutions.

IV. Investment and Terms

    A.

    B.

    C.

You will probably want to make this the last page you hand out. This way, you have had time to build your audience's perception of value, talk benefits, and impress them with your research, preparation, dedication to service, etc., before mentioning price. (Incidentally, the word "investment" sells better than "price.")

To complete your Proposed Action Plan, prepare the customary signature section in which the prospect approves your proposal.

Solution Five: Present "Options" separately

Make your recommendations based on the information you collected, then confidently ask for the business.

You may want to prepare an "Options" page that you distribute only if your original recommendations are not approved. Then, if your prospect or prospects bring up something that makes some provision of your proposal inappropriate, you can pass out the options page. However, using the options page usually makes your original proposal obsolete, so avoid issuing the options material if possible. It is simply additional firepower in case you need it.

If you do find that you must offer an options page, do your best to keep all the decision makers or those who will influence the decision on hand so you can re-hash the details of the options on the spot. Get closure and, if possible, make the changes on the original proposal as simple as possible. Get it initialed by the buyer, and you still have a sale. If the changes are too numerous or complex, don't wait long before getting back together with the group.

I was once in this situation when selling a complex corporate training contract, and I noticed it was just before lunch. So I simply said to my client, "If you'll be kind enough to provide me with some secretarial assistance, I'll have this proposal re-done as you've requested and have it ready to sign at 1:30 p.m. If we can reconvene for a few minutes just after lunch, we'll have this cycle closed." The parties agreed, and I was gone by 2 p.m. with a consummated sale.

Suggestion Six: Stand firm on time limits and expiration dates

Many people don't make decisions until they have to. If there's no sense of urgency, some people will procrastinate endlessly. I believe every proposal should have time limits, so the prospect understands that the offer presented will be obsolete and unavailable after a specified date.

Where do you put an expiration date on your proposal? I suggest at the very end, near the signature line, because that's when your prospect should be thinking about making a decision. You may want to make this a final and additional page to be handed out only if you don't get the order today.

How do you phrase the time limit? You may want to use a phrase similar to this one: "The prices of the products, services and/or delivery commitment outlined in this proposal are guaranteed by ___(your company name)___ through ___(date)___." Use your company name, not theirs. The date you specify shouldn't be more than a week or two, three weeks at the most, from your presentation, unless there are extenuating circumstances. If you put an expiration date on your proposal of 30, 60 or 90 days away, you may be sunk. You are inviting procrastination, indecision, and the paralysis of analysis.

An expiration in the near future will also protect you and your company in the event you have price increases or unforeseen circumstances that could wipe out your profits.

One other thought about timing: Make a high-quality decision as to when your presentation will take place. Ask yourself, "Is now the time when they'll be most likely to buy? And will this be a date and a time when all the key players will be on hand?"

Suggestion Seven: Plan on getting an affirmative decision the same day you make your proposal

Be sure there are no key elements missing that would prevent you from getting a positive decision immediately following your presentation. Let the buyer know what you've done to get the ball rolling as soon as the proposal is accepted. Demonstrate effective follow-through.

Somewhere in your proposal presentation you should say something like, "Several of you have told me that you need to get a decision made on this as soon as possible so that everything can be in place by the first of next month. With that in mind, I think I have covered all pertinent issues in this proposal today so that an affirmative decision will be easy and painless for you." Then smile. A pleasant smile during your closing attempt can be disarming and effective.

The creation and presentation of a pertinent, high-quality sales proposal will have a great deal to do with your perceived credibility, with your image as a professional, and also with the results you get in your sales career. Remember this: To keep sales cycles short and closing percentages high, your presentation *must* outshine your competitor's presentation.

Group and Committee Presentations

To become a high performance salesperson, we must learn to make effective presentations in a group setting. There are three vital ingredients for great presentations before a committee or group. Those ingredients are pertinence, preparation, and impact.

Pertinence

I suggest that in the opening moments of a group presentation – and it doesn't matter if you're addressing three people or ten – you should share some data with the group that lets them all know unequivocally that you've not only done your homework but done it well. Let them know that the presentation they are about to hear is completely pertinent to their situation or problem. You might say something like this: "In my data-gathering process, I learned some interesting information about your company, your specific needs, and your management philosophy. One of the things that impressed me most was your vice president of manufacturing's premise that..." Then give the relevant quote.

From this point forward, you allude to other things that reveal to your audience beyond the shadow of a doubt that they are listening to a presentation designed specifically for them. Yes, get into the detail and the information that applies specifically to their operation. You may even want to pull a line from their company's mission statement that reinforces some of the ideas and principles you present.

If you are on target in presenting ideas truly pertinent to their company and their philosophy, they'll be impressed. They should walk out of that meeting muttering to each other, "Boy, that salesperson really did some in-depth research and tailoring." And chances are you'll walk out with the sale.

While these ideas are relatively simple and obvious, 90 percent of today's sales proposals still have too much "we" and "us" and not enough "you" orientation. How long will it take for salespeople to learn this? Who knows.

Preparation

My first tip regarding preparation is to always be early for a group presentation. Check your environment to be certain that everything you will need is on hand.

Make sure the room is set up exactly as you want it to be for maximum effectiveness and impact. If you'll be using audio/visual equipment, check it in advance. Don't leave anything to chance. Additionally, do whatever you can at this point to minimize interruptions and distractions.

Have you ever had a little stage fright? It's normal, and some constructive tension can work in your favor. The more presentations of this type you make, the better your presentations are likely to become. *The Book of Lists* by Amy Wallace reveals that the number one human fear is not death by burning or drowning, as some might think. The number one fear is speaking before a group! Most of that fear is unfounded but, whether founded or not, if you are nervous and fearful as a speaker, you have to deal with it because it will be very real to you at that moment.

Speaker Cavett Robert had a excellent observation on fear and nervousness before a group. He said, "Even after years of speaking, you never totally lose the butterflies – you just learn how to get them to fly in formation!"

Well, let me tell you how to get your butterflies to fly in formation. Be so well prepared and well rehearsed that you know it's going to go smoothly. The best insurance for a confident, successful group presentation is a strong knowledge of the topic coupled with a high level of preparation.

In getting ready for a presentation, try to anticipate what your prospects want and need to hear in order to respond positively. Try to anticipate any apprehension and present ideas to eliminate it. And, as we have already discussed, be sure your focus is on the needs of the organization and the individual decision makers and influencers.

Is He For Real?

The greater the impact of your presentation, the greater the chance of an immediate positive decision.

Impact is influenced by many factors, not the least of which is your presence in delivery. You must appear confident, well prepared and, to a reasonable extent, in control.

Paul Cockrill, an executive with J. Strickland Company, told me a story about one of his company's best salespeople that is a good illustration of how to create a presentation with impact.

Harold Simmons was a territory sales manager in Florida for J. Strickland, a company that manufactures health and beauty products. Harold had one account that made up over half of his annual volume. It was Sav-A-Stop, a large rack jobber that had more than 2,000 salespeople who serviced grocery and convenience stores.

Everybody wanted to do business with Sav-A-Stop – Procter & Gamble, Gillette, all the big guys. When Harold went to the Sav-A-Stop offices, he sometimes found himself in the waiting room with 50 or more other salespeople. Harold represented a smaller company competing with the big-league companies. In order to make his message noticed and remembered, Harold knew his presentations had to be unique.

One day when he was to make an important presentation to a Sav-A-Stop buyer, Harold showed up in the waiting room wearing overalls and a straw hat, with a package of chewing tobacco in his pocket and a blade of grass between his teeth. Instead of bringing a box of samples, Harold arrived with a bushel basket filled with fresh farm vegetables and fruits. Attached to each tomato, cabbage, cucumber, head of lettuce, watermelon, etc. was a detail sheet with a photo and information about a particular J. Strickland product. Details were included that outlined how much the buyer could save if he bought each product from J. Strickland. This approach took courage!

The buyer Harold was meeting with at that first presentation was so delighted that he asked Harold to stop his presentation mid-stream. The buyer went and found other buyers and invited them to sit in on Harold's *show*. The salespeople with the big companies in the reception area could hear all the commotion but couldn't imagine what was going on. As you may have guessed, their wait was much longer than usual.

Each year since then, Harold has come up with more fresh, creative ways to make his sales calls memorable. Buyers have come to expect a special show, and Harold doesn't disappoint them. One year he rented a cap and gown and "educated" Sav-A-Stop on products. Another year he was a cowboy, complete with saddlebags, in a product "round-up."

During the time that Harold has been making his unique presentations, J. Strickland's business with Sav-A-Stop has grown from about $25,000 a year to almost $500,000 a year. Now that's what I call *impact!* Harold learned that a creative theme, well executed, can definitely enhance your presentation.

Show and Tell?

Also consider carefully the impact visual aids can have. Perhaps handout materials could help in your attempt to convince your prospects. But beware of too many handouts or providing them at the wrong time, because they tend to decrease eye contact between the presenter and the listener. You don't want to be speaking about something of importance and look up to see your prospects reading about something else in your handout, with their attention diverted from where you want it to be.

Anytime you have more than one decision maker or influencer, the selling process becomes more complex and the sales cycle is customarily longer. A high-impact presentation will eliminate some of the problems which normally go along with the complex sale. You can gain additional impact and positive response by encouraging questions and interaction within the group. Just be sure you retain control; you could lose the sale if you appear too "laid back."

A rule of thumb is that as long as you are standing up and your prospects remain seated, you are in control of the meeting. Don't abuse this accepted rule. Use that control with confident professionalism. Incidentally, it may be inappropriate to stand if your group is only three or four people or less.

I suggest you also consider the need for behavioral adaptability in group presentations. You will almost always have multiples of the behavioral quadrants represented in a given group. A presenter with low adaptability skills is going to have difficulty keeping everyone's attention and creating a high impact experience.

Generic Adaptability: Capture "Everyone's" Attention!

Let's talk about being adaptable in a generic fashion. If you assume that, in a group presentation, you'll have people from each of the four behavioral quadrants, then you will want to say things in your presentation that appeal to all four behavioral styles. If you have as many as eight or ten people in your audience, it's a good bet that you will have at least one from each quadrant – Driver, Expressive, Analytical and Amiable.

I'll give you an example of how you might capture the attention of all four behavioral types. When I make a presentation before a sizeable group of salespeople, I might use an approach like this:

"We are here to discuss increasing your closing percentage and to talk in terms of things that can make a real difference in your sales career." (*appeals to the Driver*)

"I hope, during the course of this presentation, we'll have fun and, at the same time, really get into the motivation of what will make you a higher-producing sales professional. I want you to know I'm going to get you as fired up as I can. When you leave this room, I want you to leave with renewed conviction, dedication, and a game plan for increased performance!" (*appeals to the Expressive*)

"But I don't want you to think I'm going to concentrate so much on helping you become motivated that I neglect the intricate details necessary to make the training process effective. So right now I'd like for you to open your workbooks. Today we're going to cover a lot of data and I hope you'll fill in all the blanks and take a lot of notes." (*appeals to the Analytical*)

"When we conclude this program today, I hope we will have increased our skills, had an enjoyable experience working together, and learned how to have better business relationships." (*appeals to the Amiable*)

That's an example of generic adaptability. What did I do? I used a sentence or a phrase or two that appealed to the value systems of people in all the various behavioral styles.

By learning how to tailor our group presentations to all behavioral types, we're becoming more adaptable in our process of human behavior. What does that mean to us in the marketplace? It makes us feel better about our jobs. It increases our closing percentage and thus our income. It's a win-win situation for everybody.

Successful Application 15

Featuring: Ron Tate, President, Balance Point International; Seattle, WA
(Author Interview)

Our business is developing management training programs for companies, and the customer usually is top management, very often the chief executive. I remember one time when I was presenting my proposal to an Analytical-style CEO who was highly skeptical. His doubt was not so much about our company as it was about whether his company needed management training in the first place. So it was a challenging sale.

The CEO sat stone-faced throughout my presentation, not responding much at all. When he did talk, he said, "We're a 100-year-old company, and our people have been here for a long time. We promote and train from within, and we're doing fine. So you tell me why we should be interested in your proposal."

"Most managers," I told him, "become managers in the same way we become a parent – one day we just wake up and we *are* one! We may be decent human beings, but we haven't had any training to be parents. Imagine what a difference it would make if we had!" Well, I got his attention with the parent analogy because it's true – most managers, upper and middle-level, haven't been trained to be managers.

So the Analytical CEO said, "Tell me what it is you think you can do and, if you convince me, I'll sign your contract." But that's when I used an approach that I've found works not only for Analytical types but for most every type of manager.

"If you and I sit here and decide on this training," I said, "you run the risk of alienating a large number of your managers, simply because they haven't been permitted to participate in the process. If they don't buy into this program, they'll treat it accordingly.

"The thing I would ask you to do," I said, "is to pull your managers together and, at no cost or obligation, my company will come in and meet with them. Then we'll let them tell you and me whether or not they feel they would want to make a commitment to growth and development in a program like ours. And if they like it, they will tell us. And if they don't, they'll tell us as well."

Now there was some risk in taking this approach with the Analytical CEO, who may have felt he could make the decision on his own. Maybe I could have gotten a signed contract without risking a possible rejection by the managers. Why did I use the approach I did? Because it was simply the right thing to do.

"All I ask of you," I told the CEO, "is to be there from start to finish. Hold your phone calls. Invest one hour in listening to your managers' responses. Then, after the meeting, you and I can sit down and make a determination if this is a good move for your company. Would you be willing to do that?" He said yes.

When we met with the managers, I knew how to present my case to them. I utilized an approach that had an appropriate balance of facts and emotion. First I asked them how they became a manager, and almost all said "I happened to be in the right place at the right time." The parent analogy, in other words. We spent a lot of time in interaction, getting the company's managers to give us ideas about what they felt they needed.

Then I asked the participants to take five minutes and list the managers they had done their best work for, and why. The responses were precisely the management skills we teach in our courses: good communication, providing good direction, coaching, vision. Likewise, when I asked the participants to list the managers under whom they did worst and why, they indicated communication and vision were lacking.

What happened in that meeting is that the company's managers sold the CEO on the fact that the program we were proposing was what his managers felt they needed and wanted. After the meeting, we wrote a $39,000 training contract that created a 12-month management development program. We took an Analytical CEO from real skepticism to an enthusiastic "Yes!" by letting his own people sell him on our service through a creative, interactive group presentation.

DON'S PARTING THOUGHT

A powerful proposal presentation process can provide prosperity previously only pondered, never produced.

Skill #16

✦✦✦✦✦

Closing The Sale:
Earning the Right

"If two people want to do business together,
the details won't stop it from happening; if
they don't want to do business, the details
probably won't make it happen."

—PHIL WEXLER

Have you ever heard it said that you can be the nicest person in your business... you can have the greatest personality... you can dress like a million bucks... you can even give a presentation quite well... but when you go out into the marketplace, if you can't close, you can't sell?

Do you see closing as *that* important? You better believe it is! But let me suggest to you that some new things are happening in selling. And if you are selling like you were as recently as five years ago, you are leaving bucks on the table.

It's an entirely different world from what it was a few years ago, making more creative sales strategies necessary. Our marketplace is different, and it is incumbent upon us to stay abreast of the times. One important issue is the realization that before we can successfully attempt to close the sale, we must *earn the right*.

Confrontation From Marbella To Melbourne

Try this experiment with someone in your office or a fellow sales professional. Ask that person to put out their right hand, palm out, like a traffic cop stopping cars. Now put your left palm against that person's palm. You begin to push slightly against that person's palm with your palm. Now push a little harder. Harder still. What happens? The other person begins pushing just as hard as you are, doesn't he? Pretty soon you've got high energy coming from both people as they experience physical confrontation.

I have used this exercise over 200 times with members of my audiences from Marbella, Spain to Melbourne, Australia. One hundred percent of the time, when I push someone's hand, they push back! They are preparing to go into a "flight or fight" mode. Now if we let that same kind of confrontational experience occur verbally in our sales efforts, we're setting ourselves up for confrontation, strained relationships, and lost sales.

Closing isn't something you do *to* somebody; it is an experience you have *with* somebody. Remember, salespeople have not earned the right to experience a "Yes" until they create a positive win-win environment.

Closing and "The Numbers Game"

The greatest injustice I've ever seen a sales manager inflict upon a salesperson is to fail to teach them the Numbers Game, which we discussed in an earlier skill.

Every prospect won't say "Yes." You can count on it. And if you go out into the marketplace and somebody says "No", and nobody has told you how to be mentally and emotionally prepared for that, you've set yourself up for failure and for a low closing percentage.

I have never seen a high performance closer who did not understand rejection, who did not understand the Numbers Game, and who did not have a really sound game plan for handling that rejection. If a high performance pro gets rejected – if they go out to make a call and somebody says, "I've got two orders for you: Get out and *stay* out!!" – well, that high performance salesperson will, on his or her very next call, be as good as they've ever been. I mean their very next presentation will be absolutely stellar! They bounce back. As mentioned in an earlier skill, rejection rolls right off the back of high performance salespeople. Sometimes their determination for excellence even feeds on rejection!

Why? Because a high performance salesperson has it all together. But how many times have you seen the following scenario happen to a mediocre or lower-performance salesperson:

They build themselves up. "Oh, there's this one prospect," they tell themselves. "I've got this big appointment, and I'm going to close a really big sale, and..." Their whole life centers around this one prospect! One client! One deal!

The day of the big appointment comes and the salesperson is so lathered up with anticipation that he can hardly contain himself. He goes over there only to find out – *the guy died last Tuesday!*

What I'm saying is you should never hang your feelings of self-worth, and the value of a week's or a month's productivity, on one prospect or one transaction. Anything can happen. Don't ever put yourself in the position where one customer will break you (unless your company is structured so that you only have one or two accounts). Closing is a Numbers Game – you'll win some and you'll lose some. You must be prepared to concentrate on the winning but learn from the losing.

Mentally Preparing For The Close

Now we're ready to talk about attempting to close the sale. This is one of the most sensitive areas in the selling process, and we must handle it with great care if we want to excel.

Sometimes a problem will surface because the prospect simply doesn't want to do business with you. When this happens, it usually means either he's uncomfortable with you personally or he perceives your actions or suggestions to be inadequate or inappropriate for his needs.

If he thinks your presentation is too product-based and he feels all you want to do is close him, earn a commission, and go on down the road, you have gone bear hunting with a pea shooter. Your closing skills will usually be inadequate because your sales approach is sub-standard. Hopefully, successfully performing the skills we've previously discussed will keep this from happening.

These possible roadblocks simply underscore the premise that every part of the selling process holds potential for losing the sale. A chain is only as strong as its weakest link. If the previous steps and activities in the selling process have been professionally performed and have contributed to a strong foundation, the close will often be the simple and only logical result when you reach that magic moment.

You'll periodically see a sale that miraculously closes itself (They surprise you with an early "I'll take it!"). If this happens to you, give yourself some positive strokes because this indicates you've skillfully performed the preceding steps of the selling process up to that point. In this case, you've earned the right to get that piece of business.

Many salespeople perform one or more parts of the selling process in a sloppy way and then they're amazed when things go wrong with their closing attempt. This often occurs when the salesperson tries to close before building trust with the client.

Adaptability, Not Manipulation

Earlier we talked about being versatile and adapting our styles to be consistent with the needs and comfort levels of prospects. If we learn and use that skill successfully, trust is created and positive decisions are made. If we don't learn that skill, we'll run the risk of appearing manipulative and perhaps devious or abrasive.

I was speaking at an all-day seminar on the West Coast a couple of years ago. At the luncheon break, I was talking with some other audience members when a lady came to me and said, "Don, may I chat with you for just a moment?" I said, "Sure."

"Well," said the lady, "I wanted to tell you that earlier this morning I really got into your presentation. I was taking copious notes, I was really digesting the subject matter, and I believed strongly in your ideas all the way through until just before lunch when you got into that 'adaptability' jazz." Then she said, "Do you know you totally destroyed your credibility with me when you started talking about that?"

Now that is the kind of feedback that gets a speaker's attention! Especially Expressive speakers with sometimes tender egos. If you really want to get along with an Expressive, stroke him. Tell him how wonderful he is. If you want to destroy your relationship with an Expressive, rain on his parade.

Well, this lady told me I had destroyed my own credibility. I got out my umbrella, because the rain had started.

"Don," she said, "I have a real problem with your premise. As far as I'm concerned, when you started talking about adaptability, you were talking about nothing more than manipulation. And I hate manipulation. I don't manipulate people, and I don't like for people to manipulate me. I have no intention of ever manipulating anyone. So I can't use your suggestions."

I said to her, "First, let me thank you for being so frank with me. And I hope you will give me just a moment to try to clarify the difference between adaptability and manipulation because believe me, it's not the same thing." She agreed to listen.

Then I told her that, theoretically, if I was going to manipulate someone – if I wanted to take advantage of them financially or otherwise – then I would try to be the winner in a win-lose transaction, right? Well, indeed that would be a manipulative thing to do. It would mean that I was trying to do something *to* that person, *for* me. The implication would be that I'm the winner and they are the loser, right?

In that case, there would be a lack of goal congruence. If there is no goal congruence and I'm going to try to put this deal together anyway, that's manipulative. That is not justifiable, and I don't subscribe to such ploys. Never use any of the ideas you gain in this book or from any training program to manipulate other people. If you believe in the product you are selling and in your own talents, you don't have to manipulate anybody. But you do have to be versatile. It's a totally different perspective.

The execution of sound adaptability skills is non-manipulative and builds solid trust without needless stress (Review Illustration on page 85, Skill 7). Creating a high trust level earns us the right to close. Adaptability is doing something *to* me *for* the other person. There's a great deal of difference between adaptability of this order and manipulation.

Can you accept the fact that the decision-making process is vastly different with different people? I've written a lot in this book about the variances in human behavior, and I hope you've accepted the premises in this area. People are coming from different places and it's our job to sort that out.

Good Timing and Trial Closes

Timing can be everything in closing. When the natural communications flow is present, you will often get verbal or non-verbal buying signals that indicate the prospect's readiness to make a move. Capitalize on them, and efficiently get the prospect's commitment while you can.

High performance salespeople are masters at spotting *windows of opportunity* to close the sale. If you don't get a specific verbal buying signal, look for any positive indication that the prospect is convinced of the value of your offer. Be confident and assumptive, but don't be pushy.

One way to ascertain whether it's appropriate to close at a particular point is to use a trial close. This is a question you ask of the prospect in order to determine his readiness to make a decision. It can be a casual question like, "Do you feel we're heading in the right direction to try to solve your problem?" If the prospect implies you're on the right track, try to close him soon.

Other examples of trial closes would be, "Charlie, do you think we're going to be able to do business?" Or, "Does this appear to be a product that is responsive to your needs?" The simpler and more casual, the better – that's the rule that applies in most cases with the trial close.

Don't attempt to close before earning the right. Read your prospect carefully for his response to your ideas and proposals. If you try to close too soon, get a negative response, and keep on selling, you are now faced with the difficult task of getting him to swallow his pride and *change his mind.* Use trial closes to assess his feelings. Remember that more assertive people have shorter attention spans and less assertive people have longer attention spans, requiring more time. Build trust early, keep stress low, and you'll close them sooner and with less difficulty.

Successful Application 16

Featuring: Kurt McFadden, Salesperson, Reser's Fine Foods; Bellingham, WA

Submitted by: Jerry Reser, National Sales Manager, Reser's Fine Foods; Beaverton, OR

If you'd like to watch an expert at closing in action, spend a day with Kurt McFadden, a route salesman for Reser's Fine Foods in the company's Beaverton, OR district. For Kurt, "selling" consists mostly of making recommendations and then writing up orders. But behind those "easy" sales are hours and days and months of work on Kurt's part, time spent earning the good will and confidence of his customers.

"My goal is to move every customer I call on up to the top rung of the Loyalty Ladder," Kurt said. "You want to get people to the level where they trust you so much, where they are so sure that you are looking out for their welfare, that they will follow your recommendations almost 100 percent of the time."

Moving people up the Loyalty Ladder takes time, effort and a sincere interest in your customers, according to Kurt.

"The Number One thing," Kurt said, "is to like people and to genuinely want to help them. You've got to really get to know your customers. I learn about their families, their hobbies, their social activities – everything I can know about them. You've got to demonstrate that you're not just concerned with your product – you're concerned with their life."

Kurt admits that getting interested in his customers isn't hard work for him. "I'm not a bashful kind of guy," he said. "I go into a store and it doesn't matter if it's the store manager, the assistant manager, the sales clerk or the clean-up person – I show 100 percent respect and friendship toward everyone. You never know: the boy who is unloading boxes today may own the store some day."

A new wholesale buying club opened recently in Kurt's service area, and when he went into the store the first day, he didn't know anyone. All the managers and employees had been transferred to the new store from other areas. Two weeks later, Kurt had claimed the cooler manager as his "good buddy," and he was bringing motivational tapes to the woman behind the counter in Receiving. Within a month, Kurt had won the friendship of every manager and employee he needed to do business with.

A good example of the way Kurt builds confidence is his six-year relationship with Kathy Gack, purchasing manager for the deli case in the meat department at Cost-Cutter Foods, Kurt's biggest customer. In the beginning, Kathy was a tough sell because she can buy the exact same products that Kurt sells from a buying group – and at a cheaper price. So Kurt had to sell Kathy on service rather than price.

"My approach is to show people that I'm going to work like crazy to make money for them and their store," Kurt said. "With Kathy, I come in and work my product right to the shelf. She gives me a four-foot section, I keep it full, I move things around to get maximum sales. I'm not just selling product, I'm helping Kathy and her company enjoy more sales and profit."

With Kathy, Kurt got to know her family, attended work-related meetings with her, helped her out with advice about things he has learned by watching what is successful in other stores, and worked in other ways to gain her loyalty. "Kathy isn't just a customer any more," Kurt said. "She's a friend. I really care about her success."

Kurt's loyalty-building efforts have paid off with Kathy. "Now Kathy's department no longer checks the order in; I just wheel it in there," Kurt said. "They don't even ask about the quantities I bring in. I leave back stock, and they don't question it. Kathy knows that I'm never going to leave too much. Now, she usually says to me, 'Kurt, you know what to do. Go for it!' "

Recently Reser's Fine Foods introduced a new frozen hash brown potato product. Kurt was confident of the product's quality and its value in relation to other hash brown products being stocked by his customers. "With most of my customers, I just walked in and said, 'Hey, I've got a great new item here that can make you money. Where would you like for me to put it?' It really wasn't a question of do you want it. They know that I'm not going to bring them a 'dog.' They trust me to get them the best results."

In addition to making friends with the employees he calls on, Kurt likes to meet, help, and learn from store customers. "If a customer asks me where some item is, thinking I'm a store employee, I'll stop what I'm doing and go help them find it. It gives me an opportunity to point out our products to people and do a little selling job. Also, I like to find out what customers think about other products. Then I can share that valuable information with the store owner and department managers."

Because Kurt works so hard to help his clients and their stores succeed, many customers have come to consider him a partner in their business. "The decision-making people feel that I am almost as much an employee as some people who are there full-time," Kurt said. "When they see you are working for their same goals, they come to consider you a member of their success team. And usually that means they are willing to give you that extra shelf space you can always use."

Recently one retail store jokingly proclaimed Kurt their "Employee of the Month" because he helped that store move a problem employee into a new job with another one of his customers.

"It was great because it was a win-win-win-win situation," Kurt said. "The employee won because he moved up into a management job he liked better and was better suited for. The store that hired him won because he's doing a great job for them. The store he left won because they resolved a problem that was just a personality conflict between people. And of course I won, because now the employee and both the stores are happy with how I helped them. It let me step up another notch to show that I'm always looking out for the welfare of my customers."

DON'S PARTING THOUGHT

The best way to close a sale is to have a relationship
of such high trust that your customer never gives
any resistance to your recommendations.

Skill #17

✦✦✦✦✦

Closing the Sale: Getting The Yes

“Whenever you ask a closing question… shut up!”

—J. Douglas Edwards

High performance salespeople are invariably talented closers. They have many sound techniques. They know what to say, when to say it, and how to get a comfortable, affirmative decision from prospects. Talented closers are keenly aware of the behavioral style of decision makers and of the prospect's perceptions of his needs. Using all that knowledge and then timing the closing attempt very carefully is why the high performance pro has such an impressive closing percentage (and makes closing *look easy!*).

In this chapter, I'd like to share with you some of the techniques that I've used and that I've seen other high performance pros use to successfully close a sale.

Effective Objection Handling

Some high performance salespeople do such a thoroughly effective job early on in the selling process that getting the order is often easy and natural. But at certain times we all have to deal with objections.

Objections are considered, studied, and handled far differently today than they were only a few short years ago. There are a lot of skilled salespeople today who, when they follow the "new rules" in selling, get few or no objections. This is an indication that they are doing it right. Now, if they will just make lots of calls, they will help lots of people and get rich in the process.

In the past, trainers often suggested that the selling process was debate-oriented and that the salesperson would win only if he or she had more good answers than the prospect had objections. Today the salesperson who fails to focus on the win-win transaction will simply not endure.

Before we get too far into examining objections and how to handle them, I'd like to set forth a very important premise regarding objections. The more involved we become with our prospective buyer, the more knowledgeable we are of his needs, the better we have listened to his input, and the more on target our proposal is, the fewer objections we will ever hear.

The mere word "objection" sounds confrontational. Let's think more in terms of an obstacle. Obstacles represent things that are in the way, but together the prospect and the salesperson can deal with these obstacles and clear the path to a sale.

The key here is *working together,* and that can be done only if two things are present. One, you must have an in-depth knowledge and genuine concern for the prospect's wants and needs. And two, the prospect must be willing to work closely with you, which will come as a result of your earning his trust.

Causes of Objections

Recent studies reveal that most objections come from one of six major causes:

1. The prospect lacks trust in the company or the salesperson.
2. The prospect has a natural resistance to changing either his purchasing habits or his situation.
3. The prospect questions if the funds are available to make the purchase.
4. The prospect doesn't feel a need for the product or service at the time.
5. The prospect needs more information or fails to recognize his need.
6. The prospect assigns a higher priority to the purchase of other products.

The Value of Objections

Some people have a vast misconception about objections. They think of an objection as a curse or an insurmountable roadblock. "Objections keep me from making sales. They are obstacles I have difficulty dealing with, and I don't know how to handle them," they think. But objections can be valuable if we're competent enough to know what to do with them.

Are there indeed some benefits of objections? I think so. They give you an opportunity to turn the objection into an advantage. Objections are much like an x-ray into the brain of the person you're talking with. It tells you where they're coming from, and it helps you get a better handle on their behavioral, psychological, and situational posture. I have always felt that the toughest person to sell is the one who never says anything. Give me objections any day!

When we think about the concept of objections, let's consider them our friends rather than our foes, and let's focus on how we can benefit from objections when they appear.

Forms of Objections

Objections come in various forms. They may come as an *excuse* or a *stall*. Do you know who's most likely to give you an excuse or stall in the decision-making process? Less assertive people. They're slower to take action due to the caution they exercise.

When someone gives you an objection, they may simply be asking a *question*. Some people ask questions with a negative overtone. All they're doing is seeking additional information. So don't get into a negative overtone yourself, but respond to the information they are requesting in a positive manner.

An objection can also come in the form of a *condition*. That's an objection for which there is no answer. I'll give you an example.

Let's say you are selling a high-ticket item – maybe $40,000. You discover in the qualifying process that your prospective buyers don't have any money and just declared bankruptcy last week. They have no borrowing power, no source of money at all. In that case, you have no prospect, right? Well, some salespeople might say to themselves, "Boy, I'm going to close this if it's the last deal I ever do." And it probably will be.

The objection in this case is a condition for which there is no answer. When the prospects don't have the money, you usually have no recourse but to accept their objection. That is, accept it for the time being.

But let's look at the big picture in a larger time frame. Time may be your ally. Eighteen months from now, that prospect may have (a) restored his credit, or (b) amassed some cash – a rich uncle may have just left him a bundle!

Alternative Responses

When you get an objection, what can you do about it? Well, I contend that we have some alternatives. The first alternative would be to ignore the objection.

Now I know what you're thinking. "Don, ignoring an objection doesn't sound interpersonally effective," you say to yourself. "That doesn't sound like the *highly adaptable strategy* you would believe in. You've been writing about sensitivity toward people and now you say I should ignore them?"

In only one case should you ignore an objection and that's when, in your opinion, the objection is trivial. A trivial objection may be said in a very low, insignificant tone of voice. The prospective buyer says, "Well, that's a great product and it would solve a lot of our problems, but I kind of wish it was a different color." That is probably a trivial objection.

Now, what do you do with a trivial objection? If your product comes in only one color, you act as if they didn't even say it. But if they bring it up again later in your presentation, you may have guessed wrong. Maybe it's not trivial to the prospect and you *will* have to deal with it. But most often, trivial objections will go away.

When you get an objection, another alternative is to acknowledge the objection but postpone answering it. This is what you do sometimes when you're selling to several persons or a group. You acknowledge and postpone in order to maintain a reasonable level of control and effective communications with all parties. Don't forget to address the objection when the timing is right.

"Veto Power"

Do you sometimes sell products or services to both a husband and wife? How about a small committee? Well, let's say that you're selling to a couple and you've decided that, in this particular situation, the wife is the predominant decision maker.

You're giving your presentation, the wife is giving you buying signals, and then she says something like, "Let me ask you one more important question because I know we'll have to make a decision pretty soon." You're right in the middle of answering her question when all of a sudden the husband pipes up and says, "Well, I don't think I like the terms."

You'd like to be able to say, "Bug off, turkey. I was talking to your wife, who's going to make the decision anyway." But we all know that particular response would be a bad move. Anytime you've decided who you think the decision maker is, don't ever ignore the other person because even if the guy isn't the predominant decision maker, he usually has some *veto power*.

So maintain an adaptable approach with both parties. If he says, "I don't think I like the terms of this transaction," you acknowledge and postpone. "Good point, sir," you say, "and I'm glad you brought it up. As soon as I finish answering this last question your wife asked me, let's discuss the payment options in greater detail."

You turn to the wife and orient your thinking process and your strategies back to her question. Then you go back to the husband shortly thereafter. What have you done? You haven't been overly domineering, but you've maintained a reasonable level of control over the situation and thus postured yourself for success in making the sale. You have responded to the needs of both parties.

Give Up and Buy Now – It'll Save Us Both Time!

Years ago some sales trainers were saying that all salespeople who expect to succeed had better have more answers than the prospect has objections. This philosophy actually worked pretty well (*past tense!*). Some salespeople would have so many well-rehearsed answers that they won the debate. The prospect had nowhere else to go, so they bought.

Selling is very different today. Pressure a prospect into a decision he or she isn't ready to make and that prospect *will* find a place to go – straight to your competitor!

You Wouldn't Lie To Me, Would You?

Handling objections is one of the most sensitive and challenging steps of the selling process. Your strategies here are vitally important because they must flow naturally and comfortably from your mouth to the prospect's ears. I have a couple of suggestions for handling what are some of the most common forms of sales objections.

One is the postponement. You know how it goes: "Well, it looks real good but we're not in a big hurry to make a decision. We're going to think it over. Tell you what – today's Monday, and we'll have a decision by Friday. We'll give you a call and let you know."

Have you ever heard that? Well, a survey conducted a few years ago revealed that of those people who say, "We'll think it over and we'll call you later," 89 percent never call!

I've got a suggestion for you: Don't ever plan on them calling. You'll see a young, immature salesperson go out and give a sales presentation, get a few buying signals, then go charging back to his manager and say, "I think I got 'em! Looks really good. They said such and such." The manager asks, "Did you close them?" And the young salesperson says, "Well, no... but they're thinking it over and they're going to call me on Friday. I'll let you know, boss."

All day Friday this individual sits by the telephone waiting on it to ring. It doesn't. Remember this: When people say, "We'll think it over and we'll call you," they're not going to call 89 percent of the time. The percentage may be even higher now than it was when the study was done.

Keep The Monkey On Your Back

Don't plan on them calling, because when you let them think it over, you're taking the monkey off your back and putting it on theirs. And what happens is you'll never see the prospect or the monkey again. Keep the monkey on your *back*, where it belongs.

A suggested response to a postponement might be something like this: "I'm delighted that you're interested enough to devote your valuable time to thinking this over and that you're willing to make a decision on Friday. The fact that you're willing to call me is also very much appreciated, but I'm awfully hard to catch because I'm out most of the time. I'll be happy to contact you. Would morning or afternoon be best on Friday?" "Well, I guess afternoon would be best. We'll both be in by 4:30 or 5:00". "Great, I'll contact you about 5:30, OK?" "Very good. Incidentally, if I'm not too far away, I might just stop by, is that OK?" And then you start nodding so they will too.

Make Buying Easy By Handling Objections Comfortably

The response I described above is not manipulation. That's just making it easy for people to buy. Making it comfortable for them is a cardinal rule of selling. As long as our presentation and our product focuses on the needs and the goals of our prospects, we are justified in using psychology and good communications technology to make buying an easier, more comfortable process for them.

There's another objection we hear from time to time. "Looks great, but we've decided that we're gonna buy from your competitor." Did you ever get the competition objection? There are probably lots of companies out there in the same business you are in, and many of them have good products too. Remember, the weak competitors have already failed! Only the survivors remain, and they're probably good too.

When you hear the competition objection, you need to know just how to handle it. Here's the first rule: Don't ever bad-mouth your competitors. You may have some competitors who deserve to be bad-mouthed, but don't do it. Your image will suffer more than the company or person you're bad-mouthing. It will work against you.

I suggest what's called the "praise and pass on" technique. Don't cut them down. Just say, "Oh yes, XYZ Company. They're good people *but…*" After you say the word "but", that's when you want to build the value of *your* product and company, talk the benefits, focus on the prospect's needs. After you say "But… ," you'll really get inside their head and that's when you should sell them as effectively as you know how.

If you believe in your product and are convinced it's right for them, you are doing prospects a disservice if you do not handle every objection as proficiently as you can. It's not just something that's a good idea, it's your professional responsibility.

Good Reflexive Skills Save Cash and Whiskey

Good closers have good reflexes. It keeps them from missing closing opportunities.

Have you ever missed a sale and thought later of what you could or should have said that might have resulted in a positive closing attempt? I suppose we all go through the mental exercise of developing eloquent rebuttals after the fact – effective rebuttals we *might have* used during a stressful interaction. Having good reflexive skills will not only enable us to sell more proficiently, but will allow us to be more skillful and adaptive communicators.

As a communicator, persuader, leader, or sales closer, we are only as good as our reflexes allow us to be. How's your *reflex creativity index?* A lot of salespeople have never even thought about it.

We never know when we might have a lot depending on our creative reflexive response. Consider this story that Ira Hayes recently told me:

She was an older lady, of foreign extraction, making a few extra dollars working as a salesperson in a package liquor store. The store was located in a very bad neighborhood outside of Wilmington, Delaware, in the territory that I covered as a salesman for the NCR Corporation.

Late one night, she was alone in the store when three suspicious-looking characters walked in. One stayed by the door, one went to the window, and one approached her at the cash register. She sensed immediately why they were there and what was coming next.

In a sudden flash of brilliance and adaptability, she greeted the man approaching the cash register with these words: "We've just been robbed! The police are in the back room now, collecting information. Whatever you need, please get it quickly and get out." The three turned and ran out the door.

Did the saleswoman successfully close a sale? You'd better believe it!

The Effective Use of Pressure

You can be a great closer. You can have high income. You can have a lot going for you. But until and unless you become knowledgeable about pressure, you'll never be as good a salesperson as you could otherwise be.

What is pressure? *When* do you use it? *How* do you use it? *On whom?* How much pressure is *too much* pressure? These are all questions worthy of our consideration.

Let's take the last question first. Any amount of pressure that makes your prospective buyer uncomfortable at that moment is too much pressure. And it's different with different people.

Every prospective buyer has what I'd like to call a VPT factor. VPT stands for *Varying Pressure Threshold.* The correlation is as follows: More assertive people have a higher pressure threshold; less assertive people have a lower pressure threshold.

Now is that good or bad? Neither. It's just different with different people. And to become high performance salespeople, we have to learn how to gauge and sense the VPT of our prospects.

It's In The Eyes Of The Beholder

You can be in the middle of your sales presentation with a high pressure threshold prospect, observe some buying signals, get that gut-level feeling, and you just *know* you can use some pressure with this prospect.

Maybe the guy is a salesman himself; let's say he's a stockbroker. You think to yourself, "I believe I can get away with using a little pressure right now and I think I'll try it." You turn around and you close him with what some would perceive to be a relatively high-pressure close. Then you observe his response. He's grinning at you.

Has this ever happened to you? He's grinning at you as if to say, "Hey, don't use that technique on me. I just used that on another guy yesterday." But he's not uptight about it, you see. He's going with the flow, he's smiling, no big deal. It might even be the very inducement that gets him to say, "Let's do it."

You have a more narrow range of closing techniques when dealing with low pressure threshold prospects. Let's say, for example, that you're dealing with a husband and wife. Maybe one's Analytical and one's Amiable, but you know they're both low pressure threshold people. So you're trying to tread very lightly and you say, "Well, tell me Mr. and Mrs. Prospect, how does this look to you thus far?"

They might say, "Don't you pressure us!"

That would be representative of a low pressure threshold. You didn't perceive your approach as high pressure, but they did. This underscores the fact that you must handle low-pressure prospects with kid gloves. You must be much more sensitive.

Keep in mind how you come across to other people. What one prospect sees as low pressure might be viewed as high pressure by another, so we obviously don't close everybody the same way. Again, it's our job to sort that out and deal with it appropriately. This analogy is evidence of the fact that today we can't sell everybody the same way if we want to get results.

Don't Ask Me – Ask Brad!

Let me tell you a quick story. One of the greatest sales closers I've ever known is Brad. He's in the Midwest, the top salesman for an industrial firm, and he's made a lot of money for a lot of years. Brad and I have made calls together and researched closing the sale in the field. I believe we've both learned some things from each other, but I probably learned more from him than he did from me.

One day I conducted a seminar for Brad's company, and we were standing outside their corporate offices following the seminar. It was a lovely sunny day, and we were out there discussing our favorite topic, closing the sale.

Suddenly I looked toward the front of the building and out the main entrance door came two of the company's other salespeople. They were walking toward us, grinning. Well, after more than a couple of decades in this business, I've figured out what those grins mean. They're basically grins that say, "I have a question, the answer to which I'm reasonably sure you don't have."

They walked over to us and looked directly at Brad. One of them said, "Brad, we've got a question for you. Now we'll readily admit that you know more about closing than anybody else in our company. You say the reason you make more money than any of the rest of us is that you are a powerful closer, right?" Brad nodded in agreement.

"Well, we've got a question for you Brad," they said. "And the question is this: How much pressure do you use when you close somebody?" They just knew they would have Brad stumped.

Without a moment's hesitation, Brad turned and faced them squarely, smiled, and said, "Just enough."

What a great answer! You see, we don't sell everybody the same way. We use varying degrees of pressure with people, remembering that nobody likes an over-abundance of it today.

Or You Could Ask Plato

It's been said that high performance salespeople are smooth and articulate, saying the right thing at the right time in the right way and making it all look easy. They don't put decision makers under undue pressure; they use just enough pressure to get the decision.

While these high performance salespeople make it look easy, it's normally a skill that is the culmination of years of practicing, drilling, rehearsing and studying. High performance salespeople have become students of closing, students of pressure, students of decision making. They've developed the way to do it right.

Plato said, "Knowledge is recollection. An inability to recollect is demonstrative of no meaningful depth of knowledge." High performance salespeople get a great payoff for studying, for being able to recall the right words to use at the right time. They not only recollect the words, phrases and skills needed, they use them as effortlessly as Jack Nicklaus makes a short birdie putt for big winnings.

Using Variable Assertiveness

In our discussions in the chapters on human behavior, we learned that people are coming from different places. Their behavioral styles are different. Their value systems are different. And it's to our advantage as salespeople to learn all we can about how to communicate with people who are not just like us.

If there actually is a communications gap between you and the person you're trying to sell, whose job is it to close that gap? It's your job, of course. If you go out into the marketplace to spend your hard-earned money for a suit of clothes or an automobile, you figure that it's your money and it's up to the salesperson to convince you that you should spend your money on their product, right? That's the way selling works.

Review what you've learned about the characteristics and behaviors of people and how those factors can affect customers in making decisions. Can you use this information to your benefit? I'm convinced you can. But keep in mind that we must work on ensuring the comfort level in communicating with prospects and clients. I contend that you don't use the same strategy on all prospective buyers. Remember, the more comfortable you can make a prospect, the sooner and the more surely you'll get the order. This would be an excellent time to review the characteristics of More and Less Assertive people in Skill 13.

Jim Stone's sales efforts as described in Skill 14 were masterful. Do you think he would have sold the mobile home to that lady if he had impatiently tried to pressure her into a decision before she was ready? No way.

If a More Assertive type tries to sell a Less Assertive prospect in the manner that comes naturally to the assertive salesperson, chances are good the prospect will be uncomfortable. He will see the salesperson as coming on too strong; he simply doesn't want to move as fast.

Keep in mind that you can't control how other people behave. You can only control your behavior. Because of this, it's important to assess and respond to the assertiveness in others in a manner acceptable to them.

When a salesperson is oblivious to the assertiveness scale, tension grows, trust can decline, the sales task becomes considerably tougher, and the sales cycle invariably gets longer. We lose our efficiency.

Less Assertive prospects function with limited pressure. They're risk avoiders. There's nothing wrong with that, because what Less Assertives are trying to do is assure themselves of making a higher quality decision. But if the stall or the excuse is the posture they're in and you're accustomed to making rapid decisions all your life, then you get frustrated. On the other hand, if you've always made decisions in a way similar to the way the Less Assertive person is making the current decision, then you can identify with them more readily.

The greater the variance between the salesperson's and the prospect's assertiveness factors, the more challenging objection handling and closing are. That's because there is a communications gap that is short-circuiting a comfortable interactive flow. In such a situation, the salesperson needs to back off and give the prospect some space and some time, or the sale and the relationship might be in trouble.

On the other hand, if a Less Assertive salesperson tries to sell a More Assertive prospect in a more relaxed way, that prospect may question the salesperson's conviction because he's so laid back. As you can see in both of these cases, you would be well advised to vary your assertiveness to be somewhat in sync with your prospect. This way, the decision-making process will be easier and more natural for the prospect, and he will appreciate the fact that you are adapting to his needs.

Dance to His Drummer, Not Yours

When prospects are critical of salespeople, it's usually because they've been made to feel uncomfortable about their impending decision. Develop the skill of varying your assertiveness factor and I predict you'll enjoy a higher performance level than ever. I'd like to give you a three step formula to achieve this:

- STEP ONE: Monitor the assertiveness level of the prospect. Make a decision as to whether it is high, medium, or low.

- STEP TWO: Consider how you're coming across to him. Does he see you as high, medium, or low in assertiveness?

- STEP THREE: Move into the prospect's assertiveness comfort zone, adapting your style and approach to get that prospect in the proper frame of mind for him to make a comfortable affirmative decision.

If you learn to use and continually practice this skill, I firmly believe you'll sell more and enjoy an improved level of repeat business as well.

Closing the Less Assertive Prospect

In closing the Less Assertive prospect, key in on the fact that a prospect of this type has a low pressure threshold. To try to close the Less Assertive prospect too aggressively will be futile. Give this prospect time and space; use a low stress approach and they will often come around.

Less Assertive persons simply need more time to make a comfortable decision. This is not a result of intellectual inferiority; their intellect may be superior. It's a result of his or her decision-making style. These prospects are simply not inclined to rush a decison. A soft sell approach, then, is advisable. I suggest casual phrases like, "If you're comfortable with this recommendation, I'll go ahead and write it up." This kind of approach will not short-circuit good-faith discussions.

Remember that before initiating an attempt to close a sale, we must earn the right. That means being a diligent information gatherer and assessing all individuals who may be in the decision loop. You need to talk with these people frequently, asking them what they think and how they feel. Don't use a hard sell; use positive dialogue with lots of questions.

Recommended Less Assertive Closes

Now let's look at several additional closes which will normally work well with the Less Assertive prospect.

(1) *The Special Inducement Closing Technique*
This involves anything you can say or do that might induce those people to make a decision now. Maybe their reluctance is due to a time frame. Is there something that might stir them to action?

Try an approach such as this: "Well, sir, I can understand your reluctance to make an immediate decision, but keep in mind that we will have a price increase the first of the month. And since today is the twenty-eighth, it can mean a substantial savings for you if you make a decision now."

(2) *The Related Story Closing Technique*

This is relatively simple. Recall anything you can relate in a positive vein that would induce those people to take action now.

Let's say the prospect tells you, "You know, everything sounds good but I really don't know if your product is going to solve our problem sufficiently." Then you might say, "I can understand your apprehension, Mr. Prospective Buyer. Let me tell you exactly what we did for the ABC Company. They're not in your industry, but they had a comparable problem. Let me see if I can outline the specifics of their situation and tell you how we helped them save a great deal of money when they decided to go ahead with this product."

Then you relate in detail, with total credibility and accuracy, exactly what you did in terms of providing benefits for the other buyer. If he is an Analytical, give dates, facts and numbers in your explanation. If he's an Amiable, tell him how various people in the loop were feeling during the negotiations. The related story technique is limited only by your ingenuity in relating another situation to the situation at hand.

(3) *The Call-Back Close*

This is a technique that most of us abuse. I know I've certainly abused it through the years. We use the call-back close in situations where we didn't make the sale earlier, so we go back a second time.

Remember when we said the best predictor of future behavior is past behavior? Well, if you go around again for a call-back close with nothing new and no new input, can you logically expect new positive behavior on the part of the prospective buyer? No.

We must go in with something new that will modify the prospect's evaluation, behavior, and decision-making process. What are we going to go back with? How about new benefits? How about a new product? How about new terms? I'd suggest anything new that can alter their perspective from the earlier presentation, which obviously was not strong enough to get a "Yes."

Let's suppose you return and say, "Well, you told me to come back in about three months, so I'm back. Have you made a decision?" If you're not bringing anything new with you when you return, the usual answer from that prospect will be this: "Yes, I've made a decision. The answer is still No!" If you go back in with nothing new, you can expect nothing new in terms of an affirmative decision.

Go in with some new information. With a fresh and creative approach. Maybe you say, "It was great visiting with you three months ago, and I appreciate the degree of interest you expressed. I also appreciate the additional communications we've had. Now let me tell you what has changed in perspective since we were together last. I've got some new and exciting benefits to provide for you, as well as some new solutions to certain problems we discussed." Then you return to the major points of value-building in your basic presentation, and you provide the new gems of wisdom.

(4) *The Casual Close*

Ten to fifteen years ago, sales trainers were making fun of this one, suggesting that the only close some salespeople knew was "Well, whaddaya think?" I'm convinced that such a casual approach can be very effective today with Less Assertive prospects. It is a low-key, comfortable way of asking them to make a decision. Other ways to phrase it are "How does this sound to you?" or "Does this approach make sense?" The key benefit to this type of close is that it is non-threatening.

(5) *The Forceful Summary Technique*

This is especially effective with the Analytical buyer. It's detail-oriented and involves lots of facts. What you'll want to do with the forceful summary, especially if you're involved in a complex product being sold over a long period of time, is outline the benefits very carefully and relate them as specifically and appropriately as you can to the needs, frustrations, problems and circumstances of that prospective buyer. You should probably do it in writing, providing a detailed list and forcefully summarizing the benefits of what you've got to offer.

Closing the More Assertive Prospect

The More Assertive prospect usually requires less time to close, since this type prospect tends to be more decisive and often impulsive. A little pressure doesn't seem to bother them, but don't overdo it.

You can be more direct with the More Assertive prospect. Try lines such as, "Mr. Prospect, I'm comfortable recommending that you proceed on this now while…", then state a benefit and say, "What do you think?" They'll often give you immediate approval.

Recommended "More Assertive" Closes

Now let's cover some additional closing techniques that I feel are effective with More Assertive prospects.

(1) *The Direct Request Closing Technique*

This technique has been perceived in some ways to be a high pressure close, but it doesn't seem so to me if the technique is used properly. I think it is very functional. You must always use it with conviction and with carefully-measured, limited pressure.

The direct request technique works like this: You just come out and ask for the business. I think people have a basic appreciation for salespeople who believe enough in their products and services that they are direct and lay it on the line with phrases like, "Mr. Prospective Buyer, I must tell you that, based on the input you've given me regarding your current problems and what your budget will withstand at this moment, I'm absolutely convinced that this is the product for you. The benefits we offer overwhelm the competition, our price is reasonable, and it seems a perfect solution to your problem." You then pause and smile and say, "Why don't you buy it?" And you shut up and keep smiling.

Do you know that a smile is the most singularly powerful and disarming nonverbal communication tool in existence? It's beautiful because it dissipates pressure. If you'll sit there and smile at somebody, I'll guarantee you that within 20 seconds, 9 times out of 10 that person will start smiling back at you. And now everybody is smiling. Beautiful! Hopefully, a "Yes" will follow.

(2) *The Subordinate Question Technique*

This is sometimes referred to as the secondary question. The subordinate question is any question you ask other than a direct request to buy, which ultimately leads to the affirmative decision.

For example, let's say that you're selling a product that provides a tax savings for people. And you say, "Tell me, Mr. and Mrs. Prospect, based on your current situation, am I correct in assuming that you need to take advantage of tax-saving devices to the greatest extent possible?"

"You certainly got that right!" replies the client. "We need to save any way we can." Then you say, "Great, wouldn't you agree that right now would be the best time to get started?" The subordinate question enables you to close the prospect very subtly.

(3) *The Alternate-of-Choice Closing Technique*

I must tell you that this is my favorite. Remember when we said with Drivers that we would give them options with probabilities? Working with Drivers is the perfect place to use the alternate-of-choice technique.

This method of closing was perfected during the Depression of the 1930's by Elmer Wheeler. He was retained by the Walgreen's drug chain to come in and beef up profits. In his initial research, Wheeler learned that Walgreen's was buying eggs for 13 cents a dozen and selling them for a nickel each. Now that's a pretty high profit item! Walgreen's was selling eggs in milk shakes and malts, and the chain trained every soda jerk in its entire chain to use the alternative-of-choice close.

Here's what happened. You'd come in and sit down on a stool at the soda fountain, and the soda jerk would come over to take your order. Let's say you'd ask for a vanilla milk shake. Now the soda jerk would get creative. He'd reach under the counter and grab two eggs, hold them up in clear sight and say, "Fine sir, would you like one egg in your milk shake or two?"

Those who didn't want any would often say, "Just give me one." Many times, those who wanted only one would say, "Hey, believe I'll have two." The point is, zero was not one of the choices! Terrific technique. Don't ask *if*, ask *which*.

I contend that the alternate of choice is such a powerful technique that you've got to be careful to keep from taking advantage of people with it. This reminds me of a story.

An old grouch walked aboard an airline. The flight attendant said, "Welcome aboard, sir. Could I get you a drink when we're airborne?" The old grouch barked at her, "No, I don't want a drink." Then he went back and sat down.

Soon a young, smiling businessman walks aboard. "Welcome aboard, sir. Could I get you a drink when we're airborne?" the flight attendant asked. The young businessman said, "Sounds terrific. I'll have a scotch and water." He then goes over and sits down right beside the old grouch.

After the plane is airborne, the flight attendant brings the scotch and water for the young businessman. He accepts it with a big smile. Then she turns to the old grouch and says, "Pardon me, sir, but are you sure I couldn't bring you a drink?"

The old grouch looks up, takes off his glasses, glares at her and says, "Lady, I've already told you once I don't want a drink. Let me see if I can make it a little clearer for you. I don't drink. I don't approve of drinking. I'm not going to take a drink. I'd rather commit adultery than take a drink!"

At that, the businessman handed his scotch and water back to the flight attendant and said, "I didn't know we had a choice!"

(4) *The Sharp Angle Close*

This is another close that works well with the More Assertive decision maker. The sharp angle technique is used when the prospect asks a question that you could answer with a "Yes," but you don't. You close them. Here's how it works:

Steve goes in to buy a shirt. He looks around in the men's store, finds a shirt he really likes and he says to the clerk, "Very nice shirt. Do you have it in green?" Now if the clerk in the men's store says yes, he's a dummy. The clerk should say, "Oh, you want it in green?" Steve says yes and you've got a sale, right? That's the sharp angle. Seize the opportunity.

(5) *The Automatic Close*

The last method I want to discuss is the *automatic close*. This is not only one of my favorites, it's also one of the most effective. The only problem is that it just doesn't happen often enough.

The automatic close is absolutely beautiful because when you least expect it, that miraculous moment occurs right in the middle of your sales presentation. They interrupt you and they say, "You've said enough. Sounds terrific. I'll take it." To which some salespeople reply, "Wait a minute, I ain't through with my presentation yet!" I said *some* salespeople do that. Not you, I hope.

The late great Dick Gardner had a fantastic line that pertains to the automatic close. I hope you'll never forget this line. Dick said, "If you can sell them with blah, don't say blah blah." Once you have sold something, remember that if you keep on talking, you might buy it back!

Successful Application 17

Featuring: Dave Jackson, Chairman and CEO, Rex Yacht Sales; Fort Lauderdale, FL
(Author Interview)

The fine art of negotiating often plays a vital role in getting a "Yes" from a prospect. A multi-million dollar deal that our company recently closed with a wealthy, sophisticated Eastern European client is evidence of the important role that patience usually plays in negotiating a sale.

It started with a fax inquiry. What was unusual was that the fax was in Russian! But our leading sales broker jumped right on it. He found a translator who could read Russian and learned that the fax was an inquiry about a 110 foot yacht we were advertising in the European editions of several leading yachting magazines.

We responded to the fax that same day. About two weeks later, we received another fax from the same interested party, this time in English. The second fax stated the date and time he would be arriving at our offices with his contingent from Europe to view the yacht that interested him.

When the prospect arrived, he brought along his own translator. Our staff had lined up several boats in the same category as the one he had inquired about. He zeroed in on a boat that I happened to own and stock. We had purchased it for about $2.5 million and were asking $3 million for it. We wanted to get as close to $3 million as possible.

As you may have guessed, the news that the United States was experiencing recessionary times had reached the shores of Europe. This prospect had the impression that America was on her knees economically, and the boat business was on its knees too. He had heard that in the United States, you could buy anything for 30 cents on the dollar if your terms were right. We didn't have to talk to the prospect long to realize that we had a tough sale on our hands. But it was a sale we really wanted, and we were willing to work hard to reach closure.

The European client was a savvy negotiator. He wanted to buy the boat that day, he told us. He kept reaching into his pocket for his checkbook. The price he named was about 30 cents on the dollar – a price that we would never accept. So our sales job was to build value and to bring him to the realization that, even though the market may be weak in certain areas, good value will always keep its value and will sell. In short, our task was to *re-program his value system.*

We did not accomplish that task within an hour, or a few hours, or even by the end of that day. We shared some drinks, we talked about yachting, and we each reviewed our positions dozens of times, coming at it from different angles. Our talks went on into the wee hours of the morning. Finally I announced to the group that I had to go to bed and that I'd like very much to continue our discussions the next day.

The prospect didn't call us the next morning, so we contacted him and set up another session two days later. He invited us to come down to his suite at a luxury hotel in Miami Beach. He also asked us to bring a contract to the meeting.

A less-experienced sales team may have taken that request as a signal that the prospect was ready to meet our terms, but we were more realistic. We had learned how he spent the day after our late-night session, a day we initially assumed he spent relaxing. Actually he had been in the showroom of our major competitor, shopping prices.

Another factor that kept us from assuming that this sale was a sure thing was the nature of the product itself. You don't use a yacht for commercial fishing, and you don't charter it out. So the businessman was looking at $3 million of dead capital. And you haven't finished paying for a yacht when you pay for the boat itself. With crew costs, fuel costs, and other expenses, you can push the operating budget up to about $600,000 a year. So the yacht owner has to pay about 20 percent a year for real upkeep, which means a loss of about 7 percent a year on his money.

When we arrived for the second negotiating session, I had two contracts in my pockets, the first contract very close to our asking price, and the second (my fall-back contract) at the price we were willing to accept.

We sat down, I brought out the first contract, and the negotiations began again. Not only was the European client a good negotiator, his translator was a good negotiator too! I had three people on my team – myself, our sales broker (who was handling the acutal negotiations), and our nuts-and-bolts person who could provide details about manufacturing, customization, delivery dates, and the like. We manufacture these boats in Hong Kong, and the boat that the prospect was interested in was under construction, about 80 percent complete. The yacht he had looked at while visiting our offices was a sister ship.

One of the things I've learned in negotiating is that it's always better to go through a third party. In other words, I let my salesman do most of the talking and I sat back, staying rational and as unemotional as possible. In negotiations, it's often true that he who talks first loses. I didn't have to attune my thinking to responding to the turns of the conversations; I could focus on our overall message and goal. My role was to continue emphasizing the quality of our product and our service.

The prospect began with an offer of $1.5 million. Several hours later, he was up to $2.4 million. He was dancing around the room, saying he wasn't going any higher. He had his checkbook out again and was ready to write the check. And he was suggesting that, if we couldn't come to terms, he'd have to pull out and buy from our competitor.

Another negotiating strategy I've learned is to never – never! – belittle your competition. I told him it was a very fine boat that my competition had shown him. I said some complimentary things about my competition's sales skills. But I continued to point out the superior features of my product and to emphasize my company's commitment to great service. I did not say a single word to cut down my competition.

When the discussion turned to price again, I explained to our prospect, without getting emotional, that I had some very real costs in the yacht under discussion. The freight costs to get the boat to Florida were about $120,000, I told him, and the U.S. duty was $80,000 – a total of more than $200,000. He responded by telling me, in essence, that he didn't care what the freight or duty costs were. "I'll take that boat anywhere in the world!" he said.

Now I saw some light at the end of the tunnel! If we let him take the boat in Hong Kong, we could save $200,000 in costs, which left room in our negotiations. We finally signed a contract at about 2 o'clock the next morning.

In retrospect, I realize that it was very important to our prospect to pay the price he wanted to pay. It was an ego thing, to some extent, but that's often a factor in negotiations. He was willing to take certain things out of the deal, make certain concessions, so that he could get his price. And since removing the freight and duty costs removed real costs for us, we were willing to meet that price. So it was a win-win for both parties.

There's another thought I'd like to share on negotiating a deal and it's this: When a deal is done, it's done. It doesn't matter what concessions were made in the negotiations, whether I paid their price or they paid mine. Once you sign the contract, you treat all customers the same. That chapter is over, and it doesn't need to be brought up again. The price should be forgotten the day that the deal is done; that's the day it becomes your job to start delivering on the service end of the agreement. You must always leave room in the deal to be able to provide good service to your client. If you don't, you are going to have an unhappy customer, no matter what price he paid.

Incidentally, the buyer and I have since become close friends. We even bought a ranch together in Montana. It just goes to show that when you close a win-win transaction, good things often continue to happen.

Don's Parting Thought

If one can't close, one can't sell. The better closer you are, the shorter your sales cycles will be and the more success you'll enjoy. Closing is not something you do to somebody – it's a win-win transaction we experience *with* somebody.

SECTION THREE

The Excellence Dimension: Getting The Most Out Of You

SKILL 18: Enthusiasm in Selling

SKILL 19: Goal Setting

SKILL 20: Goal Achievement

SKILL 21: Your Personal Image of Excellence

SKILL 22: Handling Conflict, Problems and Feedback

SKILL 23: Common Sense Sales Ideas

SKILL 24: Dedication to Training

SKILL 25: Gaining Career Progress

Skill #18

✦✦✦✦✦

Enthusiasm in Selling

"Nothing great was ever achieved without enthusiasm."

—RALPH WALDO EMERSON

My friend, Vernon Richmond says "Knowledge is power, but enthusiasm pulls the switch". How much do you know about enthusiasm?

For many years I've heard people say that to be an effective communicator, one must be enthusiastic. One day I realized that I had never given much thought to this important trait, its meaning or its use. So I decided to become more knowledgeable on the topic. And I learned that there's more to gaining and using enthusiasm than I had ever dreamed.

One of the things my research taught me is that enthusiasm comes in two varieties. There is *internalized* enthusiasm, and there is *displayed* enthusiasm. These two types of enthusiasm are very different, and both are quite important to sales success.

Internalized enthusiasm influences our inner feelings toward our profession, our goals, and the tasks to be achieved. It represents the eagerness with which we approach our job. It is an emotion that will often determine what we get done in a given time frame. Salespeople who possess internalized enthusiasm prosper from it, inspire others with it, and make a lot happen in a short period of time. Those who don't have it might be intelligent, capable individuals but will usually be performing at far below their capacity.

Displayed enthusiasm is the degree to which we show the excitement we feel. For some people, this type enthusiasm just comes naturally. Displayed enthusiasm seems to be part of the value system of the highly emotional person; it's just a natural part of his or her behavioral style.

Using Enthusiasm Strategically

A certain type individual will read a book, listen to a tape, or hear a speaker who tells them they've got to be enthusiastic and that person, on hearing the words, jumps right out of his or her chair and says, "Yeah! That's what I need to do. I've gotta be more enthusiastic than I've ever been before and I'm gonna do just that!" And he or she goes charging out loaded with enthusiasm, all fired up and ready to put that enthusiasm to work.

Now what happens if this person gets into the marketplace and the first person they call on is an unemotional, fact-based Analytical type whose behavior is totally opposite? How do they handle all that enthusiasm? The answer could be *very poorly*. We must use displayed enthusiasm selectively.

Some people with a low display of emotion look at the highly-enthusiastic salesperson and think, "Who *is* this loudmouth and what's he doing here?" Bad strategy on the part of the overly- enthusiastic salesperson. Wrong approach. More reserved individuals don't normally display a great deal of enthusiasm, but it would behoove them to work on it if they are a salesperson attempting to sell the highly-emotional type client.

The issue here is one of planning, strategy and adaptability. When we can make our prospective buyer more comfortable by selling them the way they like to be sold, we are on our way to shorter sales cycles and higher income.

The first lesson to learn regarding enthusiasm is this: *Enthusiasm is something that must be used at the proper time with the appropriate people and in the proper dosage.*

If enthusiasm isn't a part of a targeted strategy, it's probably going to become your adversary rather than your ally. Enthusiasm can be your greatest friend or your worst enemy. It's like your automobile: understand it, fuel it, maintain it well, and it will take you anywhere you want to go; abuse it, drive it carelessly or drunkenly, and it will be the source of your demise.

Life-Saving Enthusiasm?

You've undoubtedly heard it said that with the right degree of enthusiasm, you can sell anything. That saying reminds me of a story I heard years ago about the kid who was about to be drafted to go to Vietnam. He didn't want to go, but he needed to develop a strategy for avoiding the service. So he got creative.

This young man goes down to take his physical. He charges into the head physician's office at the infirmary, walks straight up to the doctor and says, "Doc, I want you to know that I can't wait to get to Vietnam."

The doctor looks at him with surprise.

"Doc," said the young guy, "when I get over there I'm gonna find those Viet Cong and hit 'em across the head with the butt of my gun. I'll jab my daggers through their hearts. And when I catch the really mean ones, I'll get a bead on 'em with my M16 and shoot them right between the eyes. I tell you Doc, I can't wait to get over there. I'm gonna kill 'em!"

The Doctor looks across at this young guy and says, "Fella, you've got to be *crazy.*"

And the kid says, "Put it down, Doc. Put it down right there on the form!"

This kid's method was not exemplary, but his story illustrates that a high level of displayed enthusiasm can capture attention and make things happen. Treat enthusiasm as a respected skill; use it wisely and well, and it can be a vital tool in your treasury of selling skills.

Cultivating the Inner Enthusiasm That Inspires High Performance

"Enthusiasm," Dale Carnegie said, "is as contagious as measles."

Just reading that quote and thinking about Dale Carnegie's achievements inspires enthusiasm in me. But while we are all periodically energized by articulate quotations and the observance of high levels of enthusiasm in others, I think we must look within for energy and boundless enthusiasm.

I believe the foundation that will enable us to experience enthusiasm in our daily lives is a *noble vision.* We must have a vision of something we want to achieve, a vision that allows us to set measurable daily goals and get excited about achieving them.

Those who founder sadly, functioning at less than their potential, are usually those who are unaware of what they must do today, now, in order to achieve their goals. To make one's career and life meaningful, we need a life plan that can be translated into daily requirements to energize us. As basic and pedestrian as that sounds, I know of no better way to feel genuine internalized enthusiasm for life than knowing what is required of you today in order to get where you want to go. Then you can devote your energy to fulfilling that requirement.

Admittedly, this perspective is more activity-focused than emotion-focused, but subscribing to a defined activity level reaps results that charge our emotions for greater achievement. The alternate approach would be to psyche ourselves with great emotion, which is likely to deflate rapidly if we cannot focus that energy into a specific activity and purpose.

How To Develop Internalized Enthusiasm

How do you start your day? What kind of input do you use to fuel that human computer between your ears? This will be one of the most important decisions of your day.

I have developed the satisfying habit of reading a few pages from two or three select authors early each morning. Another great source of inspiration is audio cassettes. I found years ago that this is a wonderful alternative to negative headlines or the bemoaning of this unfair world. It gives me a pleasurable reason to get up early when sleeping later might be a more joyous choice for some.

One of my favorite authors to read in the morning is Orison Swett Marden, who wrote over 40 books almost a century ago. His books include *The Victorious Attitude* and *Peace, Power and Plenty*. Marden was an early influence on my good friend Og Mandino, whose writings I also find inspiring (*The Greatest Salesman in the World, The Choice, University of Success, etc.*)

Another thinker and writer whose works I like to read in the morning is Elbert Hubbard, who was sadly lost in the sinking of the Lusitania in 1915. Hubbard's *Selected Writings* and *Little Journeys* are a true source of inspiration. His most famous work was the great article *A Message to Garcia.*

Whoever said "As your day begins, so it shall go" was on target. Get your creative juices flowing early and you are more likely to find new power and enthusiasm within yourself.

What does the word "crusade" mean to you? If you have one, you know what it does for your level of enthusiasm. Webster defines it as any activity pursued with zeal and enthusiasm, a cause to strive toward. What is your crusade? If you don't have one, you bought this book just in time! Write down your personal purpose as eloquently as you can, read it daily and be energized.

When we know what we want to achieve and feel it within our heart, then and only then will we capture the inner enthusiasm of a personal crusade. Define your values, set your goals, establish daily action requirements and attack them with crusade-inspired energy! I predict you will encounter few obstacles capable of counteracting the incredible level of inner enthusiasm you will have developed.

An Enthusiastic Decision For Success

If it's correct that we function on only 16 to 18 percent of our brain power and that 98 percent of our daily behaviors are the result of habit and conditioned reflex, we all have much room to grow, experiment, learn and progress.

Do something today that you've never done before! The best way to erase your performance barriers is to set new standards for yourself and vow to surpass previous measurable achievement levels. This is done with internalized enthusiasm that you have created for yourself.

What have you programmed yourself to achieve within the next 12 months? Why *that* amount? Is your current achievement level based on well-planned strategy, or are you just busy repeating your yesterdays one day at a time?

Erase previous barriers by knocking them down. Consciously – indeed, with a vengeance! – propel yourself with determination beyond previous sales plateaus. Become the high performance salesperson that others set their standards by, rather than the one others know they will easily surpass.

Thomas Carlyle said, "Every great movement in the annals of history has been the triumph of enthusiasm." Develop a definite game plan for your progress, then reach inward for the energy and enthusiasm to help you achieve it. What Carlyle calls "the triumph of enthusiasm" can happen to you!

Successful Application 18

Featuring: Chris Diaz, Realtor; ERA Rancho Real Estate Company; Santa Ana, CA

Submitted by: Danny Cox of Tustin, CA., Professional Speaker and former Manager with Forest E. Olson Realtors, now a Coldwell Banker company; Los Angeles, CA

She was a former tomato picker with an eighth grade education, barely five feet tall. She spoke with a heavy Spanish accent. And she was a real estate salesperson. Oh, was she *ever* a real estate salesperson! Chris Diaz, working alone, could out-produce offices of 20 or more people.

She did just that for Forest E. Olson Realtors at one time. It was the year she was our Number One producer out of 1,200 salespeople. I've never found anyone who had higher production in all the real estate companies I've spoken to around the country.

When she came to work in our offices, she was in her late thirties. She had her heart set on making the Million Dollar Club in her first year. In the late fall of that year she came to me, depressed. She needed to earn $20,000 in commissions to qualify for the Million Dollar Club and she was behind. She wanted to go to the real estate company down the street where they sold bigger houses, so she'd make more money on each sale.

I don't remember exactly what I said to her that day. Something like "bloom where you're planted." I think I told her that she'd started to establish a reputation for herself in the Hispanic community and she should keep building on it. Anyway, she left my office that day crying.

The next day she was back, working hard, smiling, bubbling like she always did when she was selling. Between October and December, she doubled the amount she'd made on sales during the first nine months of the year. She made the Million Dollar Club that year, and every year since.

Chris Diaz came to think of selling homes to the Hispanic community as her mission. She saw her work as more than selling; it was helping her fellow Hispanics get a decent home. To do that, she had her kids out working the streets on roller skates, passing out flyers, telling Hispanics that Chris Diaz would try to help them find a home. She worked hard, and when I asked her how she kept going at that pace day after day, she told me this:

"Selling real estate isn't hard work. Let me tell you what's hard work. It's bending over all day out there in those fields in July, picking tomatoes. It's drinking out of the same jug of water with all the other workers, and the jug's been sitting out in the sun all day. *That's* hard work." I always remember Chris Diaz when I hear people talking about hard work. It's all in the attitude.

Chris left our company to open her own real estate firm. Today she has her own escrow company and her own mortgage business as well. Chris has been incredibly successful, and she has really enjoyed her success. She has been able to buy the fine jewelry she had always wanted and a fabulous home with a crystal chandelier in Orange County. And she goes to mass every morning to give thanks for her blessings.

Enthusiasm and a positive attitude made Chris Diaz one of the very best salespeople I've ever known. One day I asked her, "What's your best sales record so far, Chris?" She told me that in one month she had 29 listings and sold 27 of those listings herself. She also sold 18 additional listings in the same month!

"How do you do it, Chris?" I asked her. Her enthusiastic answer: "God didn't make me with an Off switch!"

DON'S PARTING THOUGHT

Nurture and maintain a high level of internalized enthusiasm. So strong a level of enthusiasm, in fact, that you are determined that your goals and dreams will become reality. So strong that your mission compels you to plan and work more diligently than ever before.

Employ displayed enthusiasm with great finesse. Turn it on with those who respond to it, but turn it down with those who need more facts and less hype. Be thankful for the rewards and blessings you have already received and be enthused about the rewards and blessings you are creating for yourself now!

Skill #19

♦♦♦♦♦

Goal Setting

"Diligent planning leads to profit
as surely as haste leads to loss.**"**

—SOLOMON

Everybody who ever lived has been told about the importance of personal and professional goal setting. So why is it that less than one-half of one percent of salespeople today have their goals in writing?

In this chapter, I'd like to make you aware of the pitfalls, the potential and the strategies for a sound, results-oriented goal setting program. There are four important facts to remember about planning your life through goal setting:

Fact 1: Everybody knows about goal setting.

Fact 2: Hardly anybody really gets involved in an organized goal-setting process.

Fact 3: Those who *do* get involved in the process reap incredible rewards.

Fact 4: There are guidelines that can make goal setting enjoyable, rewarding and relatively simple.

There are a lot of people out there who give lip service to goal setting. They say things like, "Well, my goal is to make more money this year than I made last year." That's not a goal, that's a wish – and far too general to be very helpful.

A Full-Time Servant At No Charge?!!

I sometimes encounter people who say, "I don't need to write down my goals. They are right up here in my head, and that's good enough for me!" Some would argue that unwritten goals are better than no goals at all, but they would have overlooked the most important fact about goal setting: the human goal achievement process does not take place in the conscious mind, but in the subconscious mind.

The best way to program the subconscious mind is to write your goals down in definitive, clarified form. Do that with great care; turn it over to your subconscious mind, and your goal-setting and achievement process will begin to work as if on automatic pilot. The subconscious mind, once programmed, works for you 24 hours a day, 365 days a year, and all it costs you is a little time and energy to program it. It's hard to believe we can have a full-time servant without cutting a check!

It's not a miracle or a concept that will work without your attention and energy. The fact is that once you have properly programmed your subconscious mind, it directs the attention and energy of your conscious mind to take appropriate actions.

Free Dollars Too!

Several years ago I did a personal study of goal setting among professional salespeople. During a typical month, I'll address 8 to 14 audiences. I decided I'd single out one month and during every speech and seminar I did that month, I'd use a special vignette of material related to goal setting to further my research on the subject. I was working on the premise that everybody knows about goal setting but few people write down their goals.

Here's what I did. I went to the bank and got a handful of silver dollars (this was back when they were readily available.) It's May, and my first speech is in Chicago. I had about 200 people in the audience. I stood before my audience, clicked the stack of silver dollars in my hand, and said, "Friends, we're going to go through a little exercise, during which each of you can win one of these silver dollars. I'd like for everyone who has your personal or professional goals in writing, on your person, right now, to please stand up, come forward and show them to me. I'll give you a little token of remembrance today – one of these silver dollars."

I used that material in every speech and seminar I presented during the month. City after city. I had over a dozen appearances that month, and I was exposed to thousands of people. Do you know that for the entire month, I gave away only $3.00!

Boy, that was the cheapest investment I ever made in some good material! But wait… I'm not quite through with the story.

The Value of Being A "Quick Study"

The last day of May, I was doing a sales rally in Oklahoma City with Norman Vincent Peale and J. Douglas Edwards. We had a big crowd of nearly 1,000 people. It was a really good meeting and everything was progressing beautifully.

I was the middle speaker. I pulled out my silver dollars and I went into my spiel about everybody knowing about goal setting but not doing it.

And once again, I said, "Everybody who has your goals in writing, with you, right now, on your person, come forward and let me give you a little gift."

This one guy throws his chair back and confidently comes charging up to the front of the ballroom and says, "Here they are, Don – right here!" I glanced at his goals and said, "I'm really impressed. Here's your silver dollar." And he said, "Thank you very much, Don. By the way, it's good to see you again. Haven't seen you in almost a month, since I was in Chicago!"

Well, I had to laugh. The guy deserved a silver dollar, as much for so creatively capitalizing on an opportunity for some public praise as for having set his goals.

Anyway, this story illustrates the fact that very few salespeople put goals in writing, even though they know how important it is. And I'm making you a promise right now: If you study, develop and master this skill, your life will never be the same.

You'll be a member of the uncommon few, not the common masses, and you'll have a very real advantage over your competition. *Mastering this skill may do more to put you in the category of the high performance salesperson than any other skill we'll discuss in this book!*

Dr. Napoleon Hill described a goal as anything you want to be, have, do, or achieve. That's a very simple – and very good – definition of goal setting.

And now that you know the power of goals, I want to give you 21 ways to develop a workable, high quality goal-setting process for yourself. I call these 21 items *Goal Factors*.

Goal Factor One: Commit to a viable plan

You've heard it said that a journey of 1,000 miles begins with the first step. Well, a successful future in your sales career should begin with well-thought-out goals.

You wouldn't attempt to build a building without plans or blueprints. If you added bricks and boards at random, you'd end up with little more than a pile of brick and wood.

What if your plan doesn't work out? Well, you can always get a fresh sheet of paper and start over with a new plan. The greatest pitfall in the quest for success is not failing – it's not committing to a plan.

Right now, commit to planning your goals every year for the remainder of your sales career. I also recommend you give yourself a deadline *now* for the completion of your goal-planning and goal-setting process for the rest of this year and in subsequent years. Establish a date at which you will have completed your goal-setting process. Two to nine days is recommended, but decide *now!*

Goal Factor Two: Consider personal governing values in setting your goals

If you have a goal that conflicts with your value system, that goal will be very difficult to achieve. You should carefully consider your values and beliefs before setting any goals for your professional life.

I have included in this chapter a copy of the "Goal-Pac" form I use in training sessions when we are discussing goal setting. You will notice on the Goal-Pac Personal Success Plan (see p.266) that under each of the primary goal categories is the word *"premise,"* with a space following in which you can write a few words or a phrase that clarifies your strongest belief in that area. When you write down your carefully thought-out premise, it should reflect your values and beliefs.

Life is filled with priorities to be set and decisions to be made. The clarification of your values and the establishment of your personal premises will make life's decisions much easier to make.

Goal Factor Three: Visualization with personal authorship is essential

Too many people go through life worrying endlessly about what other people think. While you may welcome the input of other people you respect, don't let them set your goals for you. You must live your own life, reap the fruits of your own labors, endure your own pain. It's up to you to set the sail for your life's journey. If someone else authors your goals, your commitment level and belief in accomplishing them won't be nearly as strong. Don't compromise your individuality! It is one of your greatest assets.

One of the opportunities we have in a free enterprise system is the right to succeed to whatever degree we choose and earn. As long as you never lose sight of the realistic prices you must pay, you can have just about anything you believe you can have. Your goals should reflect your own unique beliefs, desires and ambitions.

Begin With Brainstorming

Goal setting, in my opinion, should begin with some quiet personal brainstorming. Lean back, close your eyes, and let your mind wander into the future. Let your imagination go. As you think of things that describe what you want to be, have, do or achieve, write them on a clean sheet of paper. You can tweak and clarify the goals later; for now, just jot them all down (the eight categories shown on the Goal-Pac can help you focus your thinking.) This is an excellent beginning procedure for the goal-setting process.

Whether you spend 30 minutes or three days on this initial exercise, it will normally get the creative juices flowing and the excitement level high for goal setting. Remember, what you visualize is what you attract.

After you have completed the brainstorming, go back and assign appropriate and realistic time frames to each goal. If one of your goals is to climb the Matterhorn, it's a good bet that it won't happen next week. Richard Halliburton did it, writing major parts of one of his great books on the way up, but he had a sound plan for climbing the Matterhorn before beginning. If you want to be the Number One salesperson in your company, carefully consider what you'll have to do and how long it might take to achieve this.

Simply put a number after each goal that signifies the number of years you expect it will take you to reach that goal. With shorter-term goals, designate months or days allotted for achievement. You are now off to a great start!

Goal Factor Four: Make your goals definite and precise

Don't allow a goal to be a simple vague wish. Wish is the sound the wind makes, and wishes often disappear just like the wind that blows by. Goals should reflect well-thought-out beliefs and aims. Wishes are usually the result of shallow perceptions.

A strong, definitive goal nurtures confidence and action. The more precise a goal is, the easier it will be to visualize and achieve. For example, if you'd like to increase your income by exactly $12,000 per year, that's obviously $1,000 per month. That is exact and precise enough to allow you to identify the activities and actions you must implement to follow through and make that goal a reality. To say "I'd like to make more money" isn't good enough. It's not precise enough to build a *plan* around.

Goal Factor Five: Make your goals attainable and personally credible

If you set a goal that is unrealistic and/or unattainable, it can become a de-motivator. An example of a typical unrealistic goal is if you say "I want to triple my income this year" versus your desire to increase your income by 20 percent.

Your goals must have credibility with you and be attuned to your abilities. You can develop a viable plan for a 20 percent increase in your income, and it will probably be achievable. But it's likely you won't find it personally credible to say you'll try to triple your income in a single year. On the other hand, if you have a well-thought-out game plan that you feel will work to triple your income this year, go for it!

No goal is too small to write down and focus on. Often the size of the goal is not as important as the positive habits you develop in the initial goal-setting and follow-up process. The achievement of even small goals can be a boon to your self image as you develop into a better goal-setter and a bigger goal-achiever.

Goal Factor Six: Evidence intense desire

Many times you'll really turn on that after-burner if you want something badly enough. Desire can be an unbelievably powerful motivator, giving birth to new levels of self-discipline and results.

Often people reach substantial goals simply because they have too intense a desire to be denied. The intensity of desire can be enhanced by pictures of the item or the end result you desire. For example, three or four strategically-placed photographs of the boat you and your family want can be very helpful. The reminder of what you are working toward can really work for you.

Goal Factor Seven: Make some of your goals significant

Many times the greatest stimulant to personal growth is to stretch yourself beyond previous performance levels. Each time you exceed previous levels of achievement, it's exciting. And it's a reminder that there are very few limits to what you can accomplish. We all have billions of brain cells just waiting to be stimulated by worthy goals!

Dreams of a significant dimension can be very helpful to you. Let them be a source of power, excitement and hope. Dreaming of a large goal will help you develop a stronger set of expectations for your life. Just remember to give yourself a realistic time frame to reach that goal. If what you're working toward really matters to you, you'll give everything you've got to make it happen.

Goal Factor Eight: Never set a goal that violates the rights of others

When your goals are compatible with the goals of significant others in your life, your support system will be stronger. The closer the relationship, the more important goal compatibility becomes in order for you to achieve happiness and harmony.

If you set a goal that's unfair or unjust to others, you're setting yourself up for failure, frustration and disappointment. Remember the win-win philosophy and high standards of today's professional salespeople, and this will never be an issue you'll have to worry about.

Goal Factor Nine: Review and revise

Revising your goals isn't giving up. It's just good business practice to find those goals that are sound, stable and realistic and then let them lead you to higher levels of productivity.

I appeared on a program with my good friend Zig Ziglar one time when he spoke about goal setting and the periodic need for goal revision. Zig asked the audience this question: " If we took off in an airliner today here in Cleveland enroute to Kansas City, and the captain realized an hour into the trip that we were two degrees off course, would he turn around and return to Cleveland?" The audience laughed at the absurdity of the question, but the point was well made. Revision is viable, and periodically very necessary.

Review your goals often, and revise the ones that seem to be off the mark. Keep stretching yourself to reasonable limits so that you will continue to grow.

One word of caution: Don't revise your goals too often. If you must revise income goals, do so quarterly but not daily or weekly. Give your goals a chance to work before you change them. Oftentimes the goal itself may not need to be changed, but the time frame you have allowed for its attainment will. Remember the words of Jerry Bresser: "There are no unrealistic goals, only unrealistic time frames!" (More on this in Skill 20.)

Goal Factor Ten: Separate materialization from strategy in your goal-setting process

Ultimate ownership of a material possession or goal may be noble or admirable, but picturing it isn't enough. For a goal to materialize, it must go through the maturation process. The most important ingredient in that process is a nurturing, committed strategy.

The presence of a strategy means you're pro-active, you're pushing forward, you're putting forth creative effort, and you have every intention of making that goal materialize. Without a sound strategy for attainment, few goals are realized.

Goal Factor Eleven: Categorize Your Goals

I recommend the following eight goal categories for your consideration. I have listed them alphabetically:

- *Career Goals.* The biggest enemy of the setting and achievement of career goals is complacency. Don't allow yourself to take opportunities for granted. Maintain a commitment to growth and advancement in this vital area.

- *Education and Personal Development Goals.* We all need new skills and continued education to improve performance and quality of life. The mere fact that you are reading this book indicates you understand the importance of this category. Be eager and positive about developing your skills, and your life will continue to get better.

- *Family goals.* To maintain a balanced, fulfilled life, you must put energy in this area at all times. Again, the payoff can be great when the family unit works positively.

  The family is also customarily the most valuable source for a strong support system. Each family member can be an integral part of the success process for every other family member. I suggest you have a periodic family meeting at which you discuss each others' goals and the progress being made toward those goals. Goals requiring the energies of all family members are especially valuable and important.

- *Financial goals.* To neglect goal setting in this area is a serious miscalculation of necessity and opportunity. In the area of financial goals, a little planning and discipline go a long way. Financial goals should focus on two key areas: net worth and income. Try not to contract what my friend Dr. Larry Markson calls the "I Need Disease." Financial progress is often based on the concept of delaying gratification. Incidentally, I don't think I have ever seen a salesperson operate close to their potential while experiencing financial problems.

- *Physical goals.* You won't achieve the things you want to in life unless you are physically able to do so. Take care of yourself. Value and have pride in your body. Become a student of weight control, nutrition, exercise and your own metabolism. The healthier you are and the higher your energy level, the more you'll sell and the happier you will be.

- *Social, hobby and extra-curricular goals.* Once again, the word here is balance. Individuals vary greatly in their attitudes and needs in this category. Become aware of other family members' goals; compatibility and overlapping in this area are often desirable. Ask yourself what hobbies and social involvements could be the most fun and rewarding.

- *Spiritual goals.* Only you can ascertain your feelings, ideals and commitment in this category. I'll simply quote Dr. Kenneth McFarland who once said, "Few in any endeavor seem to endure over the long run without a meaningful spiritual conviction."

- *Miscellaneous.* This is your catch-all category that will include any goal that doesn't logically fit into the other seven.

I'd like to suggest that you spend nine days on your goal-setting process. Devote a day to each of the eight categories just discussed. Think about a given category for a full day, make notes, crystallize your thinking and focus on where you want your life to go in that area. The last day will be the time to put everything in final, organized form on your Goal-Pac or worksheet.

Now, let's continue with the 21 factors of goal setting.

Goal Factor Twelve: Consider your time structure carefully

There are three time structures to consider in goal setting: short, intermediate and long term.

You should see short-term goals as something to reach in 90 days or less. Daily, weekly, monthly and 60-day goals fall into this category. These short-term goals will make your longer-term goals achievable, so treat them with great care.

Intermediate goals are from three months to 12 months. And long-term goals are for periods such as two, five, seven, ten or twenty years. Try to make your short-term and intermediate goals incrementally consistent with your ultimate long-term goals.

Goal Factor Thirteen: Consider your personal track record

Remember, if you don't know where you are or where you've been, it's going to be tough to accurately project where you're going. This is the reason that I recommend salespeople keep close tabs on their numbers, especially achievement levels in a given time frame.

Know your achievement statistics. If you assess and understand thoroughly your past and present successes and performance levels, your goal-setting process will be of a much higher quality. You can set goals that are more realistic and attainable if you know what you are reasonably capable of.

Goal Factor Fourteen: Make your goals measurable and time sensitive

You need to know where you are at all times to be sure you are on target. As a rule of thumb, the more specific and time-sensitive your goals, the more easily they can be tracked and measured.

If you set a 30-day short term goal and you achieve it in five months, the quality of your goal-setting process is suspect. You may need to give more attention to setting timetables for your goals. On the other hand, if you hadn't written the goal down, it may have never been achieved. So don't beat up on yourself for missing a time frame.

Monitor and measure your goals regularly with a time-sensitive focus. When you can't or don't measure your progress, it's difficult to know if you're setting goals that are too low or too high for yourself. Remember, the setting and achievement of goals are not *events* but part of a *process*. The more you work on the process, the better you will become at it.

Goal Factor Fifteen: Consider your personal comfort zones (and your willingness to leave them!)

To embrace goals that will make you a higher producing salesperson, some behavior changes will be necessary – such as getting up earlier, or doing more telephone work, or making more calls per day. Assess your willingness to change some behaviors as you establish the time frames for your goals.

You need an open-minded willingness to explore new areas and ideas, even those that will take you out of your comfort zones. It's normal to experience discomfort in the process of change, but you must be willing to deal with that if you want to reach your goals. The vital factor is your willingness. Don't *get in your own way* in this regard. Vow now to change, grow, experiment and stretch yourself, and you will undoubtedly surpass your previous performance levels.

Goal Factor Sixteen: Use goals as your personal thermostat

You know how a thermostat works – you set it at a certain level and the temperature goes to that level because the thermostat dictates the output of the system required to reach the desired setting. Your subconscious mind works similarly. Just put your goals at a particular setting, and your subconscious will dictate the output of your performance and growth. Sound too simple? It's not. It works.

Think *thermostat* and where you've got it set. People who haven't established goals that challenge their abilities have their thermostat set too low. It's at a level that doesn't demand much; they are complacent and have stifled their own growth. When such people experience one glitch in their daily system, they are subject to financial, professional or personal ruin. Don't fall into that trap. Let your goal be bigger than any personal frustration that gets in the way or slows you down.

Here's another trap: letting someone else set your thermostat for you. I'm certain many people have gone to their graves with their music still in them because they never set their thermostat, or worse yet, they let somebody else set it. Your life is no dress rehearsal. Every day is the very real here and now. When a day is over, it's gone forever, so make sure it is devoted to *your* goals.

Set your goals – and your thermostat – higher for greater success. Your subsequent achievement level will amaze even you.

Goal Factor Seventeen: See your goals as attitude enhancers

Sales professionals who have a good goal plan and a strong commitment to achieving those plans always seem more positive than those who don't. It becomes obvious that they know where they are going and their "up" attitude helps them get there. Why some salespeople deprive themselves of high achievement and incomes with low personal expectations, I'll never know.

I consider the "check off" a motivator. I'm firmly convinced that people enjoy and are gratified by achieving something on their goal list or daily planner. It simply feels good to do something and check it off. Give yourself many such pleasures because each time you check off another item, you are reinforcing not only the joy of achievement but the viability of the written goal-setting process.

While goal setting and achievement is not necessarily easy, it is relatively simple. Get excited about how much better your life can be through goal setting!

Goal Factor Eighteen: Vividly imagine your goal becoming a reality

Close your eyes and picture yourself reaching and enjoying your goal. Picture every detail as specifically as you can. Do this often with enthusiasm and conviction, and failure won't have a chance. Remember to also picture yourself as the kind of person who is worthy of the goal. Undeserving people are less likely to achieve a goal.

The process of mental imaging is one of the most powerful of all the goal factors and will serve you well by bringing your visions of the future into the present. Close your eyes and imagine vividly and in great detail, the more detail the better.

Goal Factor Nineteen: Put your goals in writing

Don't fall into the trap of believing that your goals don't have to be in writing. I'm convinced that unless your goals are down on paper, in black and white, there's no way you can be definite or committed enough to get significant results. You don't have your subconscious mind working for you adequately until your goals are written down.

When you write down goals, you tend to clarify and crystallize them. And you dramatically multiply the chances that your subconscious will implement the necessary changes in your mind. The results can be immediate and significant. Research indicates that putting your goals in writing *triples* your commitment level. Think of the power in that fact! Goals to which you're not committed stand little chance of coming about.

Now I want to introduce you to a simple but powerful process for putting your goals down on paper. It's my Goal-Pac format, which I have developed based on many models I've studied over the years. The format includes the eight goal categories we discussed earlier in this chapter, as well as time structure considerations.

Begin by using the Rough Copy format during your brainstorming process. Then follow the steps outlined on this and the following pages to complete the goal-setting process.

Goal–Pac©

STEP 1

Category	1 Year	2 Year	5 Year	10 Year	20 Year
Career					
Education / Personal Development					
Family					
Financial					
Physical					
Social					
Spiritual					
Miscellaneous					

Goal Achievement Log

Goal–Pac©

List and check off ❏ items below as you gain closure. Recognizing the achievement of interim goals reinforces progress!

List your goals in the appropriate time box.

STEP 1

Item achieved	Date	Category	1 Year
❏			
❏			
❏		Career	
❏			
❏			
❏			
❏			
❏		Education / Personal Development	
❏			
❏			
❏			
❏			
❏		Family	
❏			
❏			
❏			
❏			
❏		Financial	
❏			
❏			
❏			
❏			
❏		Physical	
❏			
❏			
❏			
❏			
❏		Social	
❏			
❏			
❏			
❏			
❏		Spiritual	
❏			
❏			
❏			
❏			
❏		Miscellaneous	
❏			
❏			

264

Goal–Pac©

STEP 2

After entering your goals, turn to Goal–Pac© Personal Success Plan and re-list your 1 year goals (step 3).

2 Year	5 Year	10 Year	20 Year

Name: _____   **Goal–Pac**©

Critical Dates:
    Start Process: _____
    Complete Planning: _____

Category	Weekly Requirement	Monthly Requirement
Career (Personal Premise:_____ _____ _____)		
Education / Personal Development (Personal Premise:_____ _____ _____)		
Family (Personal Premise:_____ _____ _____)		
Financial (Personal Premise:_____ _____ _____)		
Physical (Personal Premise:_____ _____ _____)		
Social (Personal Premise:_____ _____ _____)		
Spiritual (Personal Premise:_____ _____ _____)		
Miscellaneous (Personal Premise:_____ _____ _____)		

Personal Success Plan

Transfer one year goals from goal achievement log.

STEP 3

Quarterly Requirement	Six Month Requirement	One Year Goals

Goal Factor Twenty: Graph and chart your goals

Many people who are committed to goal setting keep graph paper and make charts to monitor their progress. This technique constantly and vividly reminds you of how you are progressing toward the achievement of a given goal.

For example, last year I had a weight loss goal. So I got graph paper and charted pounds on the left and months of the year across the bottom. I logged in my weight on January 1 and my desired weight on December 31. I drew a line from one to the other. That downward line enabled me to develop a proposed progress line.

The first day of each month I logged in my exact weight so I always knew the degree to which I was progressing toward my goal. At various times I was a little ahead of my goal or a little behind, but I always knew exactly where I was and that was important. By the way, I made my goal, and frequently reviewing that chart really helped keep me on track. This is an excellent means of monitoring progress.

I wish you luck in your progress toward mastering the art of goal setting. But luck is not really what you need. You need Goal Factor Twenty-One: A plan for action and achievement. And that's the skill we'll be looking at in our next chapter.

Successful Application 19

Featuring: Brian Klosterman, Vice President, SONY Consumer Television Products Company; Park Ridge, NJ

Submitted by: Jim Palumbo, Senior Vice President, SONY Consumer Television Products Company; Park Ridge, NJ

Do I remember my first selling goal? You bet!

I was about 12 years old, and in some magazine I read about how you could earn a real tape recorder by selling greeting cards. I was really into electronics as a kid, and I loved gismos, audio equipment, anything electronic. That tape recorder was something I really wanted.

You had to sell 78 boxes to get the tape recorder. So that was my first selling goal: 78 boxes of greeting cards. I went on foot, door to door, sold those 78 boxes of cards and earned my tape recorder. It was a great thrill, and I've been setting sales goals ever since.

Goal setting is very personal. It's not something anyone else can do for you. An ambitious, lofty goal you set for yourself might not be for everyone. So it's important to set goals according to your own standards, because you're the one who is going to have to work to achieve those goals.

When I was 18, just a kid out of high school and working in the sporting goods department at Sears-Roebuck making $2.10 an hour, I set a goal that I wanted to make $1,000 a year for every birthday I'd had. Pretty soon I had moved into a selling job in the electronics department at J.C. Penny, and I was working at Radio Shack on the side. That's where I learned about Sony products. I was very impressed with them, and I set as another one of my goals to one day work for Sony.

By the time I was 25 years old, I had to revise my goals because I was already making more than $25,000 a year. So I updated my goal: I wanted to make $2,000 a year for every birthday I'd celebrated. A few years later, I passed that goal too. I had gotten into wholesale selling and sales training, and soon I was able to update my goal to $3,000 a year and I reached that goal also.

I joined Sony when I was 31 years old, another goal achievement. Then I began setting goals regarding what I wanted to do at Sony. I wanted to be a vice president at Sony, and I achieved that when I was 33.

By this time in my life, recognition had become as important to me as dollars earned, and I no longer set my goals solely according to what I wanted to earn. Most people find, after they reach a certain income level, that dollars are just not their only motivation anymore. That usually happens somewhere between poverty and wealth, though I'm not sure just where!

Writing down your goals gives them more power. It's not enough to say, "I want to make enough money to pay the bills this month." You need to put down on paper what you want to achieve, and then figure out your game plan for making it happen. And you have to reevaluate your goals again and again. You may set down as your goal to do X, but you realize that it's possible to achieve even more, so you reach for Y.

Along the way, I've also had goals regarding my family life, physical goals and goals in other areas. If you're going to be in the Aspirer mode – aiming to be a "high flier," as I like to call it – you must have a healthy mind and body. Your goals should be to find a balance in life. God, family, and career – those are the things I try to keep in balance.

There's one more aspect of goal setting that I think is very important, and that's to share your goals with others. Share with your staff what you want to achieve in business and ask for their help. Share your goals with your family, too. I've found that when you share your goals with your associates and your family, they not only become cheerleaders for you when you win, but they are cheering for you all along the way – and that support can be a big motivator to help you reach your goals.

Today, every time I review my written goals, the process helps clarify where I am and where I plan to be in the future. We should be very careful what we put in writing about our life's goals – because I've found *what I set as my goals are what happens!*

DON'S PARTING THOUGHT

Capitalize on goal setting, one of the greatest sources of power for human progress. Set your goals with insightful prioritizing and intense motivation. Don't leave your success to luck, chance, or the whims of another. Your success is within you, and setting goals will help you get it out!

Skill #20

✦✦✦✦✦

Goal Achievement: 12 Steps To Get You from Vision To Reality

"Happiness lies in the thrill of creative effort and the joy of achievement."

—FRANKLIN D. ROOSEVELT

In his best-selling book *Release Your Brakes,* my friend and fellow professional speaker Jim Newman says something that I like about setting goals for yourself. "Goals aren't simple conveniences," according to Jim. "The human behavioral system requires goals for survival."

Even the most primitive man set goals, though he certainly didn't write them down. His first goal was to find enough food or water to make it through the day, or shelter to survive the winter storm. When his basic needs were met, he'd move onto higher goals. Like finding someone to snuggle up to around the campfire.

Those goals that we haven't consciously set but move toward anyway are what I call "absentia goals." If the only goals we have are absentia goals, then we behave precisely like Mr. Primitive. We move toward whatever has become the uppermost thought in our minds at any given time. We let the needs of the moment determine our agenda, instead of striving for well-considered, noble goals.

I've known people who behaved as though their goal was to fail. Clearly they didn't sit down with paper and write "Goal One: Failure." But by failing to establish a goal structure for themselves, they began to move toward goals that were set by the first-thing-that-pops-into-my-mind method of setting goals. And friends, that system is a first-class ticket to failure or, at best, to mediocrity.

I'll say it again: To become a high-performance salesperson, goal setting is a must. In the last chapter, you learned about the goal-planning process. Now we want to discuss how to achieve those goals once you've set them.

I've prepared a list of 12 factors that I believe influence your ability to achieve your goals. These are all factors that you can control. Hard work is required to master some of these factors, and others depend on your attitude. But I'm convinced that seizing command in these areas will help you realize your goals and enhance your sales performance.

Achievement Factor One: Practice self-discipline

High performance people are competent self-disciplinarians. They have a stick-to-it dedication to the task at hand that paves the way for success after success. Keep in mind that discipline, intense desire and persistence determine our destiny, not simple wishes.

Sales managers building a team of winners want those salespeople who subscribe to the "I'll-Make-Just-One-More-Call" philosophy. Not the clockwatchers who say, "Just one more hour and I can quit." Winners have the discipline to use every minute well.

It takes discipline to set the alarm at 5:30 instead of 6:00 a.m. It takes discipline to block out office distractions, to say "No" to the siren call of golf or long lunches or other enjoyable activities that can shorten the time you have available to spend working toward your goals.

It takes discipline to keep on keeping on, to keep pouring energy into that last 30 minutes of a long day. But high performance salespeople have that kind of personal discipline, and it makes the difference between mediocrity and greatness.

Achievement Factor Two: Set personal performance standards

Companies have performance standards, so why not individuals? Well, we should. Ask yourself these questions:

- What do I expect of myself?

- Is it more or less than I expected of myself last year?

- Is this level of sales production one that I can realistically attain?

- Will I have to *stretch* to get it done? (If not, maybe you should reconsider and shoot higher!)

Most people set their standards by the production of those people around them, rather than by what their own true potential is. Don't drag a ball and chain around. Unleash your inner power by demanding more of yourself today than you did yesterday.

Keep score! Measure your performance relentlessly. After setting your goals, begin to chart your progress. What did you accomplish this week? This month? This quarter? Ask yourself, "Did I really push myself, or did I just settle for what was easily within my grasp?" The only way to evaluate how well you are adhering to your standards is to keep score.

No one should be better at setting performance standards for you than you are. Just make sure you reach for the stars – and keep up with your progress along the way.

Achievement Factor Three:
Reject procrastination

W. Clement Stone has a simple three word motto: "Do it now." That's one of the most succinct – and one of the best – rallying cries for success I've ever heard.

Let me tell you the best way I've found to fight procrastination. Don't picture the entire task to be completed, just picture the first simple thing you have to do to get the ball rolling. Got that picture in your head? Now go do it. Right now. That's right. START! Starting is the hardest part.

Once your day is well planned, don't keep on until you plan it to death. By then, the day will be over. Get out the door. Get in the car. Get on the phone. And start the required process for making a productive day. Once you're out of the starting gate, the toughest thing is behind you.

Another way to jump-start yourself off the "On Hold" position is to decide in advance at exactly what time you'll begin a given task. Then keep your promise to yourself. At the exact time you set, drop everything else and begin to do the task you resolved to do.

Achievement Factor Four:
Feel good about your goals

You're among the uncommon few when you have goals in writing. So reward yourself with positive feelings about having accomplished something important.

That mental pat on the back felt great, didn't it? Now keep feeding on those positive feelings. They'll create momentum that will help propel you toward the achievement of your goals. And they'll help you feel good about setting goals again next month, next year and for your lifetime.

Remember, goal setting and goal achievement are processes, not singular events. What you're learning about setting and achieving goals now will be valuable to you forever.

Achievement Factor Five:
Make your goals public

You don't have to run a newspaper ad. But sharing your goals with some select individuals around you at work and at home can have a positive influence.

It's not necessary to share everything, just what you're comfortable telling. Sharing your goals increases your commitment level and decreases the possibility that you'll give up. It's also a positive when you share a confidentiality with someone who can be a good part of your support system.

When you make your goals public, you'll get some good ideas from your supporters that could be helpful in your achievement process. However, you may also get some criticism. And that leads to Achievement Factor Six.

Achievement Factor Six:
Reject the doubts of others

Don't let others shake your belief in your goals or yourself. Don't let anybody quarterback you out of your confidence and determination. Some people may not want you to reach your goals because it will make them look bad. Shake off their criticism or cynicism. Don't succumb to negative input.

Shakespeare said, "Our doubts are traitors and make us lose the good we oft might have won by making us fear to attempt." Don't make yourself a loser by listening to the naysayers who promote and nurture doubt and pessimism.

"It won't work." "It will take forever." "You could never do that." Arm yourself against such stones that try to shatter your will. Turn that negativism around and use it as stimulus. Let it make you even more determined and committed to your cause.

Achievement Factor Seven:
Review and revise

Monitor your progress toward your goals during the achievement process. Establish a time daily or at least weekly to go back over your goals and consider your progress.

Revise your goals only when you must. Circumstances can change, and you may need to change paths toward your destination. But if you put into your goal-setting process the kind of thought this activity deserves, changes will be minimized.

It's far better to revise your goals than to mentally cross off a goal because it was obviously unrealistic and unattainable. If you and your spouse or date decide to eat at a certain restaurant and along the way you lose the address or get lost, you don't give up and go home, do you? You go to a different restaurant. Or you phone and try to find the right address. You adjust. And that's the way you should treat your goals.

If it's obvious you can't get to the place you wanted to be, then aim for another worthy destination.

Achievement Factor Eight:
Resist the temptation to falter. Persist!

We often grow strongest in times of adversity. When things get hard, high performers just work harder, work longer, and work smarter. The tougher a goal is to reach, the more appreciation you'll have for it when it's yours.

Try to avoid succumbing to depression. Depression is the enemy of achievement. Avoid it by refusing to let negative thoughts take root in your mind. Depression often brings along its close cousin, the "Poor Me" syndrome. The next step is usually quitting, but not for winners.

Winners are tenacious in pursuit of their goals. They change pace, change tactics, change priorities – but always with their ultimate goal in mind. Their behavior may appear inconsistent, but it's just because they had to make a detour to get where they had decided to go. Losers, on the other hand, sit down beside the road and give up. They abandon a project or important sales goal when the going gets rough. They display shallow persistence at best.

Remember: For winners, the ultimate goal is usually a constant. It's the strategy and timing for getting there that's most often modified.

Achievement Factor Nine:
Be open to teamwork and mutual support

Do you spend time with people with whom you enjoy a mutually-beneficial relationship? I recommend it, since nobody can succeed alone. Every person you work with, your family, and your friends can be part of a support system that enriches your life with beneficial ideas and input.

One very meaningful dimension of my life has been my Mastermind group. We have a close relationship in our little group of four. We have no hidden agendas. We're willing to help each other, and we get help and support in return.

This group was started informally – in fact, accidentally – over 10 years ago. The synergy of our group has been strong. It's based on mutual respect and creativity. We listen and learn, and it's a win-win situation for everybody. If you're not part of such a group, I suggest you start one. You're likely to get valuable new ideas on how to achieve your goals. One of the best sources for ideas on the formation of a Mastermind group is Napoleon Hill's great book, *Think and Grow Rich*. Remember that for a group like this to work, total openness and a strong mutual respect are paramount to the group's success.

Achievement Factor Ten:
Make deadlines work for you, not against you

Deadlines can be a tool for achievement. They may be stressful, but they also give you that kick-in-the-seat-of-the-pants motivation you need.

Give yourself deadlines for your work and your goals. You'll find your achievement level will rise. Remember Parkinson's Law: The amount of time required for the achievement of a task is determined by the amount of time available for its completion.

Achievement Factor Eleven:
Have An Activity-Based Philosophy of Achievement

The actions and energies required to achieve most goals can be tied to specific activity levels. For example, a salesman might realize that, to reach his sales goal for this month, he'll have to make exactly seven more calls per week based on his current closing percentage. He can see, in real numbers, what's required to make his goals.

Have an Action Plan for each goal you set. Your Action Plan should list specific activities and behaviors required to meet your objective. When you accomplish an activity, it makes you feel you're on target and your goals are achievable.

Achievement Factor Twelve:
Have a positive habit structure

Career success and goal achievement are seldom instantaneous. They normally occur over a significant period of time.

When you map out the path you plan to take to reach your goals, you'll be taking the journey in small steps – minutes and hours and days and weeks that add up into years. And all during those minutes and hours and days, you'll be following habits.

Habits are the commanders of our destiny. They determine our probability for success. Is your habit structure one that will enable you to reach your aspirations?

Constantly assess and reassess your personal and professional habits. Recognize a bad habit for what it is: a roadblock on your success journey. Replace that roadblock with a well-thought-out habit that will propel you to your destination.

Here's a three-step program that can help you in your efforts to replace undesirable habits:

Step One: Write down the old habit you want to change and why you want to change it. Suppose you've been sporadic about writing personal notes to prospects after an initial call. You know it's a valuable step that will make subsequent calls much more fruitful, but you're just not writing those notes. Scold yourself in writing. Tell why changing that habit is important.

Step Two: Write down the new habit you're going to implement, and write the results you expect with this better habit.

Step Three: Write the dates you'll start to work on this behavioral change, and the date you plan to have it totally internalized. Be a realist; allow as much as three weeks for closure.

Habits are hard to change. That's why I recommend the written process. Writing it down helps you internalize your intentions and dramatically increases your chances of success. And, just as with written goals, writing down how you plan to change triples your commitment to sweep out habits that are holding you back and adopt new and better habits.

Successful Application 20

Featuring: John B. Tigrett, Entrepreneur; London, England, and Memphis, TN
(Author Interview)

One of the factors essential for goal achievement is persistence. You must continue to believe in your goals even when others around you are filled with doubt. Successful businessman John B. Tigrett is an example of the rewards that can come from daring to set high goals and then having the courage to stick with them.

John Tigrett is a distinguished entrepreneur, philanthropist, and world-class deal maker. He recently told me about one of his ventures that required a combination of extraordinary self-belief, patience, and persistence to achieve his goal.

"I had done a business deal for Armand Hammer in Morocco and had gotten to know him well. A couple of years later, when I decided to change my life and move to Europe, I asked him if he had any work I could do. So he got me to run his Occidental (Petroleum) operation in Europe."

"One of the first things I saw was that he was very limited in the oil business. He had operations in California and in Libya, but Libya was very treacherous because of the political situation. So I suggested that he try to get into the North Sea."

"Now the North Sea was not a very popular option at the time; it was regarded as too much of a gamble. They'd only found one well. But my own view about what was in the North Sea was this: an island of coal surrounded by a sea of oil."

"Another deterrent to the North Sea was that getting the right to drill there was very political – and very expensive. You had to go to the government and sell them with great detail and conviction on why you wanted this particular block of water to drill in. What we did was put two ships and a team of geologists out there and spent between $7 and $8 million finding out where we wanted to drill. We finally decided to try to get five blocks."

"Because getting the blocks was so political, I decided we needed somebody local on our team. We had Dr. (Armand) Hammer, and he had gotten Allied Chemical. I knew and had done work for J. Paul Getty, and I got him to come on board. I tried one or two local people, but they thought it was too risky and turned me down."

"While I was looking for somebody else, Lord Thompson called me. He owned newspapers all over the world, including about 70 in the United States, I think. I'd never met Lord Thompson, but of course I had heard of him. So he called me and said, 'Paul and Armand said that I need to talk to you. Come see me.'"

"I went to his place – it's like a castle – and I met this fellow, very thick glasses on, and he said, 'Call me Roy.' I asked why he had wanted to see me and he said, 'I called you because I want to be worth a billion dollars before I die.' Well, I can tell you that I'd never had anybody say that to me before! I said, 'Roy, that's an unusual proposition. Let me ask you what you are worth right now.' So Lord Thompson went over to his desk, pulled out this little drawer, looked at some papers and said, 'This morning I was worth $616 million.' I said, 'That's great. We don't have so far to go!' (By the way, I never saw Lord Roy Thompson, either at his office or in one of his homes, when he didn't know exactly how much he was worth on that very day.)"

"Then I told Lord Thompson that I only knew of two things in the world that you could make a billion dollars on: one was property, and the other was oil. That's when I thought, 'By George, this is who I could get for the North Sea deal!' So I got Lord Thompson to join us. And when I had to go talk to the government boys about getting the five blocks we wanted, instead of taking all these technicians to the meeting, which is what all the other oil companies had done, I took these old men with me. I had Lord Thompson sitting with me on the front row. Well, it worked and we got the five blocks."

"We got this big drilling platform out of New Orleans and sent it over – it was big enough to have a helicopter landing pad and a hotel – and we started to drill. Geologists told me the 'high' we drilled first was the highest high they'd ever seen. We drilled that thing for about five weeks and it turned out to be the driest hole any of us had ever seen. And when you've got a dry hole 710 feet under water, you've got a really dry hole! And nothing you can do with it."

"I had gotten Lord Thompson to put up $5 million and right away I got a call from him. 'I heard the hole was dry,' he said. 'How much did that cost us?' I told him that it cost about $8 million. He started to talk about how I had assured him we'd find oil, but I reminded him that I'd always said it was a gamble."

"From that dry hole, we went to the next one. Same partners, no change in our procedure, just moved the rig down to the next high and drilled about five weeks. That one was dry too. Moved on to the next high, drilled five weeks, another dry hole."

"By this time we had had three dry holes, and I had just about lost Lord Thompson. He was calling me every day, getting real mean on the telephone too. Dr. Hammer didn't call; I had Hammer's confidence. But even Paul Getty, who was at that time one of the richest men in the world and who had made his money in the oil business, was calling me about twice a week. "How much further are we going to go with this thing, Lord Thompson and Getty would ask." Our losses were enormous at that point. But I just kept on telling them, 'There's oil out there somewhere – and I want to keep drilling until we find it!'"

"I had this man working on the rig named Wilson. So we started on the fourth well and I said to Wilson, 'If you find oil – if you even *smell* oil – I want you to call me. Here's the phone number, and I want you to call it anytime, day or night. You see, I'm getting myself into an awful lot of trouble out here, and I want to know when my well comes in.'"

"Another three or four weeks went by, and I knew Lord Thompson wasn't sleeping at night, but I was. The telephone rang about two in the morning and it was Wilson. 'Mr. Tigrett?' he said. 'This is Wilson. You ought to know that we have just passed through 150 feet of the richest oil and sand I've ever seen in my life. What we've got here is a big one!' And it was."

"The minute I got the news about the well, I couldn't wait to phone Lord Thompson. He had just about written off that investment as a loss. I had to get through five or six of his housekeepers before getting one who would wake him in the middle of the night. I took great pleasure in reporting to him that we had hit a big well. From there we went on to develop an enormous oil field, and we hooked it up with about three other fields and it's still producing today."

"Several years later Lord Thompson was very ill and I went to see him. As a matter of fact, it was the night before he died. I went into his hospital room and he was very weak, but he motioned for me to come over and sit down. He reached his hand down, and when he raised it, he was holding his sheet of paper that told him how much he was worth. 'Well, we made it John, didn't we?' he whispered. I looked and his sheet indicated that on that day he was worth $1.3 billion."

"Lord Thompson wasn't the only one. As a matter of fact, the investors in that North Sea oil venture made about a billion dollars *each!* In this case, persistence paid off handsomely."

Don's Parting Thought

Persist! Achieve something; do the next thing; don't get sidetracked. Persist! Never give up. Ask yourself, "Is there a better way to get there?" Let adversity and set-backs fuel your determination. Persist!

Skill #21

✦✦✦✦✦

Your Personal Image of Excellence

"An organization can spread itself throughout the entire world and hire hundreds of thousands of people, but the image of that company and it's products is customarily projected through contact with *one person*."

—Anonymous

Early in my sales career, I saw a meaningful epigram framed on the office wall of a sales executive I called on in Cincinnati. The writer was anonymous, but I've never forgotten the significance of that message. Here's what it said:

> "An organization can spread itself throughout the entire world and hire hundreds of thousands of people, but the image of that company and its products is customarily projected through contact with *one person*."

Every employee could be that one person. That's why all employees have an obligation and a responsibility to look and be professional in every way. Professional image is vital today – perhaps more so than ever before. It may not be fair, but how we look is the principle means by which we are evaluated.

You're Looking Good... but Good "Enough"?

About a year before his death, I was privileged to spend about an hour in an uninterrupted visit with Lloyd Conant, the man who, along with Earl Nightingale, founded Nightingale-Conant, the world's largest producer of audio training tape programs. They are a great company with whom I'm honored to produce audio cassette albums. I learned a lot in that one hour from Lloyd.

The one idea most indelibly burned into my thinking came during our discussion on successful selling when Lloyd Conant said , "You can't send a Six or Seven to sell a Ten. It doesn't work." Loyd referenced the analogy of describing salespeople and their overall image and professionalism on a one-to-ten scale. I think Lloyd was most insightful in his remark. And it seems to me that the more expensive the item being sold and the more sophisticated the buyer, the more viability Lloyd's premise has.

When people interact, they make continuous conscious and subconscious evaluations of each other. In selling, you'd better stack up well, or the cards will be stacked against you!

Professional image is obviously vital to your success. And fortunately, it's something you can do something about. The question is, *will you?* It's so easy to get locked into your own comfort zones and feel little need to change.

I challenge you to ask yourself if you could project a more positive and professional image. Are you a Six? A Nine? A Seven? Or maybe a Ten? What do you need to be to excel in your business and your market?

Think about those things now and vow to enhance yourself and your professional image. Not only will it make you money, but you will experience new levels of gratification and acceptance in your life. High performance salespeople seem to always be upgrading their image.

Image – A Constant or A Variable?

Once a first impression is established, all future impressions are simply alterations of the first one. Image is never a constant, but an ever-changing variable.

For example, when you're talking with someone about a mutual friend, you might say, "How's our friend Sandra doing?" The other party would say, "Oh, Sandra's doing great and her sales performance is really impressive now."

Well, impressive compared to what? All descriptions of and references to people tend to be comparisons to first and earlier impressions of behaviors, performance and overall image. An admirable goal for high performance salespeople is to project the best possible first impression and to always be conscious of needed and desired image upgrading.

J. Douglas Edwards used to tell the story of a salesman in Los Angeles in the 1960's who was so strikingly handsome and looked so sharp that every sales manager who saw him drooled at the thought of making the man a part of their sales team. The first impression this man made was that of a Ten. He had no trouble getting a job. In fact, he had five sales jobs at once, pulling in five paychecks, with all his employers being unaware he was selling for anyone else. Obviously this couldn't last forever, and the man was caught.

It's not likely that could happen today, since there are more easy and distinct ways to spot a fraud. But the story underscores the fact that people evaluate others and develop biases based on how people look.

Considering The Components

Let's get to the meat of the subject of professional image. It's comprised principally of five components:

1. How you look
2. What you say
3. How you say it
4. What you do
5. How you do it

The simple truth is that your image, as presented in these five components, either turns a person on or turns them off. I hope reading this chapter helps to ensure that you turn more buyers on in the future.

How you look is the first and primary basis on which you are evaluated. Some may argue "My integrity, knowledge, and sincerity should be the first points on which I'm evaluated!" I agree that they *should* be, but they aren't. It may be unfair that we are assessed on how we look first and foremost, but that is the way it works, like it or not.

What you say is important because it reflects your understanding and knowledge of the topic being discussed. The appropriateness of your remarks and the impact they have on a listener's comfort zone will obviously influence how others see and evaluate you. Is the strategy with which you approach people perceived as one of professionalism and integrity? Or is it overly casual and sometimes sloppy? Are your remarks upbeat and on target, or do they too easily reflect negatives and mediocre expectations?

How you say it is important because your conviction and persuasiveness will influence your sales performance. Are you articulate and convincing? Do you key in on the buyer's value system and frame of reference? How's your vocabulary? Do you adapt your words to the sophistication of your prospect or audience? Good grammar is absolutely essential. A salesperson who murders the King's English is simultaneously slaughtering his or her chances of a positive impression.

A quick story here: Years ago a client firm of mine had a salesperson whose grammar was terrible. But surprisingly, he was still a fairly good producer. The manager felt that this person was a diamond in the rough with great potential. So the manager invested about $250 and got the salesperson to agree to go to a high school English teacher for tutoring for about three months.

The arrangement worked magnificently, and in a short time this guy was in the top 10 percent of the salesforce. What a great example of growth and image enhancement!

What you do and **how you do it** are also important in projecting a professional image. These components are especially sensitive when it comes to the issues of keeping promises and following through on sales contacts. I'd like to think that this entire book focuses on these two things.

Image Factors That Make A Difference

Now, let's return to how you look. I want to give you 12 image factors to keep in mind in your continuing quest for higher performance in your sales career.

Research indicates that you can project quality and improve reactions to yourself, your product, and your proposition by improving certain aspects of your style and type of dress. Many of these factors apply to both male and female sales professionals.

Image Factor One: Weight

Let's get this one out of the way first, because one's weight is a sensitive area. In most cases, a person's weight can be controlled with discipline, proper diet and exercise. My heart goes out to people with a health problem that causes them to be overweight.

Overweight people often don't realize that they're telling the world they have a problem controlling their own behavior. This lack of discipline turns people off. There's too much focus on excellence today for this to be overlooked any longer. You may wish to check a chart of recommended weights based on height and sex. If you haven't seen one for awhile, call your insurance agent and ask that he or she send you such a chart.

Are there some factors other than what the scales say that influence perception of weight? The answer is yes. For example, in both men's and women's clothing, plaids and horizontal lines as well as some patterns and styles tend to increase the weight perception. And men, be advised that even so small a thing as the length of your tie can have impact. The hem of your tie should be even with the top of your belt buckle or below it; for each inch your tie is above your belt buckle, it will add about five pounds of perceived weight to your looks.

Another reason to maintain your weight is that you'll have more energy if you aren't carrying around a lot of excess baggage. That energy can be converted into a more targeted approach to high sales performance.

Image Factor Two: Grooming, personal neatness, and posture

To look the part of a high performance salesperson, we can't take grooming, neatness or posture for granted. We are walking, talking advertisements for our company, our products, and our services at all times.

For hairstyles and sideburns length, observe newscasters on the national networks and local television stations. Management usually requires these newscasters to project an image that is inoffensive and appealing to large numbers of people. Check the grooming, neatness and posture of the most successful people in your field and you'll start to develop some standards that will pay off for you in your sales career.

Image Factor Three: Seek advice from those whose opinions you respect

I was recently involved in a corporate consulting assignment, during which I actually saw an executive pass over the best man for a sales management position because that man's appearance and image weren't up to par. This was disastrous to the man's career, and totally needless.

Let me offer this advice: Go to the individual in your organization who might have the most impact on decisions relating to your career progress. Give him an opportunity to offer you input about your dress and appearance. (Remember the power of *authorship!*) It's a fact that most people won't say what they would like to say about the way you look unless they're asked and encouraged to be candid.

You might say, "I want to make progress in this company and I thought I'd ask for your advice. What could I do or should I do to enhance my image as a professional?" That executive will probably not only give you some valuable advice but also have a new level of respect for you and your focus on the future.

I also suggest that you study the way your bosses and the most successful people in your industry dress. Ask for opinions of those you respect, and you'll be glad you did. After all, we all have blind spots that others can help us see.

Image Factor Four: Self-awareness and evaluation

Go to the mirror and look at yourself. How do you feel about the image you observe in the glass? Would *you* buy from you? Would you promote someone who looks like you into a position of greater authority? Be observant and try to be honest.

I was once on a convention roster with a well-known author who writes about personal image and dress. Even he had blind spots. He had on a nice looking suit but, to everyone's embarrassment, the shoulders were flecked with dandruff and his shoes were tired and scuffed. He was not well received because he had no credibility.

Be certain that you project the right image. Ray Considine points out that lots of people are Sevens thinking they are Tens. These people have created needless burdens for themselves.

Image Factor Five: Sincerity

There's a very high premium on sincerity in the marketplace today. It will help you take bigger checks to the bank, that's for sure. Some of the sincerity factors I think are important are your smile, your handshake, and eye contact.

Use your smile to your advantage. Let me pause here and tell you a story that occurred when I was 22.

Bill Schwarz had been in the business a year longer than me, so I asked him to sit in on and critique one of my group presentations. My presentation was a 30-minute talk to about 10 people, and I enrolled some of them in our training program.

Anyway, at the end of the meeting, Bill and I were driving away when he turned to me to say something. I thought, surely he's going to lay a few compliments on me because I did pretty well back there! He said, "Don, I just want to tell you one thing about your style and your communication skills and how you deal with people. You know, Don, you have a really pleasant smile."

Well, I was sitting there feeling pretty smug about my smile when he said, "Why don't you use it on your audience?"

Bill went on to tell me, "A good smile is a powerful thing for you to have in your arsenal of skills. In communicating with people, it's a persuasive tool. It's a commitment tool." Well, Bill changed some behavior on my part with those few words. I had been so intensely focused on what I was saying that I wasn't paying enough attention to how I was coming across.

Another sincerity factor is your handshake. A macho, vise-gripping handshake is as much a turn-off as the proverbial limp "wet fish" handshake. A moderate grip is most advisable, and for you to put your left hand over their hand while handshaking is overkill. Save that one for funerals; it's usually inappropriate in a business environment.

Eye contact is the third sincerity factor I mentioned. Salespeople who don't look into the eyes of their prospects have a very difficult time establishing trust and credibility. Look them in the eye. Be appropriately assertive and you'll maximize your credibility with those you talk to.

Image Factor Six: Take care of your mobile office

If you use your automobile in your business, remember that it is an extension of your personal image. Your car should be clean, neat and well-cared for, just like a suit of clothes. Your briefcase is a similar extension of your image, so be sure it looks professional.

Image Factor Seven: Be flexible and appropriate in your dress

One of the most vital areas of consideration when deciding on your personal image in dress is your clientele's attitudes and opinions. Different types of dress are appropriate for different types of business.

For example, I wouldn't recommend the same type of dress for a salesperson in a music store selling primarily to people under 25 as for a stockbroker who is primarily selling to older, more mature and more sophisticated business people. Your company or industry may want to do some research in this area and see what type of dress is best received by your industry and its clientele.

Image Factor Eight: Be a student of style

Understand not only the difference between conservative and flashy attire but also that their impact and messages vary greatly. Experts say that, in most business settings, *conservative* is considerably safer. Those same experts have concluded that the safest colors for men and women are dark blues and greys. Flashy is risky and turns many people off.

I'll never forget doing a sales training assignment one time for a land development company. I did two days of consulting followed by a one-day seminar. This company wanted me to find out what was causing their closing percentage to suffer.

When I arrived, I walked into their sales meeting room and I immediately knew at least one thing that was wrong. This was back in the late 1970's. Do you remember the typical dress for males in the late 70's? It was leisure suits, wide lapels, bright colors, three-toned patent leather shoes – remember those days? Well, this company's salesmen were selling lots in resort communities that they described to prospects as an investment, but they were dressed like a bunch of peacocks in heat! Their messages were totally incongruent.

The first thing I told that group was, "Tomorrow, I want you to wear your most conservative suit." And I described what I thought they should wear, which was very conservative. Well, they came in dressed conservatively on Day 2 and their closing percentage over Day 1 increased by 39 percent.

The more reasonably conservative we look, the fewer people we're likely to be offensive to. The more reasonably conservative your clothes and appearance, the more professional an image you will project in most business environments.

Image Factor Nine: Garment selection

Eighty percent of the first impression you make on people is determined by your clothing. A very successful manager of an insurance agency once told me that he had a way to influence the dress of the new recruits in his sales organization. Most of these recruits were young and had limited resources. The sales manager encouraged them to buy half as many suits as they were inclined to but to spend twice as much on each suit. In other words, he told them to opt for quality rather than quantity.

Wardrobe selection can be an important business decision. If you needed an appendectomy, you wouldn't perform it on yourself to save a few hundred dollars, would you? My point is that when it's an important issue, get professional advice. Buy from an establishment that has knowledgeable professionals on its staff, people who can give you quality advice on garment selection.

Image Factor Ten: Accessory decisions

Accessories can have as much or more impact on your image as garments so, again, make wise decisions in this area. Generally, quality pays off big in accessory selection. A valuable conservative watch, for example, enhances your image in the eyes of most people. There was a higher payoff in flashy accessories some time back than there is today. Remember that high quality advice whispered by the right persons is heard more readily and weighed more heavily than a shout from the wrong person.

I suggest you also go for above-average quality in other accessories such as pens, belts, shoes, ties, purses, briefcases, handkerchiefs and jewelry. Outerwear such as scarves and topcoats are also important decisions. By the way, experts say that among accessories, shoes and ties are the most important items in terms of impact.

Image Factor Eleven: Neatness and fit

Do you know some people who are wearing garments that look like they belong in a previous decade?

Just as some people never clean out their closets, so some people never clean out and update their *ideas* about clothing. For example, there's a tendency today toward looser fitting clothes for both men and women than was popular a few years ago. Be aware of what's appropriate in today's business environment.

Don't overlook obvious points regarding appearance – such as shined shoes and pressed suits. I'd suggest you never wear your suit coat while driving or while flying; the coat will look like you slept in it when you get up, not to mention the savings you'll realize in cleaning bills and garment replacement. Neat, well-tailored clothing of appropriate, traditional length and fit is an important part of your professional image.

Macho and Sexy Losers

I read recently that men in the business world are best received when they appear professional and well groomed, not macho. And women in the business world are best received when they appear professional and attractive, but not sexy.

Remember that people like to buy from professionals, and professionals conscientiously look their best. You have the right to dress any way you please, wear your hair as you please, weigh what you please. But your customers also have the right to assess you on any basis they please, and the place they are likely to begin is with how you look. A professional image opens doors, opens minds, and creates opportunities you wouldn't otherwise experience. If we want prospects to see us as quality people selling quality products and services, we must project a quality image in every way we can.

Successful Application 21

Featuring: Al Berzett, Manager of Wholesale Financing-Deere Credit, John Deere Company; Des Moines, IA

Submitted by: Dave Walters, Director of Agricultural Installment Lending, John Deere Company; Des Moines, IA

Like many companies today, we find our customers come in all shapes, sizes, colors, genders, and personalities. We have agricultural dealers, marine dealers, recreational vehicles (RV) dealers, industrial dealers, and consumer products dealers. Our dealer customers have a wide variety of business philosophies. Some are laid back, some are high energy. So we have to be flexible in the way we deal with them.

We are not quite so flexible, however, when it comes to our company image. As a general rule, we require our salespeople to wear coats and ties, and we have a dress code regarding hair length, personal neatness and the like. We've never tried to have our dress mirror our customers – agricultural dealers, for example, who may not wear ties in their showroom or office. We believe its important for us to maintain our coat-and-tie image so that our customers will feel they are dealing with professionals.

Many of our people out in the field are responsible for collecting from dealers. We want our dealers to feel they are dealing with diligent, hard-working business people, just the kind of people our dealers are. Proper business attire and conduct can help ensure that perception.

Not too long ago we had a sales representative down in Florida who seemed to have a Johnny Cash fixation. He liked to dress all in black – black hat, black boots, black clothes. He looked like an outlaw, which he seemed to feel would help with collecting. A tough guy image, I suppose. He's no longer part of our company. In our opinion, a dealer might not feel we are the kind of company he wants to do business with if "The Man in Black" indicates the kind of people we are.

Customers judge and evaluate a company based on the people they see day in and day out. A company may be serious and stable, but if the salesman who calls on a dealer dresses like a clown, the whole company gets a clown image in the dealer's eyes. On the other hand, if we present a highly professional image in our dress, talk and behavior, that conveys a sense of proper conduct in our business.

John Deere has always recognized the importance of image. For example, our products have been green for as long as anyone can remember; it's a link with farming and growth. We know that people get a feeling about a company and its people based on the visual images we present. So from our products to corporate headquarters, from our manufacturing facilities right down to the people we hire, John Deere is committed to presenting a cohesive image of dedicated, dependable professionals. It's just smart business.

DON'S PARTING THOUGHT

One cannot be the best they are capable of being
until they look and sound the best they can.

Skill #22

✦✦✦✦✦

Handling Conflict, Problems and Feedback

"Never argue. Even if you win the argument, you lose the sale!"

—Arthur H. "Red" Motley

Dr. Norman Vincent Peale shares a beautifully simplified version of his philosophy of life when he says, "The only people who don't have problems are in the cemetery." Since problems and conflicts are indeed realities of life, we should try to perfect our process for dealing with them.

One source of problems in relationships is the fact that many people can't relax unless other people behave in accordance with their desires or standards. Someone once said that one of the greatest gifts in life is to possess the ability to accept people as they are, not as you would like them to be. To get inside someone else's head and understand what they are like on their terms, rather than judging them on our terms, is a skill that we would do well to develop. In most cases, we would be unable to change them anyway.

This skill is enormously important in recognizing how to handle all business relationships when they begin to go south with a problematical cause. I know salespeople who have lost their biggest account with one slip of the tongue. I know a sharp corporate sales executive with a Fortune 500 company whose career-path was destroyed with one emotional statement in the presence of a senior vice president of their company.

Understanding "Bucket Dumping"

To get a handle on problems, especially the interpersonal or relationship-oriented problems that can plague salespeople, let's consider how the four behavioral styles might handle conflict or high stress. With each of the four styles, if conflict is not resolved early on, reactions tend to become exaggerated and/or variable.

Some people can be high strung and are likely to get stressed out occasionally, and it's predictable what they're going to do when they get stressed out. They go into what psychologists call "backup." The layman's term is "bucket dumping." Bucket dumping occurs when somebody loses their temper and dumps all their pent-up feelings or problems on you. When in backup, our behavioral tendencies are exaggerated.

We want to do all we can to avoid bucket-dumping environments while trying to make a sale. There are some things we can learn about "backup" and "bucket-dumping" that will help us deal with these potential problems in a way that doesn't cost us a sale.

In the first stage of "backup," the Driver goes into what can be termed an *autocratic mode.* He takes on a posture that is consistent with more assertive, less responsive behavior. Drivers say something like this: "Carl, I know exactly what I'm doing. I've considered all aspects of the deal and we're going to do it this way, do you understand?" In other words, we're going to do it *my* way.

Now let's look at the Expressives. It's predictable that Expressives, when in a backup mode, have a tendency to *attack.* We Expressives are not at our best when we attack, but we do attack. It's consistent with more assertive, more responsive behavior. We'd say something like, "Carl, this is not only a dumb idea, pal – this is *your* dumb idea!" We usually personalize our attack.

The Analyticals, in their initial stage of backup, go into an *avoid* posture. They want a little time to evaluate all of the factual data, all the available information, to decide what their response is going to be at some later point in time when they must react proactively.

Amiables tend to go into what we call an *acquiesce* mode. Their posture is basically one of keeping the peace. If something else is what's important to you, the Amiable will often offer to do it your way so that conflict and problems can be avoided.

Keep Anger Out Of It

Someone once said that you can measure a person by the size of the issue that makes him angry. The whining and wailing child can be compared to an adult with marginal people-skills whose only defense when under stress is to lose his or her temper and wail in disagreement. We need to think strategy here, not revenge. Be rational, not emotional, in an environment of conflict.

Most psychologists will tell you that it is hardly ever a good idea to lose your temper. I have found that when you lose your temper, you are out of control; when you are out of control, you become negatively emotional rather than positively rational. When people experience high levels of negative emotion, they often say things they wish later they had not said. Have you ever tried to un-say something? Case closed. Benjamin Franklin said it best: "Anger is never without a reason but seldom with a good one."

Put The Servants To Work

When you're handling complaints or conflict, one solution is to use what's known as the "Six Honest Serving Men of Clear Communications." You gather the facts by asking six questions related to the problem: Who, What, When, Where, Why and How?

If you are dealing with an irate customer, you might say, "I can understand your frustrations, sir. Now, can you tell me who made that promise to you, and when?" With this technique, what you are doing is making a conversion from an emotion-based to a fact-based dialogue, which can be very effective in keeping customers happy. The facts you gather are conducive to a rational, mature response, and this will usually short-circuit high emotion and anger. Try to have a high level of empathy and tension tolerance. Maintain positive control with a win-win spirit and get the problem resolved.

Another good way to get to the core of potential conflict in a positive way is to simply say, "This situation has created some stress that I'm uncomfortable with. Can we sit down and maturely discuss it?" This can be an excellent device to defuse an argument before it starts. It can defuse tempers and add new dimensions to resolving differences and improving relationships.

Remember this important guideline in conflict resolution: Rationality is usually a positive force and emotion is usually a negative force. It's not advisable to lose your temper, especially when dealing with prospects or clients. Invariably when we lose our temper, that out-of-control behavior will cause us to say things we will regret. Especially important here is the premise that we should keep customers happy at practically any cost. Losing your temper is not part of that formula.

How Did You Arrive At That?

Try this technique: In a potentially confrontational situation, explain your thought processes, not just your conclusions. If you merely state your conclusions without showing how you reached them, you aren't going to convince anyone. But if you explain how and why you arrived at those conclusions, you stand a better chance of influencing people positively.

The key is to be rational and to show, in logical steps, how you arrived at the conclusions that you now find so sensible. By disclosing your thought processes, you treat your listeners with respect instead of talking down to them. And there is an added benefit. Constant re-examination of your position sharpens your thinking.

Never allow anyone to become your enemy. That might be tough to do for some people, but there's a wise old saying that it takes two people to make a fight. One thing a salesperson doesn't need is enemies.

Work hard to resolve the conflicts that arise during the normal course of business. Never lose a friend or a sale by winning an argument. The price is simply too high. Most arguments begin over trivial matters, but their costs can be astronomical.

An argument is nothing more than a discussion that gets out of control. The skillful salesperson learns how to put things back in perspective by emphasizing the positives in the relationship and by being extremely flexible on the way to arriving at a solution.

Keep The Customer Happy

In his excellent book on professional selling techniques, my friend Nido Qubein says, "Never allow a customer to become an adversary. The customer may not always be right, but he is always the customer." Companies and salespeople who behave as if the customer is always right keep more customers happy.

When a customer feels that he or she must lose face to do business with you, it becomes an obstacle over which few people are willing to climb. The wise salesperson is willing to put aside petty grievances and grudges for the longer term objective of winning future sales. He makes every effort to resolve conflicts quickly and amicably.

When a conflict starts to present itself, remember this advice: Humbly respond with a high level of personal interest and a low level of emotion, keeping the emphasis on facts. An example might be this: "Mr. Prospect, I can understand your frustration with this situation. Be assured I'll do everything I can to get it resolved. Now let's re-examine some of the facts." Then you go into the facts.

I'm Right and Don't You Forget It!

Do you know anyone with an insatiable need to be right? This behavior usually results from a low self-image. People with extremely big egos often have this problem as well. Fellow sales trainer Larry Wilson says a problem is a deviation between *what you want and what you've got.* That simple definition is very good. Our task is obviously to minimize or eliminate the deviations.

I learned a terrific idea about conflict resolution from James Newton's book *Uncommon Friends,* which was about his life with Thomas Edison, Harvey Firestone, Alexis Carrell and Henry Ford.

While working for Harvey Firestone, Newton often found himself in the role of trouble-shooter and problem-solver. He became known for his exceptional ability to solve problems rapidly, with minimized stress, the fewest legal entanglements, and with a spirit of fairness. Faced with conflict, Newton liked to say, "Let's work together to find *what* is right, not *who* is right." That premise sets the stage for mutually satisfactory, efficient solutions with minimal emotion, stress and finger-pointing.

Anytime you sense conflict coming, I suggest you calmly say something like, "Charlie, this issue isn't worth getting upset with each other over. Let's look for some win-win compromises we can both live with. As I understand it, your primary need is…" Go on to brainstorm alternatives without raising your voice. If he wants to rant and scream, don't contribute to the out-of-control behavior. Try to be a calming catalyst in reaching a satisfactory solution.

The more adaptable and understanding we are in dealing with others, the fewer problems we'll have. The more we develop a habit of respecting human dignity and individuality, especially with a high sensitivity to customers and prospects, the better off we'll be. Doing this will not only give us inner *peace* but also a bigger *piece* of the action in terms of market share.

How To Kill Alligators

Problems seldom go away, so let's now talk about creative problem solving. High performance salespeople are often experts at solving problems. Whether the problem is theirs or their prospect's, they simply get it done efficiently and professionally with minimal hassle.

Whether a problem is interpersonal or more related to things and facts than people, I have an eight-step formula I'd like to recommend. Many salespeople have used this with excellent results:

Step 1: Define the problem by writing it down and evaluating it. Remember, the degree to which we accurately define a problem will usually influence the quality of the solution. Incidentally, if you can't write it down, it's not a problem – it's an anxiety.

Step 2: Assess the problem's cause, even if it takes a considerable amount of research. You will understand it better and solve it quicker.

Step 3: Interact with key players for pertinent input, information, and thoughts on solutions. (There's *authorship* again!)

Step 4: Consider the alternative solutions.

Step 5: Select the best alternative and develop your action plan.

Step 6: Implement your action plan.

Step 7: Gain commitment from key players on your solution, then monitor the action plan and implementation for positive results.

Step 8: Take further action to prevent the problem from reoccurring. (Most problems we have are problems we've had before.)

One final thought on problem solving. If the problem you are attempting to solve is customer- or sales-related, I urge you to have the customer participate in the problem-solving process (to the degree that it's beneficial, obviously.) Remember, the prospect's involvement in finding solutions and input in the ultimate proposal will work in favor of closing the sale.

The Importance of Feedback

If we said aloud everything we thought about people, we'd be living in a totally uncivilized and dangerous jungle. But we need to know to some extent what others are thinking and feeling in order to work more effectively with them. By learning how to solicit and use feedback, we can dramatically improve relationships and the quality of the communications flow in those relationships. This process will be very valuable to you in your sales career.

The feedback process has two principle dimensions: (a) how we *give* feedback, and (b) how we *receive* it.

In every encounter, you're in a position to increase the amount of feedback you get. You can do this by responding positively, regardless of whether the feedback is positive or negative. Even if you're hearing disagreeable news, don't murder the messenger. Either take it with a grain of salt or, if the shoe fits, wear it. If we receive feedback from others graciously, we'll encourage more of it as time goes by and that can be very productive.

I want to give you some examples of how you can make quality decisions about feedback, and I'll show you the importance of being highly adaptable in the process.

Highly-adaptable people give feedback to others positively and constructively, and they receive feedback graciously and appreciatively. Low adaptability people are usually critical in the way they give feedback, and they receive feedback from others resentfully.

Welcome Customer Feedback

Let me give you an example of the value of the feedback process. Suppose that, at the end of a seminar, Bob, the vice president of sales, came up to me and said, "Don, this was a fine program and you've done a great job for our company. But if you've got just a few minutes, I have two or three ideas I'd like to share with you that I think could make your presentation even better."

Now if I'm one who welcomes client feedback, I'll probably say something like, "Bob, I really appreciate your willingness to give me this feedback. Let me get my legal pad and sit down over here and take some notes, because I know you've heard a lot of speakers and I really want to gain from your experience."

All of a sudden, Bob begins thinking, "You know, this Hutson is a sharper cookie than I thought he was!"

Consider a different reaction. Again Bob says to me, "Don, this was a fine presentation and we certainly got our money's worth. But I've got a couple of ideas I'd like to share with you that I think could be of benefit and make your presentation even better."

Now if I'm the hard-headed type, uninterested in client feedback, and I have a full blown-case of *egomania,* I might say something like, "Well, I appreciate the fact that you feel it went well, and I enjoyed being with you, Bob, but you must not have been listening when I was introduced. Didn't you hear that I've done over 4,000 talks in the past 25 years? If I don't have my act together by now, I'm probably not going to. And besides, I have a flight in a few minutes. So I'll catch you later."

After that, Bob would probably say, "It's a good thing Hutson enjoyed being here today, because he's not coming back!"

Feedback can have a significant impact on allegiance, professional image and, of course, repeat business. Always welcome it and learn from it.

Learn About Yourself From Others

How willing are you to receive feedback from others? I have a promise for you. The more you welcome feedback, the more you'll experience it. And the more you experience it, the more you'll grow from it. I recommend you ask others whose opinions you respect for feedback. Receive it graciously and thank them for it.

If the feedback comes from a customer, no matter if it is positive or negative, or if it is about you or your company, I recommend you acknowledge it in a positive, complimentary manner. For example, let's suppose the customer says, "I recommend you tell the people in your company that the color selection of your product is poor. None of the selections appropriately match the decor of most modern offices today."

To that you should say, "That's good input, Mr. Bradley, and coming from you, I really value it. I'll pass that along immediately to the appropriate people. Thank you." Always end your response with a thank you. That keeps the flow positive, and it keeps the feedback coming. A follow-up note or call later on the results of his recommendation would also be very effective.

Give Others Valuable Feedback

When you give feedback to others, be it positive or negative, give it with care and humility, and people will be more likely to welcome it and act on it. If the feedback is critical or negative, present it in conjunction with some complimentary input as well, and that will help soften the blow.

Here's an example of how you might begin: "Bob, you've done an extraordinary job of spearheading this proposal. Anyone else probably would still be in the planning stage! But I think there's one vital issue which hasn't been addressed…"

Stuff It Or Address It?

Have you ever been a "stuffer"? Rather than openly discussing important issues and feelings with others, do you "stuff" it? Do you choose not to bring it up rather than to risk an unpleasant exchange or confrontation? Just remember, negative thoughts and bad feelings seldom go away. They tend to multiply.

If you decide to stuff something that should be addressed, you'll find yourself needlessly carrying around a heavy load of stress. That load just may be the thing that keeps you from being "up" when you need to make a call, or being receptive when getting valuable information, ideas, and feedback from others. It may also cost you sales as well as harmony in relationships at home and at work.

In this day and age, the vast majority of people like and respect the authenticity that is so obvious when someone comes to them and says, "Charlie, your friendship is really important to me, and I feel our relationship has become strained lately. Can we talk about it?" You will almost always get a positive response to that question, which usually paves the way for a positive end result.

With the question "Can we talk about it?" you open the door for a positive, high-quality interaction, which 19 times out of 20 will make you feel much better when it's over. Many misunderstandings result from too many people assuming too many things. The clear, open communication channel that's created through good feedback is valuable whether it involves customers or co-workers.

I recently created a Quality Communications Model which has four categories of communications. It is designed to help people say what needs to be said in a positive, professional manner. This makes for improved, authentic relationships and efficient business operations.

The four categories, from less effective to most effective, are:

1. The Apathetic Posture

2. The Passive/Aggressive Posture

3. The Unloading Posture

4. The Skilled Interaction

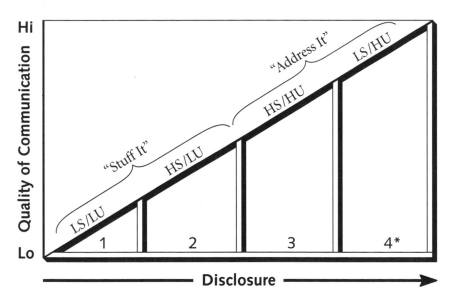

LS = Low Stress
HS = High Stress
LU = Low Understanding
HU = High Understanding

* Most desirable for positive results, improved relationships and clear communications.

Now I'd like to elaborate on the four categories shown above.

The *Apathetic Posture* is a low-stress, low-understanding, poor and often immature approach. It usually shows indifference and sometimes unprofessionalism, and this "devil-may-care" attitude will prolong rather than help solve communications problems.

The *Passive/Aggressive Posture* is hardly better. The communicator informs the other person that there is a problem or serious issue to discuss, but the information is usually communicated through hard looks, poor attitude, and a skirting of the real issues. This results in high stress but low understanding.

The *Unloading Posture* leaves a lot to be desired, since it usually involves temper loss and accompanying high stress, but at least the other party knows there's a problem that must be dealt with.

The *Skilled Interaction* is one of low stress and high understanding. This is the category that high performance salespeople always try to stay in. Communication takes place here with positive spirit and authentic interchange, even if it is on an unpleasant topic.

Have Fun With Feedback

Here's an idea I'd like for you to try. It works extremely well in our office. We have a simple phrase that we all use very positively and productively.

Someone may come into my office and say with a smile, "Don, is now a good time to give you some really high-quality feedback?" In which case I'll laugh and say, "You bet, lay it on me." The comments may be positive or negative, but the proper spirit is there with both parties, and some very good things have come from this process. It's fun, it's fruitful, and it often results in behavior changes that can lead to improved customer relations, more sales, and improved interoffice morale.

Let me give you a specific example that has happened many times in sales organizations. One member of the sales force hears by the grapevine that a certain customer doesn't like the salesperson calling on him because – well, let's say he's constantly late for appointments, something the customer is a real stickler about.

In the spirit of teamwork and a good relationship, I think the person hearing those comments should go directly to the tardy member of the sales force and tell him exactly what he heard so that the habitually late salesperson can be aware of the significance of his sloppy behavior. Instead, what often happens is what could be valuable data for the salesperson becomes ammunition for company gossip. And the poor, tardy salesperson is the last to know the impact of his behavior. That approach feeds poor morale, tears down teamwork, results in unnecessary stress in the company and often leads to a loss of business. And it's so easily avoidable.

You don't see many high performance salespeople who don't have a strong support system, a system where lots of quality feedback is taking place. It can be unpleasant at times, but the payoff is peace of mind and gratifying sales results.

Remember Basics – Like "Fly Operation"

Let me give you an example of how receiving feedback from others can help you grow. I don't do much speaking on college campuses, but I spoke before a marketing class at a college a few years ago. I was speaking in a theater-type classroom, and I had about 300 college students in the audience.

I was into my talk maybe three or four minutes, just getting on a pretty good roll, when I noticed that this young college kid sitting on the front row, maybe 19 or 20 years old, was making a gesture in my direction. It was a simple, short little hand gesture – turning up the palm, touching index finger to the thumb, then pushing the hand up in the air.

I thought to myself, "This guy is giving me a signal that… Oh, please don't tell me I'm in front of 300 college kids with my pants unzipped!" Well, I discretely checked out my zipper with my little finger and sure enough, my pants were unzipped.

Now believe me, I'm not a pervert. I don't intentionally speak on college campuses with my pants unzipped. Anyway, I realized right away that I had to do something about this. So I swung around, pointed at the illustration on the screen with my left hand, kept on talking and I solved my problem right there with little notice.

Let me ask you a question: Did this college kid on the front row do me a favor that day? I guarantee you, he did. He gave me feedback that was extremely valuable to me. I trust you'll never need feedback of exactly that nature. But you do need it. It can increase your communication efficiency and ultimately your income, and I hope you will learn to give and take feedback wisely and well.

Successful Application 22

Featuring: Woody Welch, Senior Vice President, MS Carriers, Memphis, TN
Submitted By: Mike Starnes, Chairman and CEO, MS Carriers, Memphis, TN

Some sales are tougher than others. But even the most difficult prospect is likely to respond, at some time and to some degree, when the salesperson can demonstrate he or she will work long and hard to give the customer a quality product and good service.

One of the toughest sales I ever made was to an aggressive, strong-willed manager who worked almost as hard trying to deny me his business as I worked trying to get it. The conflict that existed between his company and mine became legendary.

It was in 1980, when I was a salesman for Pullman Trailmobile, an over-the-road trailer manufacturer. I was promoted to branch manager of our office in Dallas, where the previous management team for the company had pretty well managed us right out of the market. Our business in the Dallas market area was at a disgusting all-time low.

I started reviewing our past accounts and was particularly interested in Affiliated Foods, a refrigerated operation that ran 150 or so trailers. Not only did this company buy a lot of trailers, but their maintenance work was sizeable. We had lost the Affiliated Foods account primarily because our service had gotten really sloppy. About 1977 we had delivered some equipment to them that subsequently broke. Our company didn't respond to the complaints and requests for repairs as we should have, and Affiliated took their business elsewhere.

The director of operations at Affiliated Foods was a former Texas Ranger named McIntyre. I started trying to get in touch with him and got nowhere. He wouldn't talk to me on the phone, wouldn't return my calls, wouldn't agree to see me. When I went to his office and gave his secretary my business card, she said I'd need to phone later for an appointment. But they wouldn't give me an appointment when I called. This went on and on, and I was really frustrated.

Finally one day I decided I'd just go over to McIntyre's office and stay there until I was able to see him. I took a young salesman named Jim Hagle with me, assuming this sales call might be quite educational for Jim.

I gave the secretary my business card and told her, "Ma'am, I've tried to get an appointment with Mr. McIntyre and can't. And now I'm just going to sit here in your lobby until I see him, no matter how long it takes." That was about 10 in the morning and I sat there for at least an hour and a half. I'd occasionally go up to the desk and ask the secretary to let Mr. McIntyre know I was still there.

Finally, he decided to see us. I could tell he was irritated at being put in the position of having to talk to somebody he didn't want to talk to. He led us into this conference room and it was the biggest conference room I'd ever seen in my life at that time!

McIntyre showed us to chairs, then walked all the way down to the *other* end of the table – I swear it must have been 30 feet long – and took his chair. "What do you want?" he barked.

We began trying to mend our fences and he just sat there like a bull. Soon I realized that, with me talking, we'd probably never get to the point of learning all the problems that were keeping him from doing business with us. That's when I decided to ask him a question that would get *him* talking.

"What would it take for Pullman Trailmobile to do business with you again?" I asked. Then I stopped. I sat there in silence. And I'm telling you, it was a *long* silence. I've heard of a 10-second pause in the conversation. Well, I guarantee you, we went over *two minutes* with nobody saying anything. The young salesman with me started to say something and I kicked him under the table. I wanted Mr. McIntyre to answer my question.

When he finally began talking, he was very critical, abrasive, even belligerent. The arrogance was so thick, you could have cut it with a knife. But the longer he talked, the more he calmed down. He told us all the problems that would have to be resolved before he'd even consider doing business with our company. He got everything off his chest.

That very day I went back to my office and started chipping away at solving the problems that were dividing our companies. I worked constantly, day after day, to correct all the things that Mr. McIntyre had pointed out. And I learned what his operations problems were and told him about equipment that would solve them.

Nine months later, Mr. McIntyre bought about $3 million in equipment from Pullman Trailmobile. And from that point forward, I believe I received every order that Affiliated made while I was in Dallas. My persistence, patience and determination to resolve this conflict paid off handsomely.

DON'S PARTING THOUGHT

Be happy and make others happy, not with
shallow wishes but with skilled communications.

Skill #23

◆◆◆◆◆

Common Sense Sales Ideas

"Elephants don't bite. It's the
little things that get you!"

—Joel Weldon

Legendary merchant Stanley Marcus, in discussing why his elegant retail stores had been so successful, said, "There's no detail so small that we can afford to overlook it, nor any challenge so large that we are afraid to face it."

This chapter represents a potpourri of ideas, large and small, to help salespeople conquer challenges faster. It covers everything from time management to telephone selling to making more productive sales calls. There is an undeniable trend taking place today in virtually every industry, a trend that focuses on individual efficiency and accountability. The ideas on the following pages are in tune with this important trend.

Many were shocked recently when the *Wall Street Journal* printed an article about a sizeable firm that had just completed its fiscal year and reported the greatest revenues and profits in the company's 100-plus year history – and in this same year, the company terminated 700 people! The reporter who interviewed the CEO of the company asked why. The CEO's answer was short and matter-of-fact. "Our company is now in an age of organizational efficiency," he said, "and every person in the company must make a maximum contribution." In short, it's time for lean, efficient operations from companies and individuals.

In sales, we must use every idea we can grasp to maximize our results. The only security any of us has is our competence. This skill provides ideas and perspectives on increasing our personal *sales efficiency.*

You've Got Time To Succeed!

My friend Bill Brooks, an expert in time management, says a recent study he performed revealed that the average business person wastes 45 percent of his or her time. How often do you mistake activity for accomplishment? It's very easy to do, and we all do it from time to time.

It's my belief that we should make a daily attempt to finely tune our planning and follow-through efforts as diligently as a financial planner would advise that we keep up with and wisely invest our dollars. Everyone has the same amount of time every day. The question is, how well do we manage that resource?

As a good manager must orchestrate the productivity of his people, we must orchestrate the achievement of our goals by not only working hard, but working smart. Vow to get as much positive closure as possible in the shortest period of time, and others will marvel at your success.

Let's Make this Perfectly Clear

Time management as we usually think of it doesn't actually mean managing time but *managing yourself* for maximum efficiency during a given time frame. The more efficient you are, the more you'll achieve. Territory management is really not the management of a geographic area but the management of accounts, relationships, and the potential within that territory.

The A B C's of Time Management

Now that we've established some definitions and boundaries for time and territory management, let's consider what we can do to manage ourselves and our relationships for maximum sales performance.

The number one failure factor of salespeople is time organization. To understand this fact better, we need to think about the categories of time. They are *A Time, B Time, C Time* and *D Time.*

A Time is time spent communicating with existing or prospective buyers. There's nothing any more important than A Time. One of the primary reasons some people enjoy little success and productivity is that they minimize A Time. They may put in a lot of hours, but not enough *A Time!*

B Time is time spent in preparation for more productive A Time. For example, what is your true objective for reading this book on high performance selling? I think your objective is to gain information that will help you make your A Time more productive, right? Training time is a good example of B Time, and your objective is to use B Time to enhance the effectiveness of your A Time.

We'll define *C Time* as all other time spent in business activities (paperwork, travel time, etc.), and *D Time* as personal time.

Now if you were a front line sales manager, would you rather have a salesperson working for you who put in a six-hour day with four hours of A Time – or salespeople working for you who put in 12 hours a day but only two hours of A Time? I know I'd take the salespeople giving four hours of A Time every time. Give me the salespeople who are talking to prospects!

The time management behaviors of high performers are creatively planned in advance, and their self-discipline for follow-through on their

315

plan is strong. They realize the *quality* of how they spend their time outweighs the *quantity* of time available.

Plan Your Work and Work Your Plan!

When time is well managed and tasks well organized, tension and stress are reduced and we're much more productive. It's when we poorly structure what needs to be done that we get stressed out.

The more poorly organized we are, the lower our productivity is likely to be. So we often work harder and with more intensity only to find the results still aren't what they should be.

High performance salespeople possess an inner intensity about the use of their time. They know that if a task is worth doing or a call worth making, it's better to go ahead and do it. If it's not worth doing, they forget it. They know that good time management is as much a discipline as it is a skill. High performers plan, they prioritize, and they execute. Simply put, they get on with it!

High performers have their goals set so that their year is planned from the first day. But they don't stop there. They have expertly distilled the process down to having the quarter, the month, the week, the day, and indeed every hour of the day planned. Planning your day before it starts will often be the difference between extraordinary and mediocre sales results.

Nine Principles For Improved Sales Efficiency

1. **Minimize "windshield time."** Use good planning to minimize the amount of time you spend driving your car, and you'll be able to maximize your *A Time* for increased sales results. One way to lessen driving time is to plan your calls in the sequence that will enable you to drive the fewest possible miles. Good planning can save you many hours of driving in a 12-month period.

2. **Never overlook opportunities for more creative vertical prospecting.** Continuously ask yourself, Is there more business for me at this account? Do they have other divisions or departments that I could be

selling? Is there something else within my product line that I could be selling to the same buyer? Remember to maximize account penetration.

3. **When you are involved in administrative tasks, be objective driven.** Have a "get it done, and get it done efficiently" attitude so you don't get wrapped up in what I call *administrivia*. This can consume many hours of your valuable time. Remember, shuffling papers is a camouflage for immobilization. Try to avoid performing administrative tasks during peak selling hours; do it some time other than during high quality *A Time*.

4. **Prioritize your time according to potential sales.** Categorize or rank the customers and prospects in your territory, then work diligently to invest your time where the greatest opportunities and potential lie.

5. **Make your daily calls specific and sequential.** If you can't come up with a specific purpose for a call, don't make the call. Professional salespeople always have a pre-established call objective. As best you can, know when you will do each item on your list, maintaining the flexibility necessary to keep sales at a maximum and wasted time at a minimum.

6. **Concentrate your time on decision makers.** When working by appointment, encourage your contact or key decision influencer to have other decision influencers on hand. This helps you avoid the need to schedule more meetings which will take up even more of your time.

7. **Communicate promptly and efficiently.** Whenever possible, dictate letters and send notes at the earliest possible time. This way your information flow will be more up-to-date and of higher quality, and you'll enhance your efficiency greatly. Plus, others will appreciate your promptness.

8. **When in the office, have short, efficient meetings with your associates.** Successful printing executive "Dutch" Akers has a interesting philosophy: All meetings are standing meetings! He says they stay very short. Few things are less productive than a meeting of several people who comfortably wallow around in conference chairs participating in a boring, low-intensity interchange that has no urgency.

9. **Maximize your commitment to skill building and sales training.** We all know time is money, and the more skillful you are, the shorter your average sales cycle will be. A shorter sales cycle will free you up to make more calls, more sales and more money.

As you look closely at high performance salespeople in almost any industry, you'll invariably notice that the time it takes them to make a sale is considerably shorter than the amount of time it takes the average salesperson. High performance salespeople quite simply sell more in a given time frame than others. They have learned to manage their time because they realize that it is their greatest resource.

Dominate The Interview!

It's commonly thought that good salespeople always assume dominance in a selling situation. I say "Not necessarily!"

Dominance can be easy for more assertive individuals. They naturally want to dominate and control the interview. When they read a book or listen to a tape or hear a speaker talk about dominance, those types get their juices flowing and say, "That's right! That's been my problem. From now on, I've gotta go out there and dominate!"

So they go into the marketplace and who's the first person they call on? A Less Assertive individual. A prospect who's laid back and in no hurry to make a move. In their Amiable or Analytical style, they say "What's with this pushy person? The guy's coming across like an impatient guillotine operator." What we have here is an inappropriate strategy resulting from an invalid assumption.

Do you feel you are adaptable with the use of dominance? I hope so, because it's really important in selling. Some folks have a problem with dominance; they wouldn't be able to lead a group in silent prayer! But if we want to be high performance salespeople, we have to learn how to use dominance with sensitivity and appropriateness.

The Changing Role of Dominance

The role of dominance in selling has changed dramatically in recent years. In the past, many trainers said that if you didn't dominate the interview, you'd lose control and then lose the sale. Today, prospects won't be pushed around. The strategy must be right or the sale will be lost.

Today, as a result of increased competition in the marketplace, buyers generally have more choices about who they can buy from. If you want to be the buyer's choice, you must work on creating a positive relationship instead of fighting for control of the interview. This requires an approach of greater adaptability, and it requires having your finger on the prospect's pulse in terms of needs, goals, feelings and timing.

There will also be occasions when the prospective buyer will want to maintain a dominant posture during negotiations. I recommend you let him. Don't give up your dignity and beliefs, or allow yourself to be walked on, but give him room to communicate with you from his comfort zone. In this situation, as in others, finesse and adaptability will aid you.

The American College Dictionary defines dominance as a ruling, governing, controlling, occupying or commanding position. While assuming this kind of position will often be advantageous in group presentations, it will normally work against you today in a one-on-one encounter. In that environment, I like to think that the more power you give to the other person, the more power you'll actually have.

So that you won't come across as pushy and domineering, I recommend that you open an interview with effective rapport-building, followed by soliciting the prospect's opinion, rather than making a brief introduction and then barreling headlong into a product-oriented presentation.

25 Sales Ideas For Higher Performance

I've heard it said that a pro is someone who gets above-average results consistently and makes it look very easy.

Less astute observers often think high performers are lucky. I prefer to think that the high performance salesperson is a disciplined, talented individual who does many little nitty-gritty, unromantic things very well, and this leads to above-average levels of success. Let me share with you some of the little things I've learned that can add up to significant earnings for you.

1. **Develop the habit of asking for referrals.** I'm convinced that referral prospecting is the most powerful but unused means of gaining business in the marketplace today.

   Often the best people to ask for business are your existing customers and clients. The higher people are on that Loyalty Ladder, the greater the probability that they'll come through for you. If they are pleased with what they have bought from you and the service you've given them, they'll usually be happy not only to give you leads but to allow you to use their name when contacting those leads.

   Here's the procedure I recommend: Build the request for referrals into an appropriate place in your presentation process. Don't ask too soon; first, build trust and earn the right to ask. Make it easy for the client you are talking with to think of a prospect by suggesting a group or center of influence that might produce persons to contact.

   You might say, "Mr. Shaw, who do you know in your purchasing club that you think could benefit from knowing about me and my product line?" Get as much information on the referral as possible and follow up promptly. Use the referring party's name only if you gain his or her permission to do so.

   The late Fred Herman said the best way to get a referral and appointment is to simply ask someone to get it for you! That's right – tell them when you are available and get the person you are seeking the referral from to go ahead and get you an appointment. Kinda gutsy, but it works a lot of the time.

   With the rising costs of making sales calls, this prospecting technique becomes more valuable every year. The payoff on sales calls is increased when you have the skids greased with a strong referral or recommendation.

2. **Always be prepared.** Preparation is an important key to maximizing sales. Make sure you are always ready to do business by having the essential tools at hand.

   Do you always have something to write with and write on? Do you always have business cards with you? Keep extras in several places like your wallet, briefcase, the glove compartment of your car, your luggage, your golf or tennis bag. Brochures on your product or services are always a help too. Be ready to do business or initiate business relationships at any time.

3. **Avoid the failure factors.** A few years ago I spearheaded a survey to ascertain the failure factors of salespeople. Our survey indicated that five factors are predominant in hampering sales performance. Avoid them at all costs. They are:

   a. Improperly organizing time and efforts. There are some ways you can productively use time that might otherwise be wasted. You can make phone calls while waiting to see prospects. Minimize or eliminate coffee breaks. Start earlier! Stay later!

   b. Negatively pre-judging the quality of a prospect or the outcome of a sales call. Never pre-judge. Give it your best shot every time.

   c. A low intensity of personal motivation resulting in an insufficient number of sales calls being made. (Also known as *laziness.*)

   d. Use of inappropriate sales approaches and strategies on certain prospects, or simply failing to sell them the way they want to be sold.

   e. Indifference. Yes, 68% of all cancellations, lapses, malcontents, and customer complaints are due to the indifference of salespeople.

4. **Handle detail with a vengeance for perfection.** Is record-keeping hard work for you? It's hard for most of us, but the hardest thing is the discipline of simply getting it done.

   One major difference between today's high performance salespeople and the stereotypical image of a salesman in the past is the attention paid to details. Today's pro is a master at follow-through and detail. It's a painful skill to learn, but it's vital to your success.

5. **Have positive habits.** You will do today what your habit structure dictates. Since the best predictor of future behavior is past behavior, the development of positive habits will serve you well. Remember that the chains of habit are too weak to be felt until they're too strong to be broken.

6. **Develop a reputation for trust and dependability.** These two characteristics will buy you all kinds of allegiance. Give people every reason to trust you, and give no one reason to distrust you. When trust and dependability are compromised, your customers will start looking for suppliers elsewhere.

7. **Develop a strong, understanding support system at home.** Let your family members know that you sell great products for a great company. Stress the importance of getting phone messages in an accurate and timely manner. Get all family members turned on to the idea that they are part of the team. And incidentally – if your spouse or another family member has a career, be just as supportive of his or her career as you want them to be of yours.

8. **Be a reader.** Have a global focus on your industry and your customer base. Learn all you can learn. Share valuable and timely information with your customers and associates to increase the probability that they will share important items with you. Be certain that you give customers more valuable ideas and insights than your competition does. Read not only the latest books but newsletters and trade journals to expand your knowledge of the business you are in.

9. **Be careful with your promises.** My advice on this topic is simple: Make few hard promises, but always keep them. If you'll adhere to this rule, your credibility with your customers will be high.

10. **Maximize long-term, above-average sales performance.** Never let your guard down. Keep the focus on above-average sales performance. In the final analysis, our success is determined by how many calls we make and how good we are when we do! If you'll work on those two broad areas, your sales performance should be consistently impressive. Keep sufficient pressure on yourself so that you are functioning optimally.

11. **Always have a precise call objective.** Let your prospect know what that objective is. Never use the old "I was in the neighborhood and just thought I'd stop by…" routine. The prospect would probably prefer that you not waste his or her time if you have no specific objec-

tive in making the call. Salespeople who stop by or make a call with no specific objective are not really salespeople. They are *commercial visitors,* and it's likely that they are nice to everyone except their family, on whom they have imposed a poor standard of living!

12. **Don't take repeat business for granted.** It's just as important to avoid losing a customer as it is to gain a new customer. Don't just contact your customers when you want to sell them something. Become their friend. Personal notes and birthday and/or Christmas cards are excellent tools for staying in touch.

13. **The "standing call" is best.** When making in-person calls to a prospect's office, don't sit down. If you take your seat on the waiting room sofa and wait there until your name is called, that tells the receptionist you didn't expect to promptly see the person you are calling on.

    Instead, stand or casually walk around the lobby. Your body language tells the receptionist that your time is valuable, and she will be considerably more diligent about trying to get you in promptly. I never violate this rule, and I wait less than most people. Incidentally, whether you have an appointment or not, decide before you go in how long you are willing to wait to see someone.

14. **Maximize written communications with your prospect.** Send him or her hand-written notes confirming discussions from a telephone conversation, for example. While I have never been a promoter of the paper chase, this idea is good business and will enhance the relationship dramatically.

15. **Watch your words.** Use *power words* when you can, and avoid *weasel words* that negate the impact of your sales presentation. Here are some examples of power words: excellent, vital, proven, innovative, unquestionably, results-oriented. Examples of weasel words are these: probably, somewhat, sometimes, perhaps, might.

    Avoid using negative words related to selling, such as "pitch" and "peddler." Also, profanity is likely to be very ineffective. It can do no good and may do lots of harm. On the other hand, words specific to an industry and company can be very powerful if you are able to ascertain what they are.

16. **The "cold call with letter" technique.** If you're having difficulty getting in to see someone or getting a confirmed appointment, have a letter typed to him or her in advance but don't mail it. Take the letter to his or her office, hand the letter to the receptionist and say, "Would you be kind enough to see that Mr. Bradley gets this?" The receptionist is likely to say, "I'd be happy to." Then you will say, "Thank you very much, and I'll need to wait for his response." Here's an example:

Mr. George Bradley
Vice President of Sales
The Meandering Micro Chip Company
New York, NY.

Dear Mr. Bradley:

I'm in your lobby at this time and would like very much to see you. If you'll give me seven or eight minutes, I'd like to tell you about an idea that's been proven effective in decreasing the turnover of salespeople and improving their sales results in competitive selling situations.

Thank you, Mr. Bradley, for your willingness to give me a few minutes. I'm looking forward to meeting you.

Enthusiastically,

Don Hutson

You used a unique approach and you promised a benefit. I'm not saying this technique will work every time, but I'll bet it's a new experience for the person you're calling on. There's often a high payoff for ideas that reflect creativity and individuality. Try this one and see how it works for you.

17. **Use the prospect's annual report to your advantage.** Prospects love salespeople who have done their homework and go the extra mile. You should be able to say, "Mr. Prospect, in preparing for this call today, I secured a copy of your parent company's annual report from my stockbroker and I learned..." He'll love it! Then you can say, "I'm

impressed with your company's vision for the future and your obvious high standards and goals. I'm anxious to learn more about your division and your personal ideas. I think I can contribute measurably to the achievement of those goals." Parenthetically, if you call the public relations department of any company of size, they will usually be happy to send you an annual report.

18. **Keep a smooth sequence in your presentation.** If your presentation is fractured and poorly organized, you are creating needless problems for yourself. Don't be like the salesman who rambled through a sloppy, disorganized sales presentation, then finally paused to say to his prospect, "Do you follow me?" The prospect says, "Yes, I think so... but if I knew the way back, I'd leave right now." We must do better than that!

19. **Avoid distracting and offensive sales behaviors.** Some examples of problem behaviors would be smoking, moving furniture around, giving a presentation with your topcoat on, etc. Don't do anything that will take attention away from your presentation.

20. **Don't be a clock-watcher.** Never look at your watch during the sales interview. If you want to know what time it is, glance at your prospect's watch. Or look for a clock. If you look at your watch and the prospect sees you, that interview will usually end sooner.

21. **Be careful with names.** Be sure to use the prospect's name often and appropriately. If you can't remember, write it down. Never say, "Uh..." before calling the prospect's name, as if you're having trouble remembering the name. That's a real turnoff and, amazingly, I've heard some of the world's best communicators commit that sin.

22. **Remember the law of supply and demand.** This law works for both products and for people. The more interpersonally skilled you are, the better your sales techniques and your attitude, then the more successful your sales behaviors will be and the closer you'll come to being irreplaceable. Create a demand for yourself and your services by being committed to excellence.

23. **Executive Selling.** Having trouble closing a big sale? Have you thought about asking your boss or company CEO to get in the loop by calling on the CEO of the prospect company? There is more high level selling going on today than ever before and it works.

    Sales executive and good friend Raymond Caldiero in Santa Barbara is an excellent example of successful executive level selling in action. Ray is on a first name basis with virtually dozens of CEO's at sizeable corporations, including Marriott, Northwest Airlines, Dobbs, and the list goes on. Raymond and others who operate at higher than traditional levels have proven that bigger transactions and faster actions result.

24. **Network Marketing.** Whether you are developing a strong network comparable to the one mentioned above or you are a professional salesperson who has chosen an actual network marketing organization for a career thrust, the idea is growing like a prairie fire on a windy day.

    I would say Rich Devos at Amway, Jay Martin at NSA, and numerous others doing millions of dollars of business annually have keyed in on a premise that works and works well.

    I suggest you read Fred Smith's *You and Your Network* to get some ideas on enhancing your success through the people you know and the contacts you have.

25. **Make the telephone pay.** In a previous chapter, I quoted from a study that said sales calls today can cost in excess of $200 each. You can lower that cost dramatically by learning to use the telephone effectively. Smart use of the telephone can be an extremely valuable part of your sales and marketing strategy in today's marketplace.

    Today telephone selling is bigger business than ever. Companies are opening telemarketing departments by the thousands every year. It's been estimated that telephone sales operations now exceed $30 billion in volume, and that estimate is probably low. The use of toll-free 800 phone lines alone has become an explosive development in today's business world.

    Most agree that telephone selling is a unique type of selling, but the task remains the same: to ultimately get a positive response. So let's think about how we can make telephone selling work for us. Here are 25 telemarketing tips for your consideration.

25 Telemarketing Tips:

1. **Consider your total program.** In most cases, a successful telephone campaign does not stand alone. Normally it is part of an overall marketing plan, and its success is dependent upon successful support from other areas such as printed promotional brochures, video tapes, direct mail, and in-person calls. Consider carefully every component of your telephone campaign in order to develop your winning formula.

2. **Understand the purpose of your call.** Usually there are only four reasons for making a telephone call: to give information, to get information, to make a sale, or to get an appointment or some other interim commitment. Be certain you've clarified your purpose and your strategy for success before the call is made.

3. **Follow up professionally and promptly.** Do what you say you're going to do and you'll be seen as a true professional. Sloppy follow-up can kill you in telephone selling. Show that you are eager to get their business by being timely in every respect.

4. **Understand telemarketing momentum.** If you're on a roll, keep on. Don't break the positive momentum because that's a commodity that can be very precious. On the other hand, if you are suffering from negative momentum or you're in a slump, I recommend three things. First, reassess your techniques and the scripts you are using. Alter the scripts as needed for more comfort and clarity. Secondly, increase your activity. Simply make more calls. Third, turn on your optimism afterburner. Expect results and you'll usually get results. Whatever you do, don't let pessimism and a "down" attitude be projected through the phone. That's telemarketing suicide. If you are really getting beat up, take a moment to call one of your best customers or someone else who will tell you how wonderful you are!

5. **Do your homework.** Before making the call, review all files on that account or prospect if you've contacted them before. If you know about your prospects and their agendas, you'll be more likely to get a positive response. If you can anticipate their needs and responses, your chances of success are greatly enhanced.

By the way, Joel Rice of Sales Consultants of Malibu in Angora Hills, CA (a franchisee of Management Recruiters, Cleveland, OH), told me that keeping detailed files on all prospects has been one of the chief reasons for his success in telemarketing. "I write down everything while I'm talking with a prospect. Being an intense note-taker has paid off for me many times," Joel said. After taking lots of notes, Joel keeps everything on file. "I can go back two years and call a man, then open the conversation with, 'How's your wife, Suzie?' The prospect will ask, 'How in the world did you remember my wife's name?!' It impresses people every time. Writing things down – even minute details – can really give you an edge when you reference the information on subsequent calls."

6. **Call at the best time.** You need as many factors working in your favor as possible every time you make a call. Research the best times to call in your business by charting call results. You'll soon learn when the golden hours are, and that's when you'll want to schedule your calls. Some prospects will have preferred calling times as well, so be sure to find out when they are and keep that information on file.

7. **Prepare, organize and sort your leads.** Don't wait until selling time to get yourself organized. Either the night before or early in the morning of the day you'll make telephone calls is the time to prepare yourself. Don't waste valuable selling time getting organized. Plan your day in advance.

8. **Plan your sales approach.** Just as your prospects and procedures need to be well organized, so does your sales script. The better planned your presentation, the more confident and effective you'll be. By the way, avoid at all costs a verbatim presentation that sounds memorized. This kind of presentation is impersonal and can really turn people off. And remember the value of asking some Needs Analysis questions before getting into your sales presentation.

9. **Watch your grammar and vocabulary.** In telephone communications, good grammar and an effective vocabulary are about three times as important. What you say is all that the person at the other end of the line has to go on when trying to evaluate you and your

offer, so be sure your vocabulary and grammar are error-free and appropriate to each prospect.

10. **Have a good opening.** Just as appearance is vital to the first impression on personal calls, so your opening on the telephone is essential to capturing the interest of the party listening to you. The first 20 seconds are vital, so your opening must be well-planned. You may want to have several openings you could use. Study your options and remember the importance of this aspect of telephone selling. Incidentally, "How are you today?" is the worst. That's what almost everyone says, so use something other than that in your opening remarks.

11. **Take the "curse" off the call.** Since telephone calls are often an interruption, soften any possible inconvenience early on with positive words such as "Is this a good time to discuss my recent letter to you?" Try to offset a negative response with a positive, sensitive opening. Successful training executive Art Bauer at American Media has found that saying "Is this a *bad* time to talk?" or "Did I catch you at a bad time?" often works better than saying, "Is this a *good* time to talk?"

12. **Return calls promptly.** A positive habit that I learned from Carl Carson years ago is to always attempt to return every call that you get on the day it comes in. Do this even if you have to stay late at the office to do it. Sometimes this is hard – I'm still trying to master this one – but it's professional, courteous and efficient.

13. **Keep score.** Be a good telephone record-keeper. Have an organized records sheet in front of you at all times and monitor your numbers religiously. Chart such things as times dialed, presentations given, appointments booked, sales made. With this information, you'll never be out of control or be unmotivated by feeling your strategy is in disarray. You'll always be able to ascertain your earnings-per-call and per-presentation if you'll keep score.

14. **Smile.** I don't want to insult your intelligence with such a basic recommendation, but this one is easy to overlook and the payoff is too great to forget it! I'm convinced that your smile will go right through

that telephone line. It will have a positive impact on your listener and help you maximize your sales results. If you have a problem remembering to smile, keep a mirror on your desk. When you are smiling, you are more of a pleasure to do business with.

15. **Stand up occasionally when making a call.** It's a physiological fact that we think faster when standing. Standing increases blood flow to the brain, giving you more stamina and making you more alert. A good time to stand is when making a call of above-average importance.

16. **Avoid fatigue.** Sitting at the telephone for long periods can be tiring, so give yourself frequent short breaks as needed so you'll stay fresh. If practical, a few deep breaths of fresh air can be energizing.

17. **Use conversational variance.** You will need to periodically vary your rate of speech and your accent, based on the rate of speech of your listener and their predictable receptivity to your accent. Vocabulary variance is also something to consider. Remember that your goal is to make the listener comfortable so that you can keep his attention and interest throughout your sales process.

18. **Avoid simultaneous verbiage.** The old term used by CB operators is "walking on" someone when you talk at the same time. Don't ever "walk on" anyone on the telephone. Even if that person interrupts you or begins talking when you are in mid-sentence, immediately stop talking and let them talk. The issue here is not whose turn it is to talk; the issue is clear communication.

19. **Use trial closes.** We discussed this technique as part of an earlier skill, and it may be even more important on the telephone than in face-to-face selling. Trial closing feelers such as "How does this sound to you?" or "Do you think this approach fits your needs?" are good ones.

20. **Ask for the order.** At the close of any telephone presentation or when you get any strong buying signal, ask for the order. Salespeople who wait for prospects to take the initiative to buy usually fail. Ask your prospect to buy and make it comfortable for them.

21. **Avoid "one-call psych out".** Don't ever let one particular call get you down. If you experience a vocal rejection, don't mope around or curse that person to your co-worker. Just get back on the phone and make another call. One person can't ruin your day unless you let him. Remember, every time you are rejected, you're that much closer to a "Yes!"

22. **End each call on a positive note.** This will pave the way for a better response during the next interaction with that person. It also will keep you in a positive frame of mind and motivate you to make another call right away. Good closing phrases are "We appreciate your business" or "I wish all of our customers were as much of a pleasure to do business with as you."

23. **Ask the prospect for questions.** "Do you have any questions about our special offer?" That's one way to do it. Too many telemarketers do too much talking. When you ask your prospect for questions, this will give him or her more of an opportunity to talk. And you'll simultaneously learn how they feel and what their concerns may be.

24. **Let them see you.** Some telephone salespeople have talked to customers and prospects for years without letting the customer know what they look like. This is a big mistake. Prospects feel they know you better if they see a photograph of you in a professional environment with a smile on your face.

    I have used four-color post cards for years. After I talk on the phone to someone whom I have never personally met, I drop them a post card. My son Scott is a successful salesman with the investment banking firm, Morgan Keegan Company, and he has gotten excellent mileage out of his four-color post cards as well. Scott has found using the cards shortens his sales cycle because people identify with him sooner. Prospects also respond to a non-traditional idea that may separate you from the masses.

25. **Confirm, congratulate, and clarify when you get an order.** Simply confirm that the person you called has bought something by saying a phrase like, "Fine, I'll enter your order immediately." Then congratulate the person on their decision and assure them of the positive

results they'll get from their purchase. Finally, clarify the details – such items as shipping date, recipient's address, quantity ordered, etc.

Successful Application 23

Featuring: Lew Bennett, Senior Vice President of Sales, Danek Group; Memphis, TN

Submitted by: Ron Pickard, President and CEO, Danek; Memphis, TN

When I first started as a young salesman selling sutures for the Ethicon division of Johnson & Johnson, operating room supervisors and surgeons were the decision makers. I wanted to stand out from the other salespeople selling sutures and not be just a number. One of the things I did was certainly not unusual, nor is it unusual today. But I like to think I did it unusually well.

I did a great deal of in-service training on how to prepare sutures. I learned how to use them and how to demonstrate that use. I could show my customers how to eliminate waste in the operating room, something my competitor was not doing. I learned all I could about my product and then I taught those things to the people I was calling on, so they would be knowledgeable too. This was the first step in building rapport with my customers.

Secondly, I started volunteering to speak at local meetings of medical personnel on a variety of subjects. Motivation and communication were among the most popular topics I discussed. Through these engagements, I began getting to know people.

Before too many years in medical sales had passed, I began the practice that has become my trademark. As I would call on the operating room personnel during the Christmas season, I noticed there would always be a lot of Christmas cards. Often there would be so many cards that the staff didn't pay much attention to who they were from. I realized that sending Christmas cards as a sales tool was a waste of money. However, since people do like to be remembered, I began to wonder how many of my customers got birthday cards.

I discussed this with staff members in hospitals. Without exception, they indicated they got very few, if any, birthday cards. A card from their parents, maybe from a few friends, but few other cards. So I began sending birthday cards to my customers and prospects.

I went to some trouble to make sure the first card was a surprise. I began cutting out the horoscope section of the newspaper, reading my own horoscope before tucking the clipping in my billfold. (Frankly, I've never put weight in what horoscopes said, but I found this to be an entertaining topic of conversation.) Each time I called on an operating room nurse, surgeon, or purchasing agent, I'd bring the conversation around to something – always positive – that my horoscope had said that morning. Then I'd say, "I wonder what your horoscope said today." I'd ask their birthday, tell them their sign, and read their horoscope for that day.

I'd make a mental note of the birthday during our conversation. Then out in the hallway, as I left from the call, I'd write down the date to add to my master calendar. By the time I stopped calling on operating room personnel and surgeons, I was sending well over 1,000 birthday cards a year to customers.

There are many things that make a salesperson successful. Sometimes the little things are as important as the big ones. I believe that the one single idea that helped me the most in building friendships, good relationships, and rapport with persons in the medical sales industry were those birthday greetings. Whenever I go to conventions, people still walk up to me and thank me for the cards I send them. One warm wish at a time, multiplied by thousands, added up to a winning sales idea for me.

DON'S PARTING THOUGHT

I agree with Lord Chesterfield who said, "Snatch, seize and enjoy every moment of time with no idleness, no laziness, and no procrastination. Never put off 'til tomorrow what you can do today." Success is often the successful execution of numerous simple techniques that, when used consistently over time, will put you light years ahead of your competition.

Skill #24

◆◆◆◆◆

Dedication to Training

"Learn as if you are going to live forever, and live as if you are going to die tomorrow."

—WHIT SCHULTZ

Salespeople are only as good as they know how to be. They cannot perform beyond their skill base and intellect. You can't use a sales idea you haven't learned any more than you can come back from where you haven't been.

Are you familiar with the concept known as *model training?* In model training, someone might say to you, "I want you to go work with Charlie for two or three weeks and learn how to do it just like Charlie does it. Then you can go out into the marketplace and do just what Charlie is doing – use the same words, same phrases and obviously experience the same production."

You probably sense that I have a bit of a problem with "model training." I don't think it works very well, and I'll tell you why.

I believe that one of the greatest things you have going for you is your *individuality.* Model training robs a person of his or her individuality. Words, phrases, concepts, approaches and techniques that someone else might be comfortable with could be awkward, foreign and totally unproductive for you.

Most high performance salespeople have a special individuality about them. They have their own style as a professional. They don't come off an assembly line, all cut from the same mold. But one thing they do have in common is a hunger for knowledge and an excitement about training. After reading this book or any good sales book, a high performance salesperson will be thinking, "I'm going to internalize these skills and, using all the information I've gained, I'm going to establish positive habits and an action plan!"

Process, Not Event

I enjoy asking people, "Are you as good as you're ever going to be?" They invariably say no and await my next question, which is usually, "What are you doing now to get better?" If they describe one or more acts of learning or training that are unmistakably *events* rather than part of an unending *process,* I emphasize the vital difference.

If training is to be effective, it must be part of a process, a process to which the individual is deeply committed. That process must have multiple reinforcements before the subconscious mind and habit structure of a human will have accepted and absorbed it. Then the issue of practicing and honing the edges on the skill must be addressed.

Maybe you're saying that this sounds like serious business! You're right. It's hard labor, but it pays off magnificently.

The internalization of new ideas and skills is the springboard to growth and progress. Victor Hugo said that when you open up a school, you close a prison. I wonder how many salespeople have blindly imprisoned themselves between walls of mediocrity by ignoring the many wonderful opportunities to school themselves for betterment in their sales careers.

The Process Never Ends

High performance salespeople recognize that sales training isn't a single event or exposure to one program. It's a never-ending *process* that keeps them on the cutting edge of sales excellence.

William A. Ward said, "The price of excellence is discipline, and the cost of mediocrity is disappointment." A diligent belief in training accompanied by disciplined action and follow-through are required to gain the desired results and avoid disappointments.

Our environment and our industries aren't static entities. They are ever-changing. Every 24 hours brings a new day in which being good at what you do is more challenging than the day before. Remember: When you cease getting better, you cease being good.

We need to continuously keep an open mind for new ideas to grow our business. We need proactive, positive intention coupled with a desire to put to use all the tools of effective persuasion. This must begin with a strong belief in training, followed by an action plan.

Play It Again, Sam

I once read that you must hear a word 17 times before it is a part of your vocabulary. All types of learning must have a repetitive force to be internalized. That repetitive exposure, incidentally, must be accompanied by a desire for improvement.

Repeated exposure to a technique or an idea at spaced intervals is highly effective in helping us experience quality, lasting internalization. In my opinion, the most powerful example of what spaced repetition education can do for salespeople occurs with the use of the audio cassette. As an educational resource, the training cassette has probably done more than any other single thing to magnify the income of salespeople.

The Joy of Results Overcomes The Threat of Change

Many salespeople are worried about training because they know that training will bring change, and change threatens many of us. It's a fact that the results of training can be feelings of initial discomfort or awkwardness. That's because training often alters what we say, do and believe.

As we have discussed, behavior change can be discomforting. We must accept the fact that no idea, technique or behavior change can effectively come about without repetition and reinforcement. Putting new ideas and techniques in place and changing our old habits to incorporate the new ideas we learned can be a bother. But it's worth the trouble.

I predict that whatever got you to where you are now from where you used to be isn't the same thing that will get you from where you are today to where you want to be in the future. You've got to open yourself up to new input in order to find that one idea, skill or technique – or those several ideas, skills and techniques – that are going to get you to where you want to go.

I hope you won't confuse sales training with product knowledge training. They are very different and should be dealt with differently. Product knowledge training is technical information about what you are selling. Sales training is a process of internalizing skills that will enable you to experience a higher level of acceptance from those who consider your proposition.

I recently read an article by Don Thoren that said both sales training and product knowledge training are vitally important to our success. But, this article said, for best results we should invest 80 percent of our time, training budget, and energy in sales training and 20 percent in product knowledge. The article went on to say that most companies today invest only 5 percent in sales training and 95 percent in product training.

My advice is to carefully distinguish between the two and then make high-quality, well-thought-out decisions on your involvement in and commitment to both types of training. If your company doesn't provide sufficient sales training, you must simply seek it out and gain it on your own.

It has been said that if you study an area of subject matter for 30 minutes daily, the odds are 100 to 1 that within five years, and in many cases less, you will be a recognized authority in that field. And expanding your knowledge can be rejuvenating. Learning new things can give you new energy and enthusiasm for your work.

How strong is your belief in training? You should be commended simply because you are a reader. Millions of people aren't! Reading books and listening to cassettes for sales ideas is the most basic of all training opportunities. Anyone who isn't doing this at some point in his or her career isn't trying very hard to become a high performance salesperson.

The average salesperson spends 480 hours per year in the automobile. That time on the road presents a great opportunity to listen to cassettes and gain new sales knowledge and skills. I recommend reading just as vigorously – but not while you're driving, of course!

Training Options: More and Better All The Time

An example of existing technology which, in my opinion, we will see more of in the future is training via satellite. As it becomes more cost effective, this trend is certain to grow.

In 1990, I was a featured speaker along with Denis Waitley, Zig Ziglar, Art Linkletter, and Patricia Fripp for Satellite Network Affliliates, Inc.'s exciting "Training Via Satellite" program. The live show was shot in Salt Lake City before an audience of about 200 and then satellite-beamed to Portland, Oregon, where 450 were attending in a theatre, and to Kansas City, where 800 additional people were viewing on forty-foot screens.

Doug Snarr put that program together with Hollywood backing and assistance from multi-millionaire Merv Adelson, formerly President of Lorimar (which produced the television program "Dallas") and now a board member of Time Warner. The entire production was first class, innovative, exciting, and quite successful from a training point of view.

Merv Adelson is a gracious, knowledgeable man who is fascinated with this technology. My son, Kevin, an aspiring actor living in Burbank, California, joined me as I recently paid Merv a visit in his Beverly Hills penthouse office. Merv encouraged Kevin and inspired me with his dedication to a continuing search for viable communications methods.

As an aside, you may be interested in a sales statistic from that satellite program. When the speakers offered their books and tapes to the audience, the per-person sales in the satellite cities were almost double those at our live site. Interesting, isn't it?

In my home base of Memphis, we are privileged to have the world headquarters of Federal Express. They have a satellite communications system (FXTV) that could only be described as *cutting edge*. It encompasses a daily six- or seven-minute newscast to employees, a monthly "Salesline" program to Federal Express salespeople that averages one hour, and other special programs to enhance not only the training effort but employee morale. Federal Express's satellite system efficiently speeds up both the learning and communications process.

A Time And Place For Training

Where and when you continue your training is largely a personal choice, but I have some ideas for you to consider. First, try to schedule training at times that won't infringe on your selling time.

I once had a salesman who would go home and read a sales book every time he missed a sale. His primary problem was call reluctance, and it was compounded by poor scheduling acumen. This is about as smart as sleeping all day and making sales calls during the night!

You may be interested in knowing that today he is successful, but not in selling. He chose to pursue a technical career, and he still reads a lot to stay abreast of his craft. He is probably better at scheduling now, too.

As far as timing, I suggest that you study information and develop skills that can be most valuable to you *this week* or *this month*. Think about what prospects you will be calling on and what problems or opportunities you will most likely encounter, then prepare yourself accordingly.

Acquire The Skill, Then Put It On The Street!

It's a simple fact that the more you know and the more sales skills you possess, the more you will produce. I've suggested before that no one is a born salesperson, a born listener, a born communicator or, for that matter, a born closer. Salespeople aren't born to be great; we are *trained* to be great! And after we get the training, we must put it to work to profit from it.

Now I'd like to share with you seven training factors that you should keep in mind for your growth and progress in the selling profession.

Training Factor One: Develop a training and personal development library

Since we are ultimately accountable for our own performance, we should likewise be accountable for our own growth and training plan.

If your company has a training library or periodically provides you with training materials, that's great. But don't stop there! Exceptional salespeople have their own library as well, and they take great pride in making frequent additions to it. If you only have four books and four file folders in your personal training library, that's OK. The important thing is you have begun a process.

Your files should include articles as well as notes from seminars and speeches you hear. Retain anything you see of value that you may want for future reference. Contribute to the file frequently and review the contents often.

Be diligent at taking notes whenever you are exposed to good ideas and techniques. Whenever you hear a good speaker, take time to look around you. I'll assure you that 90 percent of the people taking notes are the big hitters! Those people take training and the gaining of quality ideas very seriously, and they don't rely on their memory when good ideas are in the air. As Earl Nightingale once said, "When you hear a good idea, write it down because good ideas are like a slippery fish. You better gaff it while it's there, or you will never see it again."

Training Factor Two: Have a disciplined action plan for training

When it comes to training, many people are well-intentioned but poor at following through. Have a minimum number of books you will read and tape programs you will listen to per year. Then stick to your plan.

Here's an idea from Jim Rohn. Set as your goal to read two books a week; in ten years, you'll have read 1,000 books! Doing this will greatly influence your life, according to Jim.

"If you stride into the marketplace 10 years from now a thousand books behind, you'll be at an incredible disadvantage," Jim has said. "For some confrontations, you won't be a match; for some opportunities, your knowledge will be too lacking; for some values, your philosophy will be too shallow. You can't read too many books, but you can read too few."

If reading two books a week is too stringent a plan, make it one book. Or make it two books a month. The important thing is to have a plan and live up to it.

Make learning and training a habit. The sooner you start a disciplined, organized training procedure, the sooner you will profit from it. And don't rely on your company or your manager to provide all of your training for you. Remember that the principle of accountability is important. You are responsible for you.

I'll never forget a story I heard Dr. Murray Banks tell years ago when we both appeared at a Sales and Marketing Executives sales rally in Columbus, Ohio. He is a successful speaker and psychiatrist in New York City.

A patient who visited Dr. Banks said, "Doctor, I would really like to have a college degree. I've thought of going back to night school, but it would take me 10 years. I would be 55 years old by then." The woman was depressed and uninspired because of how long it would take her to complete the degree.

But Dr. Banks looked at her and said, "Well, tell me, how old will you be 10 years from now if you *don't* go back to college?"

That story makes an important point. We have to stay with a disciplined action plan and make it happen.

Training Factor Three:
Undergo "un-training" periodically

Occasionally we must throw out some obsolete ideas and sales approaches. Just as some people are pack rats with their closet, some salespeople are pack rats with old ideas, habits and techniques. No matter how outdated the ideas, these people just can't throw away the old tapes they recorded in their heads years before.

We must periodically un-train ourselves by flushing from our minds and notebooks antiquated ideas that once worked but don't work now. We should be endlessly analyzing methodology, learning the latest proven methods. Don't be among those who work hard but never make it because the ideas and techniques they trained themselves to use are no longer on the cutting edge of excellence. Cutting wood with a dull axe is hard labor indeed!

Training Factor Four:
Anticipate results from training

My old buddy Roy Hatten used to ask, "What is the difference between an optimist and a pessimist?" As the audience pauses to think, he says, "About 100 grand a year!"

Your personal game plan for growth through training will work, but you must *make* it work. That begins with an optimistic anticipation of results. As you gain ideas, try them. Field test them; put them on the street. Make them work for you. In your mind, correlate your improved performance with recent training activities. It will keep you more excited about your growth process.

Training Factor Five: Internalize quality ideas

To fully utilize and profit from the ideas and techniques you get from training, you must have repeated exposure to them over a period of time. Review them, practice them, internalize them. For those ideas and techniques to work consistently for you, they must be integrated into your reflexes. Yes, they must come naturally and smoothly to be effective in the marketplace.

Again, the use of audio cassettes is an excellent means to achieve this result. I'm a big proponent of formal education, but some salespeople have readily admitted that they have learned more in their automobiles than they ever did in the classroom. I'd like to convince every corporate executive that putting tape players in company cars for the salespeople will provide an enormous return on investment. It's more expensive *not* to have them, but some with *bean counter* mentality do not understand that.

Training Factor Six:
Budget training to be a profit center

Make a disciplined investment in quality training with the full expectation of results – results that you know will increase your sales performance and your income. Make sales training an item in your budget, and your financial stature will do nothing but improve. It's not a cost but an investment in your future.

Remember the words of Harvard University President Derek Bok: "If you think education is expensive, try ignorance." Yes, the dollars you put into training won't change your standard of living greatly, but the results you gain can raise your standard of living to new heights.

Training Factor Seven: Practice role playing

Take advantage of every opportunity to experience this method of practicing your skills. The most common scenario for role playing will probably be in your sales meetings. In this somewhat public setting, peer pressure will usually force you to be well-prepared and polished. If you can be competent in that setting, it shouldn't be hard to be competent with your prospects.

I have an additional suggestion for you: Work to identify your personal training need. Training will vary greatly by salesperson, and I want to suggest that you put some energy into identifying the level and degree of additional training appropriate for you.

You can best do this by gaining information in three areas. First, ask your superiors their opinions regarding where you most need to grow and learn. They'll be impressed that you're working to improve yourself.

Secondly, ask your customers. Just tell them you want to be as valuable to them as possible and are eager to seek additional training, skills and knowledge. They will appreciate your growth-oriented attitude.

Third, become introspective. What do *you* think your most pressing training needs are? The answers and input you compile could be valuable in establishing a new and eager game plan for getting better.

After developing your training plan, share the commitment you've made to yourself with your manager. You may even want to report your progress to him or her at regular intervals.

Training is our foundation for progress. Excitement and good intentions without knowledge are simply useless and frustrating. In closing, I'd like to share with you the words of Elbert Hubbard who said, "The biggest reward God gives us for the good work we do is the ability to do even better."

Successful Application 24

Featuring: Butch Crouch, President and CEO, SouthTrust Securities Inc., a division of SouthTrust Corporation; Birmingham, AL (Author Interview)

Training is the bridge that gets us from *not knowing how* to do something... to doing it! This is a journey that all high achievers love to take.

As President of SouthTrust Securities, I am trying to create a learning organization. Like many sales organizations, we want our people to become more effective by working smarter, not necessarily harder. This principle applies to training as much as any other area. So we look for easier, smarter ways to train people – ways to help people cross the bridge.

This sounds like a simple concept, but there are a lot of different ways to cross the bridge. For example: At our firm, it appears that some have crossed it purely with experience. This method is often called "graduating from the school of hard knocks." Although I certainly don't want to discount the value of practical experience, this is not the only way to learn. It's true that we must all ultimately graduate from this school in order to thoroughly internalize knowledge but, in my opinion, there are some great ways to speed up your "graduation day."

Charlie Jones, speaker and author, knew about other ways to cross this bridge. For years he has been writing and talking about one of his favorite sayings: "You'll be the same five years from now as you are today except for the people you meet and the books you read."

Years ago I cut out this quote and taped it to my desk. The more I looked at it, the more it meant to me. Charlie Jones' words sum up my philosophy about the importance of continuing to grow in your professional and personal life. I recently read that if you do not keep learning, the best you can hope for is *better sameness*. Who wants that?

First, let me talk about the people you meet. Simply stated, hang around with the masters. If you even suspect that a person of the master caliber is speaking nearby, go listen to him or her and encourage others to do the same. Many will be quick to give you advice, but you will only learn from those who have a profound knowledge of the topic you are exploring.

A few years ago I went to a lecture given by Ed Deming, the quality guru who played a large role in Japan's post-war success. As people asked him questions at the end of his lecture on various topics, he often answered with the same statement. He said over and over, "There is no substitute for profound knowledge."

At SouthTrust, we are trying to develop a training process that will help our salespeople gain a profound knowledge of the important issues related to their jobs. By the way, since we don't often have Ed Deming hanging around our firm, we have to help each other. Remember, a person only has to be a master on the topic that you desire to learn more about, so don't exclude people who are not masters at everything. This makes "masters" much easier to find.

Also remember that you don't have to meet these people personally. This leads to the second part of Charlie Jones' quote. "You will be the same. . . except for the books you read."

I suspect this quote has been around for a long time. If he were making that statement today, in addition to talking about the books you read, Charlie probably would also mention the tapes you hear, the VCR films you watch, and various other forms of media you use to learn. This opens up a whole new world of "masters" who no longer reside in our current world. May they rest in peace, but may their knowledge live forever!

Our firm encourages people to read. I personally think of books as my friends. They are everywhere in my life – in my office, in the car, at home, anywhere I might find myself with a few minutes to spare. People often ask me how I find so much time to read. My answer is that I don't have to force myself to do it; that's the way *I want* to spend my spare time. It is what I would rather be doing, in most cases. I look at this time as fun and as a great investment.

From a training point of view, you can spend most of your time learning the hard way, or you can read about others who have already been through that process and are willing to share some proven methods with you. I think that is why some successful authors feel the urge to write; they have an overwhelming desire to share their successful techniques with others. They are often trying to keep their readers from going through all the pain that they went through to glean out a bit of profound knowledge.

I find it amazing that you can sit down and spend a few hours reading about 20 or 30 years of someone's life, and often in that short time you can learn much of what it took them 20 or 30 years to learn! With adequate concentration and reflection, you can make books a turning point in your life.

Among the books that are my personal favorites is *Jonathan Livingston Seagull* by Richard Bach. This book teaches you to focus on learning skills (flying, in Jonathan's case). If you become passionate about this learning process, the by-products will often be things that others with lesser skills will have to scratch, claw and fight for.

The Path of Least Resistance by Robert Fritz taught me to start with a clear vision of success, evaluate the current position as it relates to this vision, and close the cycle of creativity by developing an action plan. *Man's Search for Meaning* by Victor Frankl taught me about making personal choices.

In the right circumstances, books can enhance or turn around a sales career. Read *Changing The Game* by Larry Wilson and *The Quadrant Solution* by Howard Stevens and Jeff Cox. Apply the principles and skills that these books offer, and you will see results!

The works I've cited above and many others have been excellent training resources for me over the years. I believe that when people are not ready to learn, there is nothing you can do to make them learn. However, the opposite of this is also true: If someone is ready to learn, the teacher will suddenly appear. It may be a book, a tape, a company training session, or a person. That's why it is important to make training resources available constantly. Training needs to be a strong part of your personal culture and your firm's culture. You never know when someone will be ready to learn!

How does our company apply concepts like those mentioned above? We begin by defining ourselves as a learning organization, and we constantly look for those who are ready to learn. We put books in their hands; we provide videos for them to watch; we encourage them to listen to cassette tapes; we send them to personal training courses. We give learners assignments that will stretch them beyond the edge of their current knowledge. And we maintain high expectations.

How is our training program working? As we expected. We have a very solid and growing core of salespeople who are "fired up" about the on-going process of training. Unfortunately, we still have a small group of people who are not ready to learn. Between the two groups are others who are becoming more interested in the training process. They are getting close to the "ready to learn" stage. They see the bridge and are about ready to start the journey to the other side.

Many times paying for training is like paying your light bill. You can't actually see what you are buying, you can only see the results. At SouthTrust Securities, we like the results we are getting for our emphasis on training. Among the by-products are increased excitement, increased innovation and creativity, increased sales, and the favorite of most CEOs – increased bottom line!

DON'S PARTING THOUGHT

Those who understand that they can become more because they can learn more are among the world's truly blessed people. Without skill acquisition and new knowledge, life simply repeats itself. Earl Weaver, Baltimore Orioles' manager, said it well: "The important thing is what you learn after you think you know it all." Train, read, study, grow – and your rewards will be great and many!

Skill #25

✦✦✦✦✦

Gaining Career Progress

"My interest is in the future because I am going to spend the rest of my life there."

—BENJAMIN FRANKLIN

It has been said that four things come not back: the spoken word… time past… the sped arrow… and the neglected opportunity. As you consider how to plan for professional growth and progress in your career, remember that these things come not back. When opportunity presents itself, seize it!

You should devote a great deal of thought and consideration to your career path and your career goals. Years ago the overriding issue for professionals planning their careers was income. That's still important today, but now the issues are far more complicated.

Are you pleased with the career progress you have experienced, especially in the recent past two to three years? Experts say that unemployment is indeed a very real problem, but mis-employment (having the wrong job) and under-employment (having a job that's below your qualifications) are, in many respects, more widespread. And they are tragic problems, indeed.

As we look around us, the people who seem to be the happiest, who are thriving in their careers, are the men and women who are in the right groove. They are right for the position they hold, and they are doing everything possible to create and assure themselves of continued positive momentum.

I suppose it's fairly simple today to spot people who are enjoying the good rewards of having the right position at the right time. Conversely, may you be spared the stress of long-term job seeking. One of the great attributes of the selling profession is that anyone who can sell, and sell well, will always have an abundance of sales opportunities from which to choose.

In discussing some of these issues in a Q&A session following a recent speech, an audience member offered an amusing career-related anecdote: "A downturn in the economy is evidenced by your next-door neighbor losing his job; a recession is when you lose your job; a depression is when you've lost yours and your spouse loses his or her job also!"

Advancing your career through a promotion or the successful negotiation of an improved compensation or commission plan may be among the most profitable sales you will ever close. We need to work on enhancing the marketability of our sales skills and communications expertise throughout our career.

A motivated, articulate, effective sales professional is a tremendously valuable commodity in today's marketplace. One of the greatest rights we have as members of a free society is the right to achieve well-deserved personal betterment.

A Career With Balance

I was amused when I heard the story about the sales manager who ran into a friend he hadn't seen for a while. "Hey Charlie, good to see you!" the friend said. "I hope your sales organization is doing well. How many people do you have working for you now?"

Charlie replied, "About half of 'em!"

Management will pay dearly today for a consistently high-producing salesperson who is willing to work hard. If you are truly serious about success, you will find the discipline to work hard on a consistent basis. It's those who are tentative about their careers and their belief in what they sell that find consistent, long-term hard work very, very tough.

You may have heard selling described as the highest paid hard work and the lowest paid easy work around. It's probably true. And the high performance salesperson is the one who makes above-average sales production look easy and natural. It's the same as the talented actor, athlete, or speaker who makes the job look easy, when in fact that pro has been honing his or her skills for years.

Should hard work and our quest for career success become an obsession? Is it possible to work, pursue one's life goals, and be a great achiever without upsetting the need for balance in our lives? I think so, but let's evaluate this issue carefully.

In the book *Type A Behavior and Your Heart,* Dr. Meyer Friedman says that "Type A" people (who are most typically workaholics) often lose that vital balance. They believe that hard work and compulsive achievement are the only things that matter. They may tie their feelings of self-worth to the number of hours they work beyond those of normal mortals. I'm convinced that when one goes this far, losing that vital balance, then high achievement becomes more difficult, not more likely.

When we lose balance in our lives, we no longer possess the essential factors of variety and stimulus in our peripheral areas. If we become so singularly focused, everything we attempt is being attempted on what is usually a less-than-stable foundation.

Decisions and Strategies

Dr. John Richard deWitt said, "Life is filled with priorities to be set and decisions to be made. If you carefully think out your priorities, your decisions are much easier to make." As you begin planning the stepping stones for your future career path, ask yourself these questions:

- Is there a desirable opportunity for me to increase my income and productivity in my present position?
- Should I seek promotion to a higher position in my firm?
- Or, is there another opportunity to consider, perhaps outside my present situation?

I had a close friend once who was promoted from high-producing sales professional to sales manager in his firm. He kept the sales manager title on his door for less than a year and went back to his old sales job. He couldn't afford the pay cut. Not all "promotions" are monetary promotions. What seems a step up to some might really be a step in the wrong direction for you.

On the other hand, monetary measurement is not at the top of the Needs List for some. Psychic income and varying sources of professional and personal gratification can come from many places. You must dance to your own music.

Do your research and learn of all the options and opportunities open to you before addressing your goals and game plan for the future. Then follow *your* plan, not someone else's.

Is it your goal to become a higher-producing sales professional or to rise through the ranks of your corporate structure? Remember, high performance salespeople do not necessarily become high performance managers. Regardless of our career goals, it will behoove us to be sensitive to the normal sequence of progress in our organizations. Frankly, I have found that high-producing sales professionals often enjoy more security than people in management. Talented salespeople will always have multiple options.

We need to be sensitive to the key players, in any case. Ask yourself this: Who will the decision makers be when my name is brought up for bigger and better things? The more significant the position or territory you're being considered for, the more important it is that you have a favorable image in the eyes of those decision makers. The more and better your values align with theirs, the more impressed they'll be with you.

Be A Team Player – And Ask For The Order!

Are you a good fit with your present organization and its leadership? The greater the philosophical differences between you and your company and its management, the more challenging it will be to progress within the company and experience genuine job fulfillment. If you are not experiencing a good fit now, what can you do to become more in line with your organization's direction, mission and leadership as soon as possible?

Always project a positive and progressive attitude and let the leadership of your organization know that you possess a willingness to change as needed for the good of the organization. Bosses love someone who is part of the team!

Are you a team player in the eyes of your superiors? Are you enjoying measurable, impressive progress in your present position? Will your performance, your image and your character withstand close inspection and scrutiny?

I suggest you schedule with your superiors conversations that are visionary and appropriately suggestive. Don't be reluctant to tell them things like, "One reason I accepted a position with this company six years ago was that I saw a progressive organization with impressive leadership that would give employees room to grow. I'm even more impressed today than I was then, and I'm dedicated to a future with this company. What, in your opinion, do I need to be doing to best be prepared for future opportunities?"

This is a great question to ask if you ask it of the right people at the proper time and in the proper spirit. You might be amazed at the input you get and how useful that input can be in helping you decide what's the next and best step forward on your career path.

If, after much research and consideration, you and your spouse or family members believe that you have a greater opportunity elsewhere, move – but move cautiously. Your best opportunity just might be the one you have right now.

While it's wise to remember that there could be untapped opportunities available in your present position, sometimes there are undeniable signals that it's time to make a change. If you feel used up… if you feel uninspired in your current position… if you are no longer excited about selling what you are selling… if you can't revive the enthusiasm you once had… then I suggest you find something else to sell. You owe it to yourself and your employer to move on.

Life is too short to be laboring over a task you can't put your heart and your head into. Whatever you do, do something! Vow to progress in your current position, go for a promotion, or respond to a new business opportunity when it presents itself. What's important is that you don't stay married to the status quo. You will be inundated by the progress and the dynamics of everything around you if you do.

An Example of Excellence

My friend Jim Augustine, an executive in banking and finance, recently told me of an applicant for a key position in his sales organization. Jim had heard about this individual's impressive performance at another firm and, when the man applied for a position with Jim's organization, Jim began to understand why this man's reputation was so outstanding. Excellence underlined every behavior.

During one of their early interviews, the applicant told Jim he had undergone an extensive process of testing and psychological evaluation so that he might better understand his own strengths and weaknesses. He provided Jim with copies of the evaluations, along with a personally prepared report of his goals and objectives for building on his strengths and eliminating and managing his weaknesses in the future.

Jim told me, "I've never been so impressed with someone's commitment to growth and progress. He was a truly focused, disciplined professional. I knew then that I wanted this man to be a part of my organization."

While their discussions were continuing, the man provided an in-depth business plan for the part he would play in the company. It was impressive and professional, and an offer of employment was made and accepted.

The last time I talked to Jim Augustine, this man's performance had exceeded his business plan, and his follow-through and contribution to the firm were both exceptional.

So... who made the sale in this scenario? The answer, of course, is that both parties were the beneficiaries of this win-win transaction. The employer was excited about this individual's potential contribution, and the individual was excited about this opportunity to be a part of a winning team and enjoy a higher income opportunity in his new position.

Can you see the difference between the proactive role this applicant played and someone who might leisurely drive to work saying, "I wonder if I'll get that job opportunity that's coming up?"

How Fast Can You Run?

In the final analysis, you are in control of your skills, your image, your performance and, of course, your career progress.

Demand a lot of yourself. Thrive on a spirit of growth. Seek and find happiness in professional achievement. The joy that can accompany these accomplishments is inestimable. It is joy made possible by using your talents to the fullest and consistently working to get better.

Now let's take a little trip inside our heads. Imagine yourself up in Canada. We're at a marina at Hudson Bay, fifty of us, and we are all in our own boats – boats that vary in their design, size, types and propulsion.

We set out at the same time and we're all going to a point on the other side of the bay. When we reach the destination, we will have our choice of 50 different opportunities for greater happiness and fulfillment. The one arriving first gets first choice, the last arrival gets the one choice remaining. The sooner we get there, the more we have to choose from. Is this basically how life works: The rewards go to the swiftest? I think the answer is Yes!

I have a question for you: How well-designed is your craft? How powerful is the power plant? How streamlined is it in terms of its ability to function smoothly and competently to get from Point A to Point B?

In this imaginary adventure, I suggest we correlate your boat to the skill and knowledge you currently utilize in your job. Are you reading and studying about the newest technology and product innovations in your field? Have you read the last five to ten books written about your field? Are you doing more than your competition to assure that your daily achievement is smooth sailing?

The other correlation I suggest we make is that the propulsion of your boat is the energy level you are currently displaying in your sales career. Are things running smoothly? Are you making lots of calls, creatively filling up that pipeline with prospective buyers, diligently working to keep sales cycles short?

These are the issues that impact on our career progress and the opportunities which present themselves. Get finely-tuned, know the best strategies for success in your business, and make haste to do more than your peers.

You see, we've got some people in this profession of selling who, if they are with us on Hudson Bay that day in their crafts, will find that their power plant isn't really hitting on all the cylinders. Maybe it needs a tune up. Maybe it hasn't had any work done on it lately, and it's not functioning with the degree of efficiency needed to be running its best.

Others in the profession of selling are out on the bay that day and their boats have power plants that are finely tuned. Their power plants are in top condition because those people have a hunger for knowledge and information and attend seminars, listen to tapes, read books – like you're doing now. They keep their power plants in tune by staying involved in the overall educational process.

Let's consider for a moment the other side of the coin whereby we might associate our human weaknesses with the anchors on our craft. We all have several anchors and some of us have our anchors pulled into the back of the boat, secured there so as to create no drag on the streamline movement of that craft through the water.

Maybe there are some of us who have a couple of anchors (weaknesses) that are hanging over the back but not all the way to the bottom of the bay, maybe just dragging in the water and slowing us down. Then there are others of us who have anchors which are not only hanging over the back of the transom of our craft – they are mired in the mud!

Do you know some people who have potential that is sky-high but performance that has sunk very low? The deviation between extraordinary potential and marginal performance in certain people is so often the result of weaknesses that those people have never addressed. Those people could easily make a conscious decision to do something about their weaknesses but, unfortunately, they have done nothing to get their anchors out of the mud at the bottom of the bay.

It's unrealistic to say that we can eliminate every weakness we'll ever have, but we can manage our weaknesses, can we not? Sometimes we need to ascertain how to get out of our own way!

As we address the issue of better managing our weaknesses, we are gradually getting the anchors into the back of the boat. Or maybe we totally eliminate a weakness, cutting that anchor free to hit the bottom of the bay, where we will never see it again.

I think one of our responsibilities as members of the human race – and more specifically as members of the great profession of selling – is to be as good as we can be. We need not only to identify our strengths but to build on them with all the expertise we can muster. If we do, we will enjoy more success than ever before.

Successful Application 25

Featuring: Dave Bronzek, V.P., General Manager, Federal Express of Canada; Toronto, Ontario, Canada
(Author Interview)

Some people consciously stop at different points along their career path to ask themselves, "Is my work really working out the way I had planned? Is all the effort I'm putting in worth it? Am I satisfied?"

Others of us slow down to make that kind of evaluation only because circumstances beyond our control force us to do so. I fall into the latter category.

I began my career at Federal Express at the bottom, as a courier driving a van and picking up packages in order to help pay my way through college. After college, I stayed with Federal Express because I liked the people, the company's philosophy, and the Federal Express work ethic. I moved into sales, was promoted to operations supervisor and then became the manager of a small station in Toledo, Ohio. In time I was promoted to manager of Federal Express operations in Los Angeles.

As my career progressed, I made a mistake made by many people who enjoy their job: I began working so much that I had little time for other activities. I developed typical Type A behavior, putting in 15-hour days and sacrificing all my outside interests. I was neglecting my family, too, even though I felt, at the time, that working hard was helping my family.

My race along the fast track was interrupted by an incident that threatened my career and forced me to examine where I had been and where I was headed. I was accused of something that, had it been true, would have caused me to be terminated by the company. I defended myself successfully against the false charges, but the incident hit me like a sledgehammer, waking me up to what I had allowed to happen. I had worked so hard, and yet it could have all been gone overnight.

That incident caused me to reexamine my priorities and put my work back into the proper perspective. I began to take more time for my family. I reclaimed time for outside interests. I avoided the job burnout that I believe would have eventually caught up with me down the road.

An amazing thing happened: Working somewhat fewer hours was actually good for my career instead of harmful. I found I was making better decisions, faster. My mind was fresher, and I had a sharper grasp of situations. I became a more valuable asset to my company. Achieving a reasonable balance between professional and personal goals benefitted every aspect of my life. I gained career progress, and my personal life improved, too.

I moved from Los Angeles to become managing director of Federal Express for Pennsylvania. Then I was promoted to my present position as Vice President and General Manager of Federal Express, Canada, with 1,350 employees working under my direction.

In 1986, I was named the top managing director for Federal Express, earning the Managing Director of the Year award. Then in 1988, I won the CEO Award as the top vice president of Federal Express Corporation.

I've been able to achieve these honors because I have a tremendous team working with me and also, I think, because I have continued to keep my career in the proper perspective.

There are two things that I believe are key to achieving professional success without sacrificing everything for your career. One is to surround yourself with absolutely the best people you can find, not only in terms of excellent skills but also in terms of integrity, ethics and dedication. Nobody who is successful gets there all on his own, and working with and through good people allows you to reach high goals and still have time left for other priorities.

Secondly, I believe if you focus on doing your job and doing it well, career progress in a sales organization will come without your having to worry constantly about promotions. A well-balanced person will invariably find it much easier to sell himself.

It's been my experience that, when you do an excellent job in a corporation, you don't have to go looking for recognition – management comes looking for you! I've seen a lot of people who were so busy working for a promotion that they didn't do their present job well, so the promotion never came. Do your job well – do it better than anyone else – and career progress will be your reward.

DON'S PARTING THOUGHT

Expect a lot of yourself. Make energized, high-quality decisions in career-related matters. Avoid counter-productive, workaholic behaviors that rob you of a balanced life. Get the counsel of influencers you respect. Earn the right to receive the rewards and opportunities you seek. Go for it with a creative thrust and an attitude that you will not be denied!

A B C'S of Time Management 315
A Message to Garcia 245
A Whack on the Side of the Head 67
Absentia Goals 272
Abundance 21, 46, 58, 350
Accessory Decisions 292
Accountability 95, 314, 342
Action Plan 12, 43, 191-192, 278,
  303, 336-337, 341-342, 347
Activity-Based Achievement 277
Adaptability 165, 167, 176-178, 198-
  199, 206-208, 221, 243, 304, 319
Adelson Merv, 339
Administrivia 317
Adversity 55, 276, 282
Advocate 144-145
Aerojet Tactical Corporation 122
Affiliated Foods 310
After-the-Sale Follow-Up 134
Alessandra, Tony 163
Allegiance 88, 149, 180, 182-183,
  305, 322
Allen, James 3
Allied Chemical 280
Allstate Insurance Company 24
Alternate-of-Choice Close 230
American Media 329
Amiables 170, 172, 179, 299
AmSouth XI
Analyticals 170, 172, 299
Anger 299
Anzalone, Jerry 32
Apathy 46, 59
Art of Listening 108, 114
Arthur Andersen and Co. XI
Asking for Referrals 319-320
Asking Questions 50, 104-108
Assertive Closes, Less 226
Assertive Closes, More 229, 230, 231
Assertiveness 165-166, 169, 224-226
Assertiveness Comfort Zone 226
Astrodome 188-189

Astroturf 189
Atlantic Building Systems 62
Augustine, Jim 354
Authenticity 97, 306
Autocratic Mode 299
Automatic Close 231-232
Averitt Express IX
Avery, Frederick F. IX

Balance Point International 200
Bale, Bob 43
Balkancar, N.A. 88
Baltimore Orioles 348
Banks, Dr. Murray 342
Bauer, Art 329
Baum, Gregory 22
Baxter Health Care 93
Beecher, Henry Ward 55
Behavior Research 163
Behavioral Dimensions 165, 169
Behavioral Styles 163, 168-169, 171-
  173, 176, 178, 184, 199, 224, 298
Bell, Dolores V
Bennett, Lew 5, 332
Berzett, Al 293
Blame 52, 58
Blanchard, Ken V
Bok, Derek 344
Book of Lists 196
Born Salesman 92, 171
Boyd, Ty V, 45
Brainstorming 173, 254, 262
Bresser, Jerry 22, 257
Bronzek, Dave 357
Brooks, Bill 314
Brown, Les 19
Brown, Michael 13
Bryan, William Jennings 187
Bryan Foods Division Sara Lee
  Corporation IX
Bucket Dumping 298

Building Trust VI, 81, 83, 85, 87, 89, 91, 93, 95, 97, 99, 101, 206
Building Value VI, 81, 151, 153-155, 157, 159
Burnout 57-60, 62-64, 358
Burrus, Daniel A. V

Caldiero, Raymond 326
Call Objectives 322
Call-Back Close 227
Career Balance VII
Career Goals 257, 350, 352
Career Progress VII, 239, 288, 349-351, 353, 355, 357-359
Carlyle, Thomas 246
Carnegie, Dale 244
Carrell, Alexis 302
Carson, Carl 329
Cassidy, Doug 93
Casual Close 228
Cathcart, Jim V, 117, 163, 172
Causes of Objections 215
Changing the Game: A New Way to Sell 68
Character 42, 96, 353
Charting Goals 268
Chase Manhattan XI
Chesterfield, Lord 333
Chevron 62
Chinese Bridges 98
Chromcraft Furniture 158
Churchill, Bonnie XI
Churchill, Winston 56
Clanton, Don XI
Client 8, 56, 59, 67, 90-91, 93, 99, 101, 105, 119, 128, 133, 144, 147-148, 156, 190-193, 205-206, 230, 232-235, 243, 286, 304-305, 320
Closed Questions 107
Closing the Sale VI, 81, 164, 203, 205, 207, 209, 211, 213, 215,

Closing the Sale (*continued*) 217, 219, 221, 223, 225, 227, 229, 231, 233, 235, 303
Cockrill, Paul 197
Cold Calls 18, 50, 142, 146, 148
Coldwell Banker International 246
Comfort Zones 260, 284
Commerce Investments XI
Commitment to Skill Building 318
Common Sense Sales Ideas VII, 239, 313, 315, 317, 319, 321, 323, 325, 327, 329, 331, 333
Competence 178, 314
Competent Self-Disciplinarians 272
Competition 35, 75, 110, 132, 138-139, 142-143, 145-147, 159, 183, 220, 229, 234-235, 252, 319, 322, 333, 355
Complacency 57, 59, 73, 257
Components of Adaptability 178
Components of Image 286
Conant, Lloyd 284
Confidant VI, 81, 141, 143-145, 147, 149
Confidence 12, 32, 52, 58, 76, 87, 90, 104-105, 129, 135, 185, 209-210, 255, 275, 281
Confirmation Questions 107
Conflict Resolution 300, 302
Confrontation 204, 306
Confucius 4, 141-142
Considine, Ray 142, 289
Constructive Tension 59-60, 196
Conversational Variance 330
Cost-Cutter Foods 210
Cox, Danny V, 69, 246
Cox, Jeff 347
Creativity 65-73, 75-77, 79, 90, 124, 149, 220, 277, 324, 347-348
Crouch, Butch 345
Crowley, Mary 55
Cullen, Charlie 55

Customer 30-31, 41, 70, 78, 83-87, 89-91, 93-101, 104-105, 114-115, 118, 122, 124-125, 128-129, 132, 134-135, 138-139, 142-145, 147-149, 153, 157, 164, 171, 182-183, 200, 205, 209-212, 235, 300-301, 303-305, 308, 310, 321-323, 331

Customer Feedback 304

Customer Goals 86-87, 145

Customer Needs 86, 95, 138-139, 164

Customer Turnover 95, 142

Customizing Proposals 190

Cutting Price VI, 81, 151, 153, 155, 157, 159

Dali, Salvador 77

Danek Group 332

Daniels, Bennie 90

Danks, Doug 93

Deadlines 277

Decision Influencers 106, 116, 119, 132, 139, 188, 190, 317

Deere Credit, John Deere Company 293

Defeat 49, 55, 66, 73, 108

Deming, Ed 346

Dependability 90, 97, 322

Destructive Tension 59

Determination 40, 46, 201, 205, 246, 275, 282, 312

Devos, Rich 326

deWitt, Dr. John Richard 352

Diaz, Chris 246-248

Dietary Products 93

Discipline 42, 46, 51, 53, 111, 258, 272-273, 287, 316, 321, 337, 351

Discouragement 50, 52

Discussion Approach 165

Disney, Walt 19

Displayed Enthusiasm 242, 244, 248

Dobbs 326

Doerr, Ronald H. VIII

Dominance 318-319

Dominating Interviews 318

Don's Parting Thought 14, 26, 35, 48, 64, 79, 102, 116, 125, 139, 149, 159, 174, 186, 202, 212, 236, 248, 270, 282, 295, 312, 333, 348, 359

Douglas, Arlene VIII

Douglas, Mike 104

Drivers 169, 171-172, 179, 230, 299

Drucker, Dr. Peter 68

Earning Customer Allegiance 182

Earning Trust 89

Easley, Mutt 19

Eastern Bank XI

Eckerd Drug Company IX

Edison, Thomas 66, 302

Education and Personal Development Goals 257

Edwards, J. Douglas 53, 213, 251, 285

Effective Objection Handling 214

Effective Sales Proposal 189

Effective Use of Pressure 221

Efficient Meetings 317

Egomania 305

Einstein 70

Emerson, Ralph Waldo 74, 241

Emmerling, John 72

Emotional Content 166

Enthusiasm in Selling VII, 239, 241, 243, 245, 247

ERA Rancho Real Estate Co. 246

Ethicon 332

Examination of Priorities 358

Excellence Dimension VII, 239

Executive Selling 326

Expressives 170, 173, 179, 299

Failure Factors 321
Family Goals 258
Fatigue Avoidance 330
Fear of Failure 66, 73
Federal Express 99, 123, 339-340,
    357-358
Federal Express of Canada 357
Feedback VII, 130, 156, 179, 207,
    239, 297, 299, 301, 303-311
Feedback Process 304
Financial Goals 258
Firestone, Harvey 302
Fisher, Walter C. VIII
Flavil Q. Van Dyke & Associates 47,
    101, 137, 168
Florida Farm Bureau 91
Follow Up 139, 142, 192, 320, 327
Following Up 75, 133-134
Forbes Magazine 108
Forceful Summary Technique 228
Ford, Henry 83, 302
Foreman, Ed 5, 55
Forest E. Olson Realtors 246-247
Forms of Objections 216
Foster and Kleiser Outdoor
    Advertising 108
Frankl, Victor 347
Franklin, Benjamin 299, 349
Friedman, Dr. Meyer 351
Fripp, Patricia V 339
Fritz, Robert 347
FXTV 339

Gack, Kathy 210
Gardner, 'Brother Dave' 161
Gardner, Dick V, 27, 232
Garment Selection 292
Generic Adaptability 198-199
Getty, J. Paul 65, 280
Gillette 197
Goal Achievement VII, 239, 250,
    269, 271, 273-275, 277-279, 281

Goal Congruence 85, 207
Goal Consistency 85-87
Goal Factors 252, 262
Goal Planning 252
Goal Setting VII, 48, 55, 239, 249-
    259, 261, 268-270, 272, 274
Goal Structure 272
Goal-Pac 253-254, 259, 262
Goals, Definition of 252
Golden Rule 177
Good Luck 145
Gove, Bill V, 58, 67, 99, 131
Governing Values 253
Grammar 286, 328-329
Green, Dr. Paul 58
Gretsky, Wayne 71
Group and Committee Presentations
    195
Guilt 25, 52, 54, 58, 90, 106
Guyer 163

Habit Alteration 278
Haggai, Dr. Tom 20
Halliburton, Richard 54, 254
Hammer, Armand 279-280
Handling Anger 299
Handling Conflict VII, 239, 297,
    299, 301, 303, 305, 307, 309, 311
Handling Postponements 219
Handly, Bob 60
Hard Science 162-163
Hard Science vs. Soft Science 162
Harris, Sidney 52
Harvard University 344
Harvey, Paul 11, 55
Hatten, Roy 343
Hayes, Ira V, 5, 11, 67, 220
Healthco International 21, 147
Hearst, Frank 113
Hegarty, Christopher V, 137
Herman, Fred 104, 320
High Quality Feedback 308

Hightower, Linda V
Hill, Dr. Napolean 252
Hoffines, Judge Roy 188
Holst, Art V
Hopkins, Tom 6
How The Best Is Won 20
Howard, George 114
Hubbard, Elbert 49, 245, 344
Hugo, Victor 337
Human Behavior in Selling VI, 81,
    161, 163, 165, 167, 169, 171, 173
Humor 61
Huntington Bank XI
Hurst, Allan V
Hutson, Kevin 339
Hutson, Marvin Lee III
Hutson, Scott 331
Hutson, Sara Summers III

IBM 137, 139
Image VII, 12, 17-24, 29, 50, 71, 75,
    92-93, 131, 152, 154-155, 178,
    180, 182, 194, 220, 239, 255,
    283-295, 305, 321, 352-353, 355
Image Factors 287
Image Variability 285
Imagination VI, 20-23, 55, 65-77,
    79, 254
Improved Sales Efficiency 316
Indifference, The Price of 134
Indifference 95, 134, 308, 321
Individuality 13, 19, 74-75, 96-97,
    171, 174, 253, 302, 324, 336
Inner Enthusiasm 244-245
Inside Influence 129-130
Integrity 89-90, 92-96, 102, 124, 137,
    170, 286, 358
Interactive Flow 225
Internalized Enthusiasm 242, 244-
    246, 248
Introspection 54

J. Strickland Company 197
Jackson, Dave 232
Jackson, Ted 88
James, William 12, 89
Jewell, Everett 61
Jewell Building Systems 61-63
Jewett, Dr. James E. 99
John R. Wood & Associates Realtors
    47
Johnson & Johnson 332
Jones, Charlie V, 61, 69, 177, 345-
    346
Jones, Randolph W. 13
Joy of Results 338
Jung, Dr. Carl 163

Keeping Promises 287
Kentucky Jet Trip 154
Keppler, Al 113
Killing Alligators 302
Kitchen Cabinet Manufacturers
    Association IX
Klosterman, Brian 268
Kluge, John VIII, 108-109
Kraft Food Ingredients IX
Kraft Foodservice 93
Kruse, Daniel 7
Kruse, Dean 7

Lambert, Harry W. IX
Laughter 61
Law of Supply and Demand 325
Laziness 46, 321, 333
Lefton 163
Less Assertive Behavior 165
Less Responsive Behavior 299
LFO Linoleum & Carpet 113
Linkletter, Art 11, 339
Listener Distraction 111
Listening Skills 108-112
Little Journeys 245
Loeffelbein, Roger IX

Losing Temper 60
Low Closing Percentage 171, 176, 205

M. S. Carriers 310
Maltz, Dr. Maxwell 71
Man's Search for Meaning 347
Managing Yourself 315
Mandino, Og 245
Manipulation 93-94, 206-208, 219
Mann, James L. IX
Mannington 113
Marcus, Stanley 314
Marden, Orison Swett 11-12, 31, 37, 245
Margin Protection 157
Markson, Dr. Larry IX, 258
Marriott 326
Mars, Ross 56
Marson 163
Martin, Jay 326
McCall, Ron 90
McFadden, Kurt 209
McFarland, Dr. Kenneth V, 21, 258
McMorris, Jerry VIII
Measuring and Tracking Goals 260
Memphis State University 180
Mental Imaging 262
Mental Locks 67
Mercedes Benz 14
Merchandising 76
Merrill, Dr. David 163
Metromedia, Inc. VIII, 109
Michael, Martin 158
Miller and Herman 129
Mills, Stanley 147
Mobile Office 290
Model Training 336
Monsanto 188-189
More Assertive Behavior 165
More Assertive Closes 229
More Responsive Behavior 299

Morgan Keegan Company 331
Motivational Tapes 47, 57, 210
Motive Assessment 132
Motive Defined 133
Motley, Arthur H. "Red" V, 297
Moynihan, Pat 24
Mundy, Gerry 21, 147
Murphy's Law 60
Mutual Support 277

National Association of Friends of Rare Porcelain 79
National Linen, Division of National Service Industries 123
National Speakers Association 19, 22, 96
National Steel Corporation VIII
NCR Corporation 67, 221
Needs Analysis Defined 119
Needs-Based Benefits 153, 157
Needs-Based Presentation VI, 81, 129, 133, 139, 188
Negative Goal Setting 55
Negative Pre-Judging 34
Negative Self-Talk 72
Network Marketing 326
Newman, Jim V, 272
Newton, James 302
Nicklaus, Jack 224
Nightingale, Earl 11, 284, 341
Nightingale-Conant, Inc. 284
Nissan Forklifts 88
No-Limit Assumption 70
Non-Congruent Goals 85
Northwest Airlines 326
Numbers Game 27, 29-33, 35, 205

O'Toole's Law 60
Oakwood Mobile Homes 184-185
Objection-Free Selling 118
Observing Human Behavior 167-168

Occidental Petroleum 279
Offensive Sales Behaviors 325
One-Call Psyche Out 331
Open-ended Questions 107
Organizing Leads 328

Palley, Reese 76, 78-79
Palumbo, Jim 268
Passive/Aggressive Posture 307
Path of Least Resistance 347
Patterson, John H. 67
Peale, Dr. Norman Vincent 10, 298
Peddler 323
Performance Barriers 246
Performance Measurement 273
Personal Excellence 19
Personal Performance Standards 273
Personal Styles and Effective
    Performance 163
Personal Thermostat 260
Personal Training Need 344
Personally Handwritten Note 134
Physical Confrontation 204
Physical Goals 258, 270
Piazza, Tony XII
Pickard, Ron 332
Pitch 129, 323
Planning 24, 35, 47, 100, 173, 243,
    249-250, 253, 258, 306, 314,
    316, 350, 352
Platinum Rule 175, 177
Plato 223-224
Plumb, Charlie V
Positive Habit Structure 278
Positive Habits 47-48, 255, 321, 336
Positive Self Talk 50
Possibility Thinking 66
Power Words 323
Pre-Sale Follow-Up 133-134
Prentiss, Carol 5
Prentiss, Jim 5

Preparation 21 192, 195-196, 315,
    320
Presentation VI, 29-30, 32, 41, 43,
    50-52, 81, 85, 87, 106, 118-119,
    121, 125, 127-133, 135, 137-139,
    153, 158, 167, 177-180, 188,
    190-191, 194-202, 204-207, 217,
    219, 222, 227-228, 232, 289,
    304-305, 319-320, 323, 325, 328,
    330
Presentation Sequence 325
Presentation Uniqueness 132
Pressure 56, 62-63, 89, 218, 221-226,
    229, 322, 344
Price of Excellence 337
Price-Cutting 157
Pricing 77, 124
Prioritizing 270
Problem Solving Formula 303
Problems VII, 4, 7-8, 13, 38, 54-56,
    63, 75, 84, 88, 97, 102, 115, 121,
    127, 129, 132, 138, 147-148,
    198, 217, 228-229, 239, 258,
    297-299, 301-303, 305, 307-309,
    311-312, 325, 340, 350
Procrastination 12, 46, 194, 274, 333
Procter & Gamble 197, 279, 281
Productive Energy Curve 59
Professional Image 284-287, 290,
    293-294, 305
Proposal, Sequence and Structure
    191
Proposal Distribution 190
Proposal Options 193
Prospect 9, 29-30, 33-34, 41, 45, 50-
    51, 53-54, 56-57, 60, 67, 70, 85-
    87, 89-90, 96-97, 99, 104-107,
    111-112, 114, 118-122, 128-133,
    135, 142-144, 146, 148, 152-153,
    164, 171, 173-174, 176, 179-180,
    182, 188, 190-193, 205-206, 208,

Prospect (*continued*) 214-220, 222, 224-235, 286, 301-303, 310, 318-331
Prospect's Perceptions 152, 214
Psychocybernetics 71
Pullman Trailmobile 310-312

Quality Communications Model 307
Quality Listening 112-113
Qubein, Nido V, 301

Raphel, Murray 76, 142
Reflexive Skills 220
Reid, Roger 163
Reid, Scott 114
Rejection VI, 7-9, 28, 49-57, 59, 61, 63, 133, 146, 201, 205, 331
Rejection Response 51
Related Store Close 227
Relationship-Enhancing Questions 107
Release Your Brakes 272
Reliability 95, 152, 184
Remembering Names 113-114
Repeat Business 182-183, 226, 305, 323
Reser, Jerry 209
Reser's Fine Foods 209-210
Responsiveness 165-167, 169
Results-Oriented Goal Setting 250
Revising Goals 256
Rex Yacht Sales 232
Rice, Joel 328
Robert, Cavett V, 4, 11, 96, 196
Rohn, Jim 57, 341
Role Playing 344
Roosevelt, Franklin D. 271
Roosevelt, Teddy 66, 73
Ruth, Babe 55
Ryan, Mike 16

Sales and Marketing Executives 342
Sales Consultants-Management Recruiters 328
Salesline 340
Sasser, Gary D. IX
Satellite Network Affiliates 339
Sav-A-Stop 197-198
Scarcity 58
Schulhof, Mickey 72
Schuller, Dr. Robert 11, 66
Schultz, Whit 335
Schumacher, John 123
Schwarz, Bill 289
Sebastian, Charles 122
Selected Writings 245
Self Pity 54
Self-Awareness 289
Self-Discipline 41, 255, 272, 315
Selling Strategically 179
Shakespeare 275
Sharing Your Goals 275
Sharp Angle Close 231
Shergold, Craig 109
Show and Tell 198
Shulte, Will 158-159
Simmons, Harold 197
Simon, Paul 72
Simultaneous Verbiage 330
Six Honest Serving Men 300
Skilled Interaction 307-308
Smith & Nephew Richards 114
Smith & Nephew Richards Orthopedic Division 114
Snarr, Doug 339
Social, Hobby, & Extra-Curricular Goals 258
Soft Science 162
Solomon 249
SONY XII, 72, 268-269
Southern Farm Bureau Life Insurance Company 90

SouthTrust Securities, Inc., South
    Trust Corporation 345
Spiritual Goals 258
St. George, Nick 184
Starnes, Mike 310
Steil, Dr. Manny 114
Steps To Good Listening 111
Stevens, Howard 347
Stone, Jim 184, 224
Stone, W. Clement 11, 74, 274
Strategic Enthusiasm 242
Stress VI, 17, 30, 49, 51-61, 63-64,
    84, 89, 110, 171, 181-182, 208-
    209, 226, 298-300, 302, 306,
    308-309, 316, 322, 350
Stress Management 56
Stuffing 306
Subconscious Mind 20, 250-251,
    261-262, 336
Subordinate Question Technique
    230
SUCCESS magazine 74
Sun Bank XI
Sungard Data Systems, Inc. IX
Suspect VI, 32, 81, 141, 143, 145,
    147, 149, 260, 345-346

Talaski, Randy 147
Tate, Ron 200
Teamwork 131, 277, 308-309
Telco Research Corporation 99
Telemarketing Momentum 327
Telemarketing Tips 326-327
Telephone Presentations 330
Telephone Record-Keeping 329
Temper 60, 298-300, 308
Tension 56, 59-61, 106, 179, 196,
    225, 300, 316
TGI Friday's XI
The Cold Call With Letter Technique
    324
The New York Times 77

The Standing Call 323
Third Party Impact 129
Thompson, Lord Roy 280
Thoreau, Henry David 15
Thoren, Don 32, 145, 163, 338
Threat of Change 338
Tigrett, John B. 279
Time Management 47-48, 314-316
Timing 54, 106, 152, 194, 208, 214,
    217, 276, 319, 340
Titus, C. Richard IX
Tonning, Dr. Waylon V
Track Record 30, 66, 259
Tracy, Brian V, 53
Training VII, 10, 28, 50, 57, 88, 94-
    95, 107, 109-110, 123, 130, 134,
    137, 163, 167-168, 180, 191,
    193, 199-201, 207, 239, 253,
    269, 284, 289, 291, 315, 318,
    329, 332, 335-348
Training Library 341
Training Options 339
Training Process 199, 346, 348
Training Tapes 57
Trial Closes 208-209, 330
True, Dr. Herb V, 61
Trust VI, 30, 56, 81, 83, 85, 87-93,
    95-101, 119, 132-133, 179-180,
    182, 184, 206, 208-209, 211-212,
    215, 225, 290, 309, 320, 322
Tunney, Jim V
Twain, Mark 70
Type A Behavior and Your Heart
    351
Type A People 351
Types of Questions 107

Un-Training 342
Uncommon Friends 302
Unloading Posture 307-308
Unrealistic Goals 22, 257

Value of Negative Events 55
Value of Objections 215
Value/Price Perspective 153
Van Dyke, Flavil Q. 137
Variable Assertiveness 224
Varying Pressure Threshold 221
Vertical Prospecting 316
Veto Power 217
Viland, Joseph H. VIII
Virgil 76
Vocabulary 72, 286, 328-330, 337
VON OECH, Dr. Roger 67
VPT factor 221

W. Clement and Jesse V. Stone
     Foundation 74
Wabash Alloys VIII
Waitley, Denis 339
Wall Street Journal 314
Wallace, Amy 196
Walters, Dave 293
Ward, William A. 337
Ward C.L.U., Ben 89
Watson, Jack IX
Weasel Words 323
Weaver, Earl 348
Weird Prospects 164
Welch, Woody 310
Weldon, Joel 313
Welsh, Candace 47
Westervelt, Steve 24
Wexler, Phil 203
Wheeler, Elmer VIII, 127, 230
Williams, Mike 71
Willingham, Ron 191
Wilson, Larry 68, 163, 302, 347
Wilson Learning 168
Windows of Opportunity 208
Windshield Time 316
Winninger, Tom V
Wonder, Stevie 72

Worry VI, 42, 49, 51, 53, 55-57, 59,
     61, 63, 75, 256, 358
Written Communications 98, 323
Written Goals 270, 279

Zenith Corporation VIII
Ziglar, Zig 6, 11, 151, 256, 339